Barcode in Back

MW01121271

LIFE
AFTER DEATH

LIFE
AFTER DEATH

Widows and the English Novel,
Defoe to Austen

Karen Bloom Gevirtz

DELAWARE

Newark: University of Delaware Press

Associated University Presses
2010 Eastpark Boulevard
Cranbury, NJ 08512

The paper used in this publication meets the requirements of the American National Standard for Permanence of Paper for Printed Library Materials Z39.48–1984.

Library of Congress Cataloging-in-Publication Data

Gevirtz, Karen Bloom, 1969-
    Life after death : widows and the English novel, Defoe to Austen / Karen Bloom Gevirtz.
        p. cm.
    Includes bibliographical references and index.
    ISBN 0-87413-923-6 (alk. paper)
1. English fiction—18th century—History and criticism. 2. Widows in literature. 3. Capitalism and literature—Great Britain—History—18th century. 4. Women and literature—Great Britain—History—18th century. 5. Defoe, Daniel, 1661?-1731—Characters—Widows. 6. Austen, Jane, 1775-1817—Characters—Widows. 7. Capitalism in literature. 8. Sex role in literature. I. Title.
    PR858.W5G48 2005
    823'.509352654—dc22
                    2005003462

PRINTED IN THE UNITED STATES OF AMERICA

I find Widows are confounded insupportable witty Devils.
—Aphra Behn and Thomas Betterton,
The Counterfeit Bridegroom

Contents

Acknowledgments

I HAVE BEEN PARTICULARLY FORTUNATE TO HAVE INCURRED DEBTS TO the people and institutions mentioned here. In addition to the help that has made this project possible, I owe them thanks for many satisfactions experienced during my research, thought, and composition.

I would first like to acknowledge the generosity of the Earl of Devon, who graciously allowed me access to the Courtenay papers and granted permission for their use in this work. Permission has been given by the Managers of the Retired Ministers' and Widows' Fund (successors to the Aged and Infirm Ministers' Fund and The Widows' Fund) to quote from their records now on deposit at Dr. Williams's Library, London. I would also like to thank the many archivists at the Devon Record Office, the Wiltshire and Swindon Record Office, and the Somerset Record Office for their help in tracking down materials and their permission to use them. Lastly, portions of chapter 2 appeared in *Intertexts* 7:1 and are presented here with the kind permission of the editors.

Kathy Dalton of the Blough-Weis Library of Susquehanna University and the staffs at the Public Record Office of London, England; Walsh Library of Seton Hall University; Butler Library of Columbia University; and the New York Public Library, especially Elizabeth Wyckoff, connected me with materials both current and obscure. Warren Funk and two committees at Susquehanna University provided research grants for work in England and in New York City. I am also grateful to Rachel Abram, Mary Balkun, Laura Beard, Elizabeth Bloom, Martha Bowden, Susan Bowers, Martine Watson Brownley, Laura Callanan, Martha Carpentier, Don and Stephanie Friedman, Sharon Diane Nell, Jennifer Poulos Nesbitt, Pamela Pagliochini, Laura Runge, Helene Solheim, Angela Weisl, Amy Winans, and several anonymous readers at *Intertexts*.

On the personal front, the Ofer family's warmth and generosity converted a difficult research expedition into a wonderful adventure. My extended family—the Blooms, Franks, Gevirtzes, and Weinsteins—provided tremendous and unstinting support, and they are to be forgiven if they never wish to hear another word about widows, the eighteenth century, or the novel. Without Stephen, of course, nothing would have been possible.

LIFE
AFTER DEATH

1
Introduction

THIS IS THE STORY OF THE WIDOW IN THE EIGHTEENTH-CENTURY
English novel. It is a story about sex and money, vast country estates
and crushing urban poverty, greed and benevolence, good mothers
and vicious kidnappers, exuberant thieves and repentant sinners,
empire and the domestic hearth. It is the story of two of the most
compelling events of the eighteenth century: the development of
capitalism and the invention of the novel. The widow figures in
each.

The eighteenth century in England was a period of tremendous
change. This is the century, after all, of a profound shift from an
agrarian economy to one based on manufactures, commerce, and a
global market. Traditional social networks were threatened with dis-
integration, reevaluation, or reorganization. These networks included some of the most fundamental human relationships, such as those
between rich and poor, landowner and tenant, and parent and child.
The pressing question of what it means to live in such a system arguably provoked some of the most significant modern cultural developments, including the emergence of the novel. The novel facilitated the exploration of issues arising from these developments,
such as whether morality exists in an unregulated economic system;
who, in a time of rapid social change, should be allowed to participate in that system; and the cost, real or conceptual, to English institutions.[1]

People of the age recognized that this cost was potentially high.
In addition to dislocation and unemployment, for example, the rise
of a commercial economy brought into question traditional notions
of identity. In a commercial society people could change class
through the acquisition or loss of wealth, sometimes rapidly and

sometimes more than once in a lifetime. It also became possible to simulate class as markers, such as certain clothes or a carriage, became available to anyone with sufficient money, and as money was decreasingly attached to birth. Where you were born or worked or traveled also lost the power to determine identity, although place itself continued to exert considerable influence on the cultural imagination.[2] And the explosion of economic opportunity seemed open to all, male or female, thus profoundly changing gender expectations. Anyone living at such a time can be forgiven for being anxious, and for seeking order somewhere in the chaos.

After decades of incisive scholarship, it is no longer a mystery why the novel arrived in England at this moment. It was, to simplify a bit, the child of changes to print culture, cultural discourse, and economic opportunity. Novelists brought their creation to maturity by engaging with the cultural and economic forces of the day, legitimating form and content by reflecting as well as shaping eighteenth-century life.[3] Simultaneously, the widow became an aspect of the novel's discussion of these issues. In any consideration of gender roles in the new economy, the widow stood squarely on the fault line. Possessing the same rights and privileges as a man, as well as experience and often money and property, the widow was, of all women, the best situated for making full use of the new economic opportunities. Not surprisingly, there was much debate about the role of women in commerce. Writers, whether they liked or disliked the new economy, joined the cultural project of regulating women's participation in it, and in this effort they repeatedly used the figure of the widow. The representation of the widow, regardless of her economic situation, consistently articulates and affirms the notion that women should be excluded from active and public participation in mercantile capitalism.

Widows are of particular interest because the widow's position in society was unique. Widows could own property; they ran their own households, they made their own decisions, and they were unmarried but sexually experienced. The legal system also protected widows' independence. Until 1833, English law guaranteed widows their dower: one-third of the husband's estate. Marriage contracts sometimes included jointures—annuities—which the widow disposed of as she saw fit. Once she inherited, in theory, the widow controlled her inheritance and, sometimes with it, the family finances. Gentlemen's widows inherited money, goods, and property and because they were also less likely to remarry than other widows, they often removed significant assets from circulation.[4]

Widows could do as they pleased in another sense, as well. With the right to make contracts and to go into business, a widow could earn sufficient money to improve her status and that of her children. The widow's right to control her property and her self (by deciding whether, and whom, to marry) challenged conventions for constructing womanhood; as Barbara Todd puts it, "The woman heading her own household contradicted patriarchal theory; the ungoverned woman was a threat to the social order."[5] The extent to which the widow could in reality threaten the social order depended upon her wealth, but in theory, all widows had the same right that men had to take advantage of the system.

The role of widows in society was not a new topic to the eighteenth century. The independence of widows has for centuries interested English writers, who generally have revealed ambivalence about if not outright hostility to it. Geoffrey Chaucer's attitude, for example, seems less conflicted than those of his contemporaries, yet his representation of the Wife of Bath in *The Canterbury Tales* reveals profoundly ambiguous attitudes toward women of independence and power. Four hundred years later, the widow of Restoration drama was a comic but menacing figure who threatened the power structure through her control of property. J. Douglas Canfield has pointed out that the landed estate was "both the emblem and the reality of power in late feudal England." Estates held by aristocratic families before the Civil War had been given to others; with the Restoration of King Charles II in 1660, the disposal of those estates posed a highly charged question about who should hold the property and with it, the nation's wealth. Restoration dramatists answered these challenges to the ruling class by reinscribing the power of the aristocracy through marriage. If Restoration comedy "ends in the right couple set to inherit the estate, which is the center, at least symbolically, of late feudal political economy," however, then there is little room for autonomous women.[6] In Restoration comedy, rebellious girls submit to marriage with willingly reformed rakes, and widows who refuse to remarry receive their proper punishment of insult, assault, and worse.

Perhaps one of the best examples of how Restoration comedy used the widow to reinforce a male-dominated system is Widow Blackacre in William Wycherley's *The Plain Dealer* (1676). Widow

Blackacre personifies the many threats posed by the widow to the patriarchal order: she controls herself, she refuses to be commodified in the marriage market, she controls the estate, and she controls her son. "The widow, as the play recognizes, is thus a problem and an anomaly in the world in which she is constituted," Helen Burke notes.[7] Widow Blackacre exposes the problem of the female desiring subject, that is, the free woman, in a male-dominated system. The Restoration's patriarchal society portrayed a woman's desire to use that freedom as greed or wickedness, in an effort to contain it. By condemning Widow Blackacre's refusal to hand over the estate to her son, Wycherley asserts that women, property, and women of property need to be controlled by aristocratic men. Restoration drama makes explicit connections between property and power and between widowhood and disruption.

It is important to underline that it was widowed women, not women in general, who triggered these fears about autonomy, property, and sexuality. Aphra Behn and Thomas Betterton's play *The Counterfeit Bridegroom: or the Defeated Widow* (1677), a revision of Thomas Middleton's *No Wit, No Help like a Woman's*, illustrates that powers that are transgressive in widows are not transgressive in married women. One of the main characters, called simply the Widow, manipulates men, resists marriage, and controls property. By the end of the play she has fallen in love with a woman dressed as a man, suggesting that she is represented not just as a sexual stereotype (the older widow who falls for a younger man) but also as sexually deviant (a woman who is attracted to a woman). She also has been publicly humiliated and forced to resign her property in favor of the aristocratic family that held it before her late husband obtained it.

Mrs. Hadland, the protagonist, also manipulates men and actively seeks to acquire property. She seems sexually transgressive as well, for she dresses as a man and seduces another woman. Unlike the Widow, however, Mrs. Hadland is considered virtuous and clever, since all of her actions are taken to preserve not herself, but her family, whether of marriage or birth. She manages men, but with their blessing, and she seeks the property to restore her birth family's estates and her brother's fortunes. She cross-dresses and attracts the Widow with the approval of her husband and brother. She does not resist marriage in order to pursue her own desires and independence; on the contrary, she acts within marriage and family to support those institutions. Hence, while the Widow is ultimately punished for her behavior, Mrs. Hadland is rewarded for hers. The widow is forced to return to marriage and patriarchy; the wife is applauded for remaining within them.[8]

The eighteenth century is economically and socially, and one could argue literarily, very different from previous periods. To manage the economic explosion that characterized the age, eighteenth-century society regulated male and female behavior by conceptualizing separate "spheres" of existence—the public and the private, the commercial and the domestic, and so on—and gendering the public, the commercial and related realms of experience and opportunity, male. The behavior and values that business required, such as enterprise, aggression, education in certain kinds of knowledge and skills, self-possession, and ambition, came to be considered masculine. In turn, English womanhood came to represent the reverse of this notion of masculinity; if men were strivers in the public world and producers of goods, women were guardians of the domestic sphere and consumers of goods. Femininity, according to Mary Poovey, became an enabler for economic behavior, as it was defined in antithesis both to masculinity and to business acumen.[9] This conceptualization did not actually create separate spheres; historical research shows that such a distinction between male and female existence was more a convenient than accurate description of reality. But it created a framework for defining and regulating male and female behavior and, by extension, identity in the world of mercantile capitalism.

Efforts to control female economic activity permeated eighteenth-century society. As definitions of property changed in the eighteenth century, for example, definitions of "woman" and ideas about women's roles changed as well, since women had been viewed not only as the carriers of property in marriage, but as property themselves. Traditionally, women's roles in marriage facilitated the circulation of wealth, but in a rapidly developing economy with changing class structures, this role could also make women the agents of economic and social instability.[10] Efforts to preserve social stability appear in legislation such as the Hardwicke Act of 1753, which imposed new definitions of legal marriage to maintain male control over property, to limit class mixing through marriage, and to support the propagation of a stable workforce for the empire.[11]

Similarly, economic opportunity contracted drastically for women during this time. Generally speaking, women were barred from investment opportunities, such as partnerships in new or emerging businesses. Furthermore, working women, including widows, were pushed out of economic niches that they had previously occupied. At the start of the eighteenth century, widows served in all branches of trade and in all sizes of business. They operated inns, shops, taverns, and boarding houses. They opened schools, went into service, and sold domestic skills such as spinning and washing to earn money. Widows were known to take over family businesses in timber, coal, and smelting. They ran the family farm, managed real estate, and became moneylenders.[12] Widows who ran businesses could take on apprentices in their own name.

By century's end, all that had changed. While cottage industry continued throughout the century, its importance was diminishing. Occupations such as law and medicine became during this period the professions they are today, but their organization and consolidation excluded female practitioners; it was the eighteenth century that saw the replacement of midwives with man-midwives, for example. Where once women had been bakers, coffee-sellers, vintners, grocers, butchers; clothiers, weavers, hosiers, linen-drapers, and milliners; tallow-chandlers, cordwainers, cutlers, and scissors-makers; bricklayers, carpenters, blacksmiths, gunsmiths, goldsmiths, pewterers, and clock-makers, one hundred years later, they were no longer. Millers, barbers, and apothecaries, other groups that included women practitioners, also came to exclude them. As women were prevented from entering some occupations and were pushed out of others, they saturated the much smaller labor market that remained, driving down pay as well as opportunities. Wages for women fell steadily from 1750 onward.[13] Wages for women and men doing the same work had never been equal, and with the greater importance of cash in the economy, waged labor was more highly valued than unwaged work, often domestic in nature. By the nineteenth century, women's economic position had been greatly eroded.

The print media also contributed to efforts to limit women's economic activity. As Laura Brown explains in *Fables of Modernity*, literary culture "is a collective enterprise which, through its collectivity, engages with the most vital, problematic, or prominent aspects of contemporary experience. This engagement links literary culture with the major forces of historical change." Eighteenth-century literary culture engaged with the emerging commercial economy by depicting women in ways meant to advocate their exclusion from mercantile capitalism. Terry Mulcaire observes, for example, that from early in the century in text and image Commerce was portrayed as a woman, often threatened sexually when there was a trade crisis brewing, and Brown persuasively argues that the image of Lady Credit linked old notions of "mystery, imagination, and the female body" with the new and equally mysterious and changeable "credit-based economy."[14]

While the economy itself might be capriciously female, however, females themselves were not to engage with her. Cartoons from 1720 depict women engaging in stock trading as sexually depraved or ruined and compare "Our greatest Ladies" with "Young Harlots, too, from Drury-Lane." Kathryn Kirkpatrick describes similar strategies in conduct books, which promoted the idea that correct gender and class behavior were inextricably linked and equally untransgressable. Conduct books recognized that "propriety" was a commodity and limited the ways it could be used.[15] In so doing, they limited the behaviors that would enable women to change their class without being considered transgressive.

Women's sexuality, especially motherhood, was of particular importance in this separating and gendering of the public and private, the commercial and domestic. Like the definition of femininity, the definition of maternity was one of the tools that eighteenth-century society used to understand itself. As Toni Bowers explains, emerging notions of motherhood were "critical to the construction of models for legitimate power and allegiance in Augustan England, a society where relations of authority on all levels were undergoing revision." Maternity was one place where women could claim a special authority, which made it vital to the reorganization of a male-dominated society to inscribe maternity within patriarchy, not as a resistance or exception to it. In the eighteenth-century, "natural" motherhood became "all-engrossing tenderness, long-term maternal breastfeeding, personal supervision and education of young children, complete physical restriction to domestic space, absence of sexual desire, withdrawal from productive labor"; everything else was "unnatural" motherhood and was "coldhearted, cruel, avaricious, cowardly, fraudulent, and lascivious."[16]

This revised notion of maternal identity coincides with the restriction of women's participation in England's growing capitalist economy. By century's end, appropriate maternal identity was about producing heirs—for specific families, for the army, for the empire, and so on. Women could generate wealth, but only by producing Englishmen. In rejecting the possibility of independent existence for mothers, eighteenth-century thought excluded women from one of the primary principles of the new commercial society: that the individual is a subject with intrinsic value and has the right to look out for his own best interests.[17]

Efforts to constrain women's ability to participate in the economic and social expansions included specific attempts to limit the powers attached to widowhood, including expectations of what constituted acceptable widowed behavior. Historical evidence certainly suggests a disconnect between the realities of widowhood and the gender expectations that were developing in response to economic change: there are many examples in the archives of widows who worked their way to a more secure life through commercial enterprise. Mrs. Gaddener of London inherited a tavern from her husband and with it, a crushing debt. When the creditors agreed to give her time to operate the business and pay off the debts, she managed to make the business sound. There are similar stories outside London. Rachel Welby of Sussex managed to escape dependence by opening and running a boardinghouse. In Somerset, Elizabeth Phelips restored the family estates and raised the family's income; Frances Hamilton of Wells was a brilliant farmer and businesswoman; and Ursula Venner deftly managed her father's and her brother's affairs in addition to her own.[18] And of course widows, like anyone else, could write, as the explosion of female-authored literature during this period attests. Between Mary Davys at the beginning of the century and Elizabeth Inchbald at the end, there were many women who made their way by the pen.

The realities of widowhood also conflicted with developing definitions of female sexuality and maternity and intensified the sense of widowhood as a transgressive state. The old discomfort about the connection between female sexual experience and appetite lingered, as did concerns about the connection between sexual and material rapacity. These concerns were now exacerbated by the idealization of woman as the passive enabler of capitalism—the consumer and homebody rather than the producer. The business-minded widow was problematic, defying as she did the construction of woman as recipient of the fruits of empire, and a plethora of measures were adopted to restrict widows' rights and opportunities. The legal right of widows to inherit and to control their inheritance was gradually but inexorably eroded until 1833, when the Dower Act effectively eliminated dower, a widow's automatic entitlement to one-third of her husband's estate. Legislators argued that jointure—in effect, an annuity—was more secure than one large inheritance upon the husband's death, but in practice, widows (like other heirs) did not always receive the full amount of their jointures. Overall, the substitution of jointure for dower appears to have been more about limiting women's inheritance than about providing for their security.[19] As a result of such efforts, the business-minded and maternal widow became such a contradiction of conventions that she could only be an aberration.

Attempts to control women's economic behavior appear in novels published throughout the century. Liz Bellamy, Gillian Skinner, and April London have shown that the genre proved particularly useful for exploring views about gender and property, since novels evoke whole value systems, which came into play in redefining female virtue and economy during this period.[20] Arguably the most pervasive of eighteenth-century popular ideologies was sensibility. Most simply defined, sensibility is the idea that society is held together by bonds of sympathy, "fellow feeling" for other people that promotes benevolence and generally moral behavior.[21] Emotion is highly valued, and in sensibility's more extreme and corrupt manifestations at the end of the century, people put a lot of energy into proving their worth by finding any excuse to dampen their handkerchiefs. Originally, however, as articulated by David Hume and the Earl of Shaftesbury in the 1740s and 1750s and by Edmund Burke and Adam Smith in the 1750s and 1760s, sensibility was a moral system designed to create connections among humans tempted by the allure of self-interest in an unregulated commercial system. To succumb to this temptation would be to degenerate into what Hobbes in the seventeenth century might have considered a state of "Warre," where all people are fighting for what they can get for themselves.

The novel proved a particularly effective medium for expounding sensibility, both by modeling it in fictional characters and by generating feelings of sympathy in its readers. Works such as *Robinson Crusoe* and *Caleb Williams* demonstrate that sensibility was not novelists' only response to economic questions. Nevertheless, sensibility's influence on the eighteenth century was profound, since for so much of the century it provided people with a framework for understanding themselves, the people around them, and behavior both real and ideal. Richardson's novels of the 1740s, which were published at the same time as Hume's seminal essays, are often credited as the first manifestations of sentimental thought in narrative, and fifty years later, novels still were exploring human relationships and changes in society from a sentimental perspective. How characters dispose of their money, for example, defines correct sentimental behavior at the same time that it defines class differences and financial values. The novel's representation of the widow therefore is significant in light of its ability to participate in the social and economic debates of the day and generally, the eighteenth-century novel participated by encouraging women to avoid using the power inherent in widowhood, and with it active, commercial activity. Specifically, the novel's virtuous widows tend to eschew profit-oriented commercialism or employ commercial activity for altruism or dependence.

In light of the novel's reputation for defying strict definition and for exploring complex and often thorny issues, such consistency seems unlikely. Furthermore, scholars have maintained for some time that male and female authors drew on different experiences and concerns to compose their novels. Such a conservative attitude also seems odd in women novelists who were taking advantage of the opportunities generated by a commercial economy. Remarkably however, despite appearing at very different historical moments and despite their authors' very different personal philosophies, Daniel Defoe's *Moll Flanders* (1722), Henry Fielding's *Tom Jones* (1749), Frances Burney's *Evelina* (1778), and Clara Reeve's *School for Widows* (1791), for example, all use widows to model virtuous female behavior in opposition to selfish, or at least self-interested commercial activity. Some of the novels examined in this study endorse the commercial economy and some do not, but they all try to make sense of the staggering social and economic changes taking place, including the changing roles of men and women within the new order.

As a result, readers will find side by side in this study discussions of works with different takes on the economy. Where authors' individual attitudes or experiences affect their novels and their characters, the discussion will consider them. Those experiences are often less important, however, than the shared experience of social and economic change. Similarly, male- and female-authored works are discussed together. The experience of this transition from agriculture to commerce, from basic social stability to social movement, and so on, was not limited to men or to women. Certainly, where distinctions between how men and women handled the material are noteworthy, they are remarked upon. For all these reasons, this study takes a broadly inclusive approach to texts and authors.

It also seems paradoxical that a period in which the nation was transformed by a population boom, technological inventions, political upheavals, and conceptual revolutions produced such a consistent set of attitudes in the novel toward the widow. The answer to this paradox lies in the perspective used to resolve it. Certain characteristics such as lasciviousness or bad mothering carried over from earlier literature, such as Restoration drama, because the stereotypes and their associations remained useful regardless of whatever economic or social changes were taking place. Once such characteristics were adopted by sensibility, it would require the rejection of sensibility to dislodge them from the literary vocabulary. Since sensibility influenced the emerging novel for at least sixty of the one hundred years between 1700 and 1800, it is not surprising that its traits or devices would appear in so much of the literature of the eighteenth century.

At the same time, however, this generalization about virtuous widows includes very real nuances that reflect developments over the course of the century. Novelists introduced an important innovation by using widows of all classes to explore the intersection of gender, economics, and society. There are few working widows, poor widows, or criminal widows in English literature before the eighteenth century, but the early novel certainly provides examples from these unprivileged populations. Each group of widows may have shared certain characteristics—asexuality as a sign of virtue regardless of wealth and occupation, for example—but their function in expressing anxieties or proposing solutions to social dilemmas differed. The novel's poor widows, discussed in chapter 4, served to reaffirm the social hierarchy very differently than the novel's affluent widows, the subject of chapter 2. The anxiety produced by a working widow, examined in chapter 3, is related but not identical to the definition of a criminal widow, outlined in chapter 5.

A similar tension between the broad temporal approach and a more nuanced understanding of developments over the course of the century appears in this study's handling of chronology. In many ways, the issue in the representation of widows has less to do with specific moments in the eighteenth century than with the ongoing social and economic conversion taking place. As Brown demonstrates in *Fables of Modernity*, it is possible to trace representations of a cultural consciousness or "cultural fables" without regard to the "various movements, forms, genres, and modes of eighteenth-century English print culture." Cultural fables, which are marked by recurring images and figures that address the "most vital, problematic, or prominent aspects of contemporary experience," engage with the issues and anxieties provoked by emerging modernity such as the effect of mercantile capitalism on gender and society.[22] They are about and arise from the experience of becoming a modern society, and therefore transcend the particulars of a historical event just as the emergence of modernity transcends any given moment or event. The representation of the widow in the eighteenth-century novel is also part of what Brown calls the experience of modernity, and as a result, while particular novels or characters may be tied to a specific event or year, overall the widow is used to express ideas that concern anyone experiencing the century's changes.

That is not to ignore the role of specific moments such as the French Revolution or the South Sea Bubble in the shaping of economic attitudes and their appearance in the novel, however. Where it is appropriate to register the influence of a particular event, I do so. Furthermore, sensibility's influence changed over time and its forces, such as the novel, reflect that. A look at the novel's widows shows how sensibility developed over the century as the economic system changed and took hold both practically and in the popular imagination and ethos. Widows show these changes in sensibility and confirm that its economic elements are as important as, if not inseparable from, its moral elements. As part of these changes, the figure of the widow suggests that sensibility's influence changed between 1740 and 1790, rising to a cultural and novelistic peak by the 1770s.[23] While it would be tempting to organize this study by time rather than by economic situation, to do so would shift the focus to the development of sensibility and away from the function of the widow as a response to economic developments. Since each group of widows articulates a different response to economic and social change, this study is organized around those groups.

The treatment of the widow in narrative fiction reveals much about how the novel took its place among the powerful discourses of English culture. It also says much about anxieties relating to the position of women within the society. Writers had long used widows to express ideas about gender, autonomy, and economics. The widow appears in the novel as the ambivalent figure she had always been, but now as a lightning rod for the immediate fears and hopes generated by an emerging commercial economy. We can see in the eighteenth-century widow questions about women, solvency, and power that are not far from our own. The novelistic widow offers invaluable insight into the eighteenth-century literary and economic world, important aspects of which we have inherited and are living with today.

2

Fear and Property:
Affluence and the Widow

> Madam Clement clasped her in her arms, and kissing her with
> all the eagerness of maternal affection, 'Yes, (cried she) fair crea-
> ture, heaven hath bestowed upon me an heart to compassionate,
> and power, I hope, to lighten the burthen of your sorrows.'
> —Tobias Smollett, *The Adventures of Ferdinand Count Fathom*

IN "THE REVOLUTION IN LOW LIFE" (1762), OLIVER GOLDSMITH
took aim at the distribution of wealth in Great Britain. Drawing first
the picture of a village destroyed by a "Merchant of immense fortune
in London" who was converting it into a "seat of pleasure for himself," Goldsmith concluded, "Let others felicitate their country upon
the increase of foreign commerce and the extension of our foreign
conquests; for my part, this new introduction of wealth gives me but
very little satisfaction." Goldsmith famously reiterated these complaints against mercantile capitalism in his 1770 poem, "A Deserted
Village," in which he lamented "a bold peasantry, their country's
pride" disbanded by the avarice and selfishness of the "man of
wealth and pride," who with "trade's unfeeling train / Usurp[s] the
land and dispossess[es] the swain."[1]

Authors like Goldsmith responded to the tremendous growth of
mercantile capitalism during the eighteenth century in novels as
well, and not always positively. The novel's representation of affluent
widows, by which I mean women who did not have to work and who
could afford to keep at least one servant, reinforced emerging notions of femininity. Novels promoted a model of virtuous, affluent
widowhood as maternal, benevolent, and community oriented. Such

widows are interested in gain for the family and for the community, but not for themselves. The novel's virtuous widows may engage in commercial activity, but only under certain conditions very unlike those under which men could act. Later in the century in particular, when mercantile capitalism had a much stronger hold on society, the novel's virtuous affluent widows could pursue business provided they eschewed attitudes associated with trade, such as willingness to speculate, self-interest and self-promotion, and aggressiveness. As Maaja A. Stewart puts it, "When the concentration of rights, privileges, and property depends on the exclusion of women, any woman in fiction who inherits property does so at her peril."[2] In this way narrative's virtuous affluent widows may exemplify either a rejection of capitalism as a system, or of women's participation in it.

The management of whatever she inherited was, not surprisingly, a defining aspect of a widow's virtue, both historically and novelistically. A primary characteristic of virtuous affluent widows is the use of resources for others rather than for themselves. This included trying to improve the estate that she inherited, since that would be considered self-interested and commercial. As Gillian Skinner explains, when women owned property, "it was assumed that their interest in it would be purely as a means of support. They were not expected to manage it in such a way as to increase revenues or expand their influence; on the contrary, they were assumed to lack the ability to do so, for such an ability would be out of keeping with contemporary ideals of femininity, particularly as the sentimental ideology developing from mid-century figured women as creatures of emotion rather than reason." Another aspect of these expectations is the use of her inherited resources to do good for others. Although "benevolence" is usually read as a watchword of sensibility, which became culturally dominant after midcentury, the idea that virtuous widows are generous predates and antedates sentiment. Tobias Smollett's Madam Clement in *The Adventures of Ferdinand Count Fathom* (1753), for example, is a "merchant's widow in opulent circumstances" who, as the epigraph explains, uses her considerable wealth to help the romantic heroine, Serafina. Smollett labels her motives both "true benevolence" and "maternal affection," and Serafina calls Madam Clement "mother" long before her widowed father proposes to the widow.[3] Madam Clement's benevolent and maternal impulses promote the repair of several significant relationships and communities: the marriage of the hero

and heroine, the reunion of the heroine with her father, and the social and moral redemption of the father after his initial sins against
family and society. Her care for others makes the restoration of family and community, and therefore much of the happy ending, possible.

Similarly, Clara Reeve's *School for Widows* (1791) features Mrs.
Strictland, who uses her considerable, estate-based resources to nurture others and to establish relationships and communities. The
novel opens with Mrs. Strictland's determined effort to reforge emotional connections with her old friend Mrs. Darnford. Throughout
the narrative, Mrs. Strictland looks after men and women, giving
good advice, money, and shelter to anyone who needs it. Eventually,
although she has her own children to raise, she adopts the grandson
of a ruined tradesman, Mr. Balderson.[4] She installs the old man in
one of the cottages she has built for poor tenants, who include a pair
of sisters, one of them widowed (2:92, 2:96–97). The cottages themselves are an important indicator not just of the nurturing, but of the
constancy of the nurturing performed by benevolent widows. When
a virtuous merchant wishes to buy the cottages from Mrs. Strictland,
she refuses to sell them: "They are consecrated to the service of the
deserving and the unfortunate—they shall never be alienated from
this purpose—I will secure them to it," she declares (2:268). Although this merchant is a good man, Reeve avoids even the hint that
Mrs. Strictland herself might benefit monetarily from her cottages
by keeping those cottages in the widow's possession, and for benevolent motives. The novel's epistolary structure also emphasizes the
formation, restoration, and continuation of supportive communities, since epistolary novels require the interaction of letter writing
among otherwise isolated individuals. The story itself becomes a collective effort, instigated by Mrs. Strictland.

This sharing of a character and her function across time and between authors indicates the widow's usefulness to authors concerned
about values and behavior in the emerging system, and about
women participating in it. Smollett and Reeve are dissimilar in significant ways, most obviously by gender. Their novels were separated
by forty years, and therefore manifest different engagements with
and different concepts of sensibility. Smollett's early work is at best
incompletely sentimental, employing aspects of a more rational sensibility than later novelists would use. Like Smollett's, Reeve's sensibility is pragmatic and moral, but it also reacts to the profoundly

emotional brand of sensibility that developed in the intervening years. Reeve and Smollett are both didactic social critics, however, and they shared concerns about the effect of mercantile capitalism on society: its promotion of the individual over the community and its encouragement of self-interest over thoughtful, conscientious participation in society. While they might handle women very differently in their work (Madam Clement is a much smaller presence in her novel, although her effect is great, than Mrs. Strictland is in hers, for example), their opinions on correct female behavior are in many ways significantly alike, as their treatment of widows and wealth indicate.[5] Both authors use women to demonstrate trade's threat to the traditional order and the ways that gender can be used to oppose this threat. This fundamental similarity in their views on economics and women despite other differences recurs in novelists throughout the century, from Tory Henry Fielding to radical Eliza Fenwick, suggesting that even radicalism reached a limit when it came to autonomous women and commercial activity.

Madam Clement and Mrs. Strictland also show how much of the virtuous affluent widow's community orientation in the eighteenth-century novel is disguised as benevolence to a particular person. This duality typifies the benevolence of wealthy widows: they help particular figures in their narratives, and in so doing, they also help the community at large, including the most marginal members of society. Wealthy widow Madame Du Maine's generosity to Cornelia in Sarah Scott's *The History of Cornelia* (1750) enables Cornelia to look after the poor as well as after several friends who are suffering at the hands of despotic relations. This behavior becomes even more significant in later novels, such as Frances Sheridan's *Memoirs of Miss Sidney Bidulph* (1769) and Sarah Scott's *Millenium Hall* (1762). When Sidney Bidulph takes Patty Main as a servant, she undertakes a lifetime of service to Patty's family, patronizing Patty's brother's shop and arranging a good marriage for him with the pretty, young, and modest Miss Price.[6] Miss Price and her father have been rescued from poverty and prison and restored to health by Sidney already, so Sidney might be said to have created the society in which the relationships and a microeconomy of trade, education, and marriage take place. This little society appears to mirror the larger commercial society, but with one significant distinction: it all falls under the benevolent supervision of Sidney herself. In that sense, the circulation of wealth in novels like *The History of Cornelia* or *Memoirs of Miss*

Sidney Bidulph remains paternalistic and hierarchical, rather than commercial and volatile.

Sarah Scott's *Millenium Hall* focuses on this idea, expanding the role filled by Madame Du Maine in her earlier novel to make the widow and her benevolence central to the narrative. Mrs. Morgan, a widow, and the other ladies of the hall create a refuge for "poor creatures who are rendered miserable from some natural deficiency or redundancy" and establish a mutually respectful relationship between themselves and the physically-challenged people behind the hedge.[7] They found schools for girls and boys and initiate a system of patronage, where employers from the area consult the ladies of the Hall when seeking apprentices and servants (150–51). They also encourage marriage among the peasants and "lower rank of people," providing couples with the wedding service and looking after young brides until the newlyweds are comfortable running their own establishment and maintaining their own marriages (115, 119–20). As Ruth Perry observes, *Millenium Hall* is an economy designed to promote "the sharing of resources" rather than "growth and expansion" and as such, "intervenes in both the labor market and the marriage market" to accomplish its ends and pursue its ideals.[8]

The exercise of benevolence is not simply charity in action, however; it is also the reinforcement or restoration of class divisions. This aspect of sensibility is particularly clear in Scott's works, which overtly propound sensibility as an outwardly oriented benevolent force and are full of widows. Only after Madame Du Maine learns that Cornelia is wellborn does she give Cornelia a "present of bonds, amounting to the value of five thousand pounds, offering to receive the interest and remit it to her" (Scott, *Cornelia*, 101). In several side narratives to *Millenium Hall*, wealthy widows such as Lady Lambton, Mrs. Thornby, Mrs. Alworth, Lady Sheerness and Lady Brumpton rescue impoverished and orphaned young women, returning them to the class and frequently, the family from which they were exiled by loss. Lady Mary Jones, for example, is rescued by two widowed aunts, one after the other, each one arriving in the nick of time to save Lady Mary from destitution or worse, service (Scott, *Millenium Hall*, 126, 142). In the main narrative, the ladies of Millenium Hall itself, including these formerly rescued female relatives, reinstate those who have been displaced by poverty, such as a clergyman's widow (149). Millenium Hall's servants, from laborers to musicians, are all "under some natural disadvantage": the housekeeper cannot use one hand, "the cook cannot walk without crutches, the kitchen maid has but one eye, the dairy maid is almost stone deaf, and the housemaid has but one hand." Why these people? Because "gratitude, and a conviction that this is the only house into which we can be received, makes us exert ourselves to the utmost" in serving the ladies of the Hall, as the housekeeper attests (120–21). By employing the disfigured, the women can be sure that their servants are always motivated by gratitude and a sense of inferiority. Regardless of whether such women are interacting with family, friends, servants, or utter strangers, eighteenth-century novels' virtuous rich widows disperse or maintain resources, not accumulate, in the preservation of class and a stable social hierarchy.

Widows who use their position for personal rather than benevolent purposes are treated more critically by eighteenth-century novels. These widows are often charged with crimes such as the use of money and influence for selfish ends, the exploitation of other human beings, and conspicuous consumption—that is, a love of luxury. Scott's Lady Sheerness spends her fortune on entertainment, leaving her dependent niece penniless, and Lady Brumpton's vanity "led her into expenses, which though they did not considerably impair her fortune, yet so far straitened it that she frequently had not power to indulge the generosity of her mind where it would have done her honour and have yielded her solid satisfaction" (Scott, *Millenium Hall*, 142, 146). Deplorable widows may also use emerging economic practices. Reeve's Mrs. Batson keeps up the appearance of comfort, which she can well afford, for example, but she insists in reality upon a miserly existence for herself and her servants. She is

> as covetous as old Elwes. She loves nobody but herself: yet she loves good living, but will not let others have their share. She has sometimes a chicken, or a bit of fish; a single sole, or a flat fish of any kind; or half a pound of salmon, or any thing that is nice. . . . She keeps three maid-servants, and two men; but the coachman is at board-wages, and lives with his family. She buys a quarter of mutton every week, and has it cut into pieces as it is wanted; so they live upon mutton and mutton through the year. She has a large sideboard of old-fashioned plate, which is set out every day, as if for a feast; but it serves only to put you in mind of good dinners, and create an appetite without gratifying it. (*School for Widows*, 1:224–25)

Her sin is not fiscal responsibility, but a refusal to use her financial resources to maintain a dignified household. Her servants are unnecessarily ill-fed and ungraciously treated because Mrs. Batson prefers to hold on to what she has rather than use it to care for her dependents. In other words, Mrs. Batson prefers to hoard her resources like a businessman, rather than distribute them like a landowner.

Novelists expressed anxiety about a less tangible part of a widow's estate as well: her experience. The eighteenth-century novel struggled with the role of experience in older widows, particularly when it was combined with sufficient wealth and leisure to gratify the desires that experience could generate. Arlene Fish Wilner points out that for the eighteenth century, "Experience, because it can expose her to risk, sully her reputation, and foster inappropriate ambitions is inadvisable for a female." Such a resource can render widows dangerous to others. As early as 1733, the anonymous *The Finish'd Rake* featured a London widow whose experience as a licentious, unfaithful wife warps her judgment when it comes to caring for her ward. The aunt, "having been marry'd in the Prime of her Years, for Interest, to a Man of threescore, had been easily tempted to be false to his bed"; as a result, "being conscious therefore of her own Frailty, and not willing her Niece, for whom she had a great Love, should be guilty of the like, she kept a very watchful Eye over her Conduct" with the opposite effect, inciting both Rake and niece to misbehave.[9] The aunt does not see beyond her own experience to distinguish her niece's life from her own; everything is really about the aunt and her past. This inability creates the Rake's opportunity to victimize the innocent female.

In later novels, this problem of experience's effect on judgment is compounded, heightening not just the tragic impact but also the sense in which life experience in a widow, because it is inevitably tainted by sexual experience, is corrosive. Sheridan's *Memoirs of Miss Sidney Bidulph* and Matthew Lewis's *The Monk* (1796) exemplify the way later novels show experience's damaging effects on the innocents in the widows' care. Like the Aunt in *The Finish'd Rake*, Lady Bidulph in *Sidney Bidulph* and Elvira in *The Monk* have been so affected by a sexual past that they cannot use good judgment to preserve the well-being of their daughters. Sheridan turns the mental workings of her widows, Lady Bidulph and eventually Sidney, into the mechanisms of tragedy. Lady Bidulph's mismanagement of events, a mismanagement, as Margaret Anne Doody points out, based on Lady Bidulph's own history with a man, destroys her daughter's chances for married happiness with the right man, Orlando Faulkland. As Doody explains, "Lady Bidulph's story is no mere interpolated episode. Her experience and her reaction to it, that action so long antecedent to the time of the novel's story, really form the major action of the story. From this event all else springs."[10] Lady Bidulph was left at the altar in favor of another: her fiancé, originally betrothed to a different woman, abandoned that first woman for Lady Bidulph. Overcome with guilt for deceiving the first young woman but unable to accept unhappiness with her, he cannot allow himself happiness with the second young woman he deceives either, and this dilemma eventually drives him mad. Lady Bidulph, in turn, marries her merely adequate late husband.

Lady Bidulph's experience is central to the book, even if the story is named after her daughter, because Lady Bidulph's interpretation of the world shapes the significant events and decisions of the protagonist's life. This fact would not be shocking on its own, but the central experience that shapes Lady Bidulph's interpretation is of men. Experience has taught her that men are not to be trusted, so she repeatedly rejects opportunities to learn the full story and thereby repeatedly blocks her daughter's chances for a happy marriage. Her son, Sir George, tries to explain the accusations against Faulkland, but Lady Bidulph replies, "I told him there was a terrible fact alleged, of which I could not conceive it possible for him to acquit himself," assuming that to be accused is to be guilty (39). When Faulkland comes to explain his side of the situation, Lady Bidulph relives her past and sees only a "plausible man" possessed of "looks, full of pretended sorrow, but *real* guilt" and an "artful story" he had "prepared" with her own son's help "to impose on" her (41; Sheridan's emphasis). With the belief that all men are seducers and that Faulkland's situation must repeat the injustice she encountered years before, Lady Bidulph pushes Sidney to give up Faulkland and to marry Mr. Arnold. Lady Bidulph even employs the noxious influence of other experienced widows, Lady Grimston and Lady Grimston's widowed daughter, Mrs. Vere, to enforce her interpretation of events and force her desired outcome. As Sidney herself writes after her mother dies, "I know that the memory of my mother's own first disastrous love wrought strongly on her mind," and although she adds, "I entirely acquit my dear mother, in regard to her whole conduct," she concludes, "However I have suffered by it" (317).

Sidney's sufferings extend beyond the death of her mother because Lady Bidulph has taught Sidney to see the world as Lady Bidulph saw it, to make the same decisions based on the same moral code. Ultimately, Sidney has internalized her mother's self-centered view of the world so well that she gives over all chance of happiness with her real love, Faulkland, to promote his marriage to Miss Burchell, whom he has allegedly seduced, and whose dubious characteristics Sidney and her mother determinedly overlook. From Lady Bidulph's insistence on a morality and ethics that legitimates and derives from her experience with men, a key to any widow's status, rises the tragedy of the novel and the destruction of its hero and heroine, Faulkland and Sidney.

Doody's explanation of the dangers of memory and experience in *Sidney Bidulph* applies more broadly to the question of the eighteenth-century novel's older widows. All widows have some experience, considered a dangerous asset in a woman, and because widows used to be married, their experience is associated automatically with sex. Traditionally, the idea of an unmarried, sexually experienced woman like the widow was sufficiently threatening to be represented in marginalizing terms, from the comic to the monstrous. Not all novelistic widows manifest corrupted judgment, but when novelists deliberately explore the role of experience in shaping their judgment as mothers, their affluent widows tend to judge badly. *Sidney Bidulph*'s widowed Mrs. Vere also has learned to see the world in terms of what it means to her. For her own benefit, she capitulates to older, richer widows and promotes marriage for convenience, pressuring Sidney into doing what is useful to the other widows rather than good for herself. Even Sidney, widowed twice if one counts the accidentally bigamous marriage to Faulkland at the end of the novel, spends her energy preparing "their young minds against the vicissitudes of fortune" by teaching her daughters how to live based on the model of her own experience (430). As the narrator points out, however, this preparation is wholly inadequate for what lies ahead.

Matthew Lewis's Elvira, Antonia's mother, is another example of a well-meaning widow whose sexual past has derailed her good judgment.[11] Like Lady Bidulph, she only wants the best for her daughter, but because of her past with men, she can only act to ensure the worst. Elvira, perhaps because she is neither sentimental nor female-authored, is more ambivalent a figure than Lady Bidulph, however.

Unlike Lady Bidulph, she does get to marry her first choice in suitors, the son of the Marquis de las Cisternas. Unfortunately, the wrath
of his father at the young man's marrying a shoemaker's daughter
drives Elvira and her husband to abandon their son and flee to
Cuba. While Elvira acts to remain with her husband, she also acts to
leave her son in the clutches of his hostile grandfather. This unmaternal behavior reaps its reward: the son later kills his mother and
rapes his sister, although unaware of their relation at the time. Elvira's effect on her husband has not been salutary, either. Instead of
thriving in married life, he suffers in exile, sinking into a depression
exacerbated by the deaths of almost all of his children and eventually succumbing to disease and self-pity.

From her own life Elvira concludes that beautiful poor girls can
marry handsome rich men, but they will not achieve complete happiness without the blessing of the rich man's family. She also concludes that knowledge of the world is both helpful and emotionally
painful. As a result, Elvira's behavior is highly equivocal. She is ambitious and maternal enough to hope Antonia and Lorenzo do marry,
but she vacillates between promoting and curtailing this possibility.
She manipulates her daughter to confess her affections, then uses
this confession to warn Antonia away from Lorenzo: "I perceive easily that your affection is returned," Elvira tells her, but "Even should
Himself mean honourably, his Uncle never will consent to your
union; Nor without that Uncle's consent, will I. By sad experience I
know what sorrows She must endure, who marries into a family un-
willing to receive her" (204–5). Simultaneously, Elvira discourages
her daughter and encourages Lorenzo. Elvira "was perfectly satisfied
with the conversation, which had past between [Lorenzo and her-
self]. She looked forward with satisfaction to the prospect of his becoming her Son-in-law; But Prudence bad her conceal from her
Daughter's knowledge, the flattering hopes which Herself now ven-
tured to entertain" (219). By judging the situation entirely through
her own experience and without consulting the differences in character or situation in the younger generation, Elvira ultimately ensures Antonia's unprotected state. After all, Antonia is the daughter
of the late Condé de las Cisternas, not a shoemaker of Cordova, and
therefore occupies, or is entitled to occupy, a very different social
niche. At the time of Elvira's death, Antonia and Lorenzo are unmarried, he does not feel the obligation of an engaged man, and Antonia does not feel entitled to call on him for help.

Furthermore, as in *Sidney Bidulph*, it is not just situation but perspective that the experienced widowed mother inflicts on her
daughter. Elvira's knowledge of human nature pains her so, like the
aunt in *The Finish'd Rake*, she takes pains to keep Antonia innocent.
The highly censored edition of the Bible that Elvira gives her, for example, means she has very little idea of how men and women interact, or what they might do and why (259–60). As a result, Antonia's
ignorance of human behavior, so carefully cultivated by her mother
despite her failing health and Antonia's "Friendless and unprotected" state, leaves the young girl exceedingly vulnerable to Ambrosio's advances (310). Admittedly, worldly wisdom could not have
saved Antonia from the sorcery Ambrosio uses to kidnap her or
from the physical strength her uses to rape her, but Ambrosio is a
bully and afraid of women who understand the world and therefore
understand him. When Elvira tells Ambrosio that she will not need
him any more after she discovers him molesting her daughter, he
prepares to protest but "an expressive look from Elvira stopped him
short" (264). Knowledge, which Elvira and Matilda both have and
which puts off Ambrosio, would have to have protected Antonia better than the ignorance her mother encourages.

The paradox for these widows is that they mean to be benevolent
but can only act to the detriment of the young women in their care.
Neither woman distinguishes between knowledge and experience,
although the two are not necessarily the same or involve the same
type or degree of emotional anguish. Such widows' insistence on
viewing the world through marital and therefore sexual experience,
and their inability to distinguish between knowledge and experience, also suggests a profound, however accidental, selfishness. They
appear to be thinking of their daughters, but really they are only
thinking of themselves.

This threat of widows' experience to sentimental heroines also
can be understood as a larger threat to the family. Self-centeredness
in the widow exacted a toll on the members of her family, and even
on the idea of the family. According to Toni Bowers, mothers could
commit two "crimes" in the eighteenth century: being overindul-
gent and therefore enervating, and being neglectful.[12] The key to
this formula is the idea that mothers should love neither too much
(overindulgence) nor too little (neglect); by extension, they should
love all their children, and equally. Such an understanding of motherhood does not treat the mother-child relationship as reciprocal.

Maternal attitude and behavior alone determine the relationship between the two, which is why the regulation of selfishness in the mother is crucial. In Charlotte Smith's *The Old Manor House* (1793), Mrs. Somerive's older son, Philip, ruins the family, drives his father to heartbreak and death, and compels his mother to move to London, which she hates, when he sells the family estate out from under her. Mrs. Somerive faces a significant maternal dilemma: to be angry at Philip is to prefer herself and her other children over him, but not to be angry at Philip is to disregard his effect on his younger siblings and the family as an institution. Smith carefully and repeatedly balances Mrs. Somerive between these emotions and positions. "But still that half-broken heart had all the tenderness of a mother within it for this her eldest child," the narrator reports, and later explains that Orlando, her good son, "dared not yet ask her to receive and forgive a son, who, though she still loved him, had given her so much cause of complaint—as well since, as before his father's death."[13] When Philip at last dies of dissipation, although "He had too plainly evinced, that to his own selfish gratifications he would always sacrifice the welfare, and even the subsistence of his family; yet, in his repentance on the bed of pain and languor, his mother forgot and forgave all she had suffered from him; and when he died, she wept for him as the child of her early affection, whose birth and infancy had once formed her greatest felicity" (506).

A similar dilemma faces Matilda, Countess of Athlin in Radcliffe's *The Castles of Athlin and Dunbayne* (1789). In order to save the life of her son, she must marry her daughter to the man who would murder him and who had murdered her husband, no simple decision: "Honour, humanity, parental tenderness, bade her save her son: yet by a strange contrariety of interests, the same virtues pleaded with a voice equally powerful, for the reverse of the sentence." Crucially, it is the pain of "choice, though forced upon her by the power of a tyrant," that "harrowed up her soul almost to frenzy."[14] Fortunately for Matilda, she commands an army and a loyal and able general, so military reprisal and rescue turn out to be a third viable option. The virtuous mother is not allowed to act against any child, even when one threatens the family. Elvira's abandonment of her toddler for her husband is therefore morally, or at least maternally criminal, since she is not even choosing between children, but rejecting the only one she has.

It is not simply the departure of the mother, but the manner in which she departs that is the difference between acceptable and unacceptable behavior for eighteenth-century novelists. Wives owed loyalty and service to their children and to their husbands, after all, and finding a solution when these obligations conflict is a sign of the virtuous woman. Like Lewis's Elvira, Mrs. Thornby, Louisa Mancel's mother in *Millenium Hall*, leaves her infant to accompany her husband to the colonies. Unlike Elvira, she arranges for her daughter's care with a loving and reliable relative, and spends the next twenty years worrying about the daughter to whom she cannot yet return. When they are reunited accidentally, Louisa's mother "exclaimed, My child! my child! and sinking on her knees, with eyes and hands lifted up towards heaven, poured forth a most ardent thanksgiving, with an ecstacy of mind not to be described. Her first sensation was that of gratitude to the Almighty Power, who had reserved so great a blessing for her; maternal tenderness alone gave rise to the succeeding emotions of her heart; she threw her arms round Louisa" in proper and approved motherly fashion (Scott, *Millenium Hall*, 100, 99). Louisa, Baroness Malcolm from *The Castles of Athlin and Dunbayne* also leaves her children at home to accompany her husband, placing them in the faithful and capable care of a nurse, rather than in the unprepared and vengeful hands of an enraged father-in-law. She does not choose between them, nor does she choose the welfare of her married life and her husband instead of the welfare of her children (Radcliffe, *Castles*, 148). To consider carefully who deserves love or forgiveness is to ration maternal resources, which is unacceptable in virtuous mothers, especially for those who also can ration money or other forms of wealth.

The manipulation of resources, whether they be children or qualities such as love and forgiveness, raises the specter of commercial activity and self-interest. Were Mrs. Somerive to see her son Philip only as a provider for his family, she would be viewing him only as an economic resource. She must appreciate him as her firstborn at least as much as she appreciates him as an asset or liability in order to escape opprobrium. When widows manipulate resources such as their family for their own benefit or gratification, they become guilty of neglect, favoritism, or both. Madame De La Roche in *The History of Cornelia* uses education, money, and affection to manipulate her family for her own satisfaction. She favors Henrietta, her daughter by her first marriage, and in so doing, creates a selfish, stupid brute.

She also slights Lucinda, her daughter by her second marriage; Bernardo, her second husband's son; and Cornelia, a foster child who comes to stay with her. So determined to have her own way is Madame De La Roche that she forces Lucinda into a convent, throws the friendless Cornelia out of the house, and cuts off Bernardo's allowance, finally bringing false charges against Cornelia and Bernardo and sending them to prison. Her schemes ultimately shatter the family unit. Bernardo, Lucinda, and Cornelia all abandon her while her favorite, Henrietta, remains at home, depressed, unmarried, and self-centered.

While overindulgence usually appears as irrational behavior in widowed mothers, it sometimes derives from corrupt logic. In William Godwin's *Caleb Williams* (1794), Mrs. Tyrrel spoils her son out of an inordinate pride in the Tyrrel family. "Mrs Tyrrel appeared to think that there was nothing in the world so precious as her hopeful Barnabas," Caleb reports. "Every thing must give way to his accommodation and advantage; every one must yield the most servile obedience to his commands. He must not be teased or restricted by any forms of instruction; and of consequence his proficiency, even in the arts of writing and reading, was extremely slender."[15] Mrs. Tyrrel is herself a very minor figure, but the result of her behavior is anything but: because of his upbringing, her son has mastered only a reptilian logic that causes him indirectly to murder virtuous Emily Melville, and eventually catalyzes his own death and the end of the Tyrrels. Unlike Scott and her indulgent Madame De La Roche, Godwin uses Mrs. Tyrrel as part of an indictment of the aristocracy and the social hierarchy. That he uses the same tool for his commentary—the inadequate widowed mother—is significant, however. Even for Godwin, this figure proved a useful embodiment of corruption, a source of English society's problems.

Conversely, widows' selfishness can lead to the destruction of the family through neglect. Mary Davys' Lady Galliard from *The Accomplish'd Rake* (1727) is self-centered even before she becomes a widow, but afterward, when there is no check on her behavior, her selfishness becomes even more pernicious. She announces early on that "as I am resolved to be always Mistress of my own Actions, I shall never think myself obliged to account for them to any body." As part of her interest in her own activities, she refuses to look after her children. "And for Lady *Galliard*," the narrator reports, "she was too positive, too proud, and too careless, either to be perswaded by her

Friends, or to joyn in Concert with reason for the Good of her Child," in this case, Sir John, the protagonist.[16] Consequently, both son and daughter become ignorant, egotistic, and self-serving, and both narrowly escape destruction.

The problem posed by Davys' Lady Galliard and widows like her goes beyond the mere fact that they desire, and desire men who are not their husbands. Because they are wealthy, they have the power to do something about that lust, even when resisted, and with impunity. Davys' Lady Galliard is so consumed with passion for her footman that in addition to instigating an affair with him, she dismisses her entire staff in order to hire him back without scandal. She may even be his wife's murderer. Henry Fielding's Lady Booby in *Joseph Andrews* (1742) threatens both Parson Adams and lawyer Scout with her financial and social power in her pursuit of her footman, Joseph, and while Adams resists, Scout and the local magistrate capitulate rapidly.[17] Tradition has long associated the widow with lust. The category "widow" carried with it the fear that because widows know about sex, they are more lustful than never-married women or women whose knowledge is addressed by their husbands. The image of the unattached, lust-crazed widow becomes more fearsome as the widow becomes capable of satisfying her desire, a concern that in a market economy becomes overtly linked to economic, not just social means. Women like Lady Galliard and Lady Booby are lecherous and free to indulge it because they are widows; they are socially and economically able to do so because they are affluent; and they are wicked because they use that ability for those ends.

Here again it is worth commenting on the surprising similarity in the depiction and function of the wealthy widow in novels written by authors with considerably different sociopolitical outlooks. Like Smollett and Reeve, Scott, Godwin, Davys, and Henry Fielding were separated by time, gender, life experience (Davys was a poor, poorly educated, Irish widow, for example) and, more even than Smollett and Reeve, political ideology. Nevertheless, these authors all use the affluent widow to limit autonomous female behavior, particularly as it was related to economic behavior and commercial values. It is no surprise to find a Tory like Fielding presenting a cautionary tale of wealth gone amok in a particular way: Tories were traditionalists and they distrusted, at best, the emerging economy. Limiting female economic activity and therefore female social activity would appeal to people worried by the potential of the new economy. But reformers,

Whigs, and radicals like Scott, Davys, and Godwin? Although as chapter 1 and chapter 3 explain in more detail, there was plenty of precedent for women's economic activity in the past, it usually didn't allow the gratification of desire and the social instability, including instability in the gender hierarchy, as it did in emerging capitalism. Davys' personal desire to emphasize her respectability is simply one instance of an author's internalized social anxiety about limiting the commercial explosion, regardless of his or her view of other aspects of that explosion.[18] Even Godwin accepted the stereotype, however briefly.

Consistently then, although the new economy offered all sorts of opportunities, this freedom and the use of resources to satisfy desire meets its limits in the widow, particularly when old fears about the widow's freedom meet new fears generated by the freedom made possible by emerging mercantile capitalism. With the power to consummate their unleashed desires, wealthy widows can afford to reject marriage, the proper domestic institution for containing women. Who knows what an unmarried but sexually aware and experienced woman might do? Indulge her awakened baser nature, evidently. When Sir John Galliard discovers that his mother is sleeping with her footman, his tutor observes that all women's "Passions and Inclinations" once "let loose without a Curb, grow wild and untameable, [and] defy all Laws and Rules." To restore Lady Galliard's "Passions and Inclinations" to their appropriate bounds, he recommends that Sir John force his mother to dismiss the footman and "persuade her to marry" someone suitable (Davys, *Accomplish'd Rake*, 137). In Frances Burney's *Camilla* (1796), Mrs. Arlbery derives much of her enjoyment in life from gathering men around her and ordering them about. Even when an officer is looking after Camilla, who is Mrs. Arlbery's guest, "he was not, therefore, exempt from the assiduities required by Mrs. Arlbery, for whom the homage of the General, the Colonel, and the Ensign, were insufficient; and who, had a score more been present, would have found occupation for them all." Lady Palestine, an older and experienced widow in Sarah Fielding's *The History of Ophelia* (1760), becomes a courtesan after the death of her husband, exploiting her lovers to maintain a style of living to which she is accustomed. Henry Fielding's Lady Bellaston from *Tom Jones* (1749) is notorious in London for keeping young men. As Nightingale explains, "Don't be angry, Tom, but, upon my honour, you are not the first young fellow she hath debauched. Her reputation is in no danger, believe me" and the narrator adds that Lady Bellaston is "whom everyone knows to be what nobody calls her."[19] These are not women who pursue men to marry one of them, but quite the contrary. It is the variety and number of men, and the looseness of the bond that appeals to such women.

In fact, the definition of pleasure as an autonomous pursuit of "young fellows" requires the rejection of marriage. Nightingale tells Tom Jones of a "young fellow whom [Lady Bellaston] kept formerly, who made the offer to her in earnest, and was presently turned off for his pains," and while Tom observes that "she may be less shocked at this proposal from one man than from another" (678), her instant rejection of Tom's letter, including her fury that she "could, from its coldness and formality, have sworn that [he] had already the legal right [he] mention[s]," reveals that she would have to be, as she puts it, "out of [her] senses" to "deliver [her] whole fortune into [his] power, in order to enable [him] to support [his] pleasure at [her] expence" regardless of who proposes (679-80). It is the independence to support her own pleasures that Lady Bellaston desires. "I am not married, I promise you, my dear," she assures her cousin, Mrs. Western. "You know, Bel, I have try'd the comforts once already. And once I think is enough for any reasonable woman" (719). As Gary Gautier explains, in Henry Fielding's universe, marriage and family are "not optional and incidental to one's happiness, but essential to it" as well as to "Christian redemption," so Lady Bellaston's behavior is particularly appalling.[20] Her keeping young men for sexual gratification underscores the danger of ungrounded female sexuality, the freedom of a woman empowered by money, circumstance, and nature to pursue her desire.

Widows' sexuality, however, also posed something of a paradox for eighteenth-century novelists. While an unmarried, sexually aware woman was certainly worrisome, the prospect that such a woman would be all too eager to marry again was equally troubling. Lady Booby makes her first pass at Joseph a mere week after her husband's death (H. Fielding, *Joseph Andrews*, 24). What did it say about her uncontrollable desire that she sought another mate? And what did it say about men that their widows replaced them so easily? Davys' Lady Galliard dispenses with grief almost immediately:

Lady *Galliard* had too much resolution and Courage to struggle with Grief, but like an expert Fencer gave it one home Thrust and silenced it for ever, hardly allowing so much as the common Decorum of a Month's Confinement to a dark Room, though her wild Behaviour told the World she was but too well qualified for such an Apartment for ever. (*Accomplish'd Rake*, 129)

Late-century novels in particular indicate that the freedom attendant on widowhood could be more than ample recompense for the bereavement that accompanied it. One of Madame Duval's most unfeeling gestures in Frances Burney's *Evelina* (1778) is giving up her weeds after three months.[21] Similarly, Bernard the maid repeats the advice of the London-based widow Mrs. Vernon to Julia St. Laurence, the heroine of Mary Robinson's *The Widow* (1794). "Besides, you should leave off mourning," Bernard explains; "why, no body minds losing a husband now-a-days, and widows never wear weeds above three months." Later, vicious Mrs. Vernon will observe of Julia St. Lawrence that "her deep mourning heightened her beauty astonishingly," adding ominously, "*Weeds* are delightfully becoming; I lamented the hour I left them off, and hope that, one day or other, I shall have the felicity of wearing them *again*."[22]

Novelists, especially those writing after sensibility consolidated its hold on English culture, often encoded a widow's lust as a desire to remarry. Elizabeth Griffith's highly sentimental novel *The Delicate Distress* (1769) features the "duchess dowager of H———," who, "Though her age more than doubled his," marries an impecunious but handsome young man. Laurence Sterne's Widow Wadman from *Tristram Shandy* (1759–1767) more clearly exposes the way sex and marriage shaded into each other in representations of affluent widows.[23] Widow Wadman's behavior is entirely dictated by her "love" for uncle Toby, but of course in Sterne, the word "love" has an unstable set of meanings. She reveals that she is "in love" with Toby by refusing to have her nightgown pinned shut below her feet, a decision that certainly raises questions of emotional openness, but also of physical access.[24] Her "love" is repeatedly represented in military terms, and her efforts to flirt with him and generate love in return are called "attacks." Walter Shandy accuses her of wanting Toby only so long as she can't have him; once she has "gain'd her point," he announces, "her fever will be pass'd it's height" (492). And her famous concern with the nature and location of Toby's wound, made ridiculous with Toby's cartographic explanation, is hardly the tender solicitude that Toby interprets it. When she thinks that he is going to show her the place on his body where he was wounded,

Mrs. Wadman blush'd—look'd towards the door—turn'd pale—
blush'd slightly again—recovered her natural colour—blush'd worse
than ever; which for the sake of the unlearned reader, I translate
thus:

> "L——d! I cannot look at it—
> What would the world say if I look'd at it?
> I should drop down, if I look'd at it—
> I wish I could look at it—
> There can be no sin in looking at it.
> —I will look at it." (523)

Shocked she may be, but interested she is as well. Sterne resolves
Widow Wadman's curiosity with a bold acceptance of a sexual moment: she reasons herself into justifying her own desires—"There
can be no sin in looking at it" directly following "I wish I could look
at it"—suggesting that in the widow, sexuality can overwhelm reason
and faith. She has no first name, just the title "widow" or occasionally
"Mrs.," underscoring that for Sterne and his characters, Widow Wadman is representative as well as individual and derives from the old
stereotype about lecherous widows.

Nevertheless, that Widow Wadman finally seduces Toby with an
eye that says, in the "last low accents of an expiring saint—'How can
you live comfortless, captain Shandy, and alone, without a bosom to
lean your head on—or trust your cares to?'" (482), suggests that despite the pervasiveness of the sexual humor and sexuality associated
with Widow Wadman, there is at least some aspect of companionship
and consolation associated with her. And that it is this, not the physical proximity of gardens, fingers, or legs in the sentry box, that finally strikes Toby with love, suggests that while Widow Wadman does
draw on plenty of the old stereotypes about widows, she also possesses some of the new constructs of femininity and the domestic. As
long as her interest seems to include someone else—"captain
Shandy"—Widow Wadman passes muster. Furthermore, Widow
Wadman's ability to evoke but also to escape the stereotype of the
lecherous widow for more sentimental realms reinforces the notion
that for Sterne as for other sentimentalists like Goldsmith, mainstream sensibility's dichotomies between passion and reason or sensibility and sexuality do not accurately represent the full range of
human experience and human nature.[25]

Socially, money was the only acceptable reason for a widow to
seek remarriage, and then only if the widow had insufficient fi-

nances to maintain herself and, more importantly, her family. Remarriage for social or economic ambition was equally frowned upon. Where resources were sufficient, a widow was only respected as long as she "remained piously faithful to the dead." For the eighteenth century, sexual desire was a masculine trait, so remarriage was either a sign of idiocy, "gross sensuality," or both.[26] As the example of Widow Wadman suggests, novelists usually addressed this issue by depicting remarriage to gratify desire, of whatever kind, as anything from ridiculous to villainous. Scott's "widow marchioness" in *The History of Cornelia* is "very rich, young, and handsome: advantages she values highly; and which she turns, as much as possible, to her entertainment," and she is comically stunned when Bernardo rejects her (240). A woman like Madame De La Roche from the same novel, "haughty, passionate, and self-interested," is also "inclined naturally to covetousness." Combined with "her hypocrisy and cunning" and the "violence of her temper," these unattractive qualities enable her to extract such large portions from her husbands that the novel condemns her as the "richest widow in France" (103, 104). Out of passion for Ferdinand, an unnamed widow in Smollett's nearly contemporaneous *Ferdinand Count Fathom* says cruel things about her daughter and deliberately seizes Ferdinand's attentions from that young lady (257-58). Later in the novel, a young, well-to-do widow agrees to marry Ferdinand because he is handsome and she possesses "a very sanguine disposition, which her short trial of matrimony had not served to cool" (269). Unlike the first widow, she has no children to abuse in her pursuit of the man, however, and she lives, although not before being forced to resort to a very unpleasant lawsuit to extricate herself from her marriage to Ferdinand.

The condemnation intensifies as the century progresses. Eliza Fenwick, hardly a conservative on social or gender issues, has Mrs. Ashburn in *Secresy* (1795), a woman whose "love of flattery" leads her to take a second husband for his charm, beauty, and dependence. Mrs. Ashwood in Charlotte Smith's highly sentimental *Emmeline* (1788) is particularly efficient when she remarries, doing irreparable damage to her daughters; to her brother's family, the Staffords; and to Emmeline's uncle's family, the Montrevilles; and nearly irreparable damage to Emmeline Mowbray herself. Radcliffe's Madame Cheron marries the villain of the book, Montoni. Mrs. Vernon, "whose depraved mind, was perpetually employed in forming schemes for the destruction of others" herself becomes a "victim to the snares of a congenial spirit; she married a foreign adventurer, of the vilest character, who dissipated her fortune; reduced her to misery; and, finally broke her heart" (Robinson, *Widow*, 2:181).[27] In remarrying not out of necessity, but out of desire and conceit, women like Mrs. Ashwood, Mrs. Vernon, and Mrs. Ashburn exemplify vanity, lust, and greed, for each is quite wealthy enough to live on her own terms for the rest of her life. These widows are driven not by a need for companionship, but by appetite. Their pursuits are selfish and frequently, even when they acquire the object of their passion, their success becomes a warning by ending in disaster.

By conflating sexual, material, and financial interests, eighteenth-century novels suggest that the control of desire is related to the control of property. Fenwick's Mrs. Ashburn and Radcliffe's Madame Cheron's wealth enables each to control others and to desire to control others, for example. In removing Emily further and further from the mountains and valleys that the girl loves, Madame Cheron consults her own rather than her niece's happiness. She also distances Emily from control of her inheritance and her identity, leaving the properties in the hands of servants or cruel, distant relations and leaving Emily at the mercy of her aunt and stepuncle, the villain Montoni. In contrast, when Emily finally controls her estates, the good girl passes them to her husband, Valancourt. As Benedict points out, "Emily, indeed, expressly desires them only in order to return them to male hands."[28] Emily, the sentimental heroine, not the widowed guardian, conforms to social expectation in desire and in deed. It is despite Madame Cheron's actions rather than because of them that Emily's inheritance is preserved and the young heroine is finally married to the partner endorsed by herself and the text.

Furthermore, as people of the period increasingly came to face the idea that in a commercial system, property can mean people, so the widow's control and potential abuse of property for her own satisfaction, especially her own sexual satisfaction, took on even more wide-ranging implications. In Fenwick's novel *Secresy*, for example, Caroline Ashburn observes that her mother "will assuredly marry to prove to me her power and pre-eminence" over Caroline, suggesting that there is something inappropriately, incestuously competitive about the mother's desires for a second husband (165). Similarly, Radcliffe, although more conservative than Fenwick, has Madame Cheron hound Emily and steal her wedding, using the decorations originally planned for Emily and Valancourt's ceremony as the decorations to her own marriage feast: "'I shall now celebrate my marriage with some splendour,' continued Madame Montoni, 'and to save time I shall avail myself of the preparation that has been made for yours'" (Radcliffe, *Mysteries of Udolpho*, 142). Barbara M. Benedict argues that Madame Cheron's sexuality is an aspect of her materialism, so her "lust for power [is] an unnatural appetite fed by her possession of her own estates." Evelina is not only shocked to discover herself the unwitting rival to her grandmother, Madame Duval, for Monsieur Du Bois' affections, but also outraged to discover that her grandmother wants to marry her to crass "young Branghton" to get Evelina out of her way (Burney, *Evelina*, 237). In such cases, the widow regards the sentimental heroine as competition, an unmaternal and inappropriate interpretation of their relationship with each other and with the larger society.

As such episodes recognize, desire objectifies the desiree, and in a commercial society, that object can be exchanged according to its valuation. In *The Widow*, Mrs. Vernon confesses that she wants to bring Julia St. Lawrence to London to use her to write letters and read aloud—Julia is a useful tool to Mrs. Vernon, not a person (Robinson, 2:28). Eighteenth-century novels often specifically castigate the translation of individuals into a cash value. Sarah Fielding's Lady Palestine agrees to help Lord Dorchester seduce Ophelia because she needs money (*Ophelia*, 1:156–59, 2:179–80). Lady Griskin in Smollett's *Humphry Clinker* (1771) and Madame Duval in *Evelina* are both interested in the young lady because of the possibility of marrying her to money. Madame Duval's primary interest in Evelina is to marry the girl off and to extract a dowry from Evelina's estranged father, Sir John Belmont. When Evelina resists her grandmother's attempts to take her to France to sell her to the most affluent suitor, it is to property interest, not family affection, that Madame Duval appeals, threatening that "she would instantly make a will, in which she would leave all her fortune to strangers, though, otherwise, she intended her grand-daughter for her sole heiress" unless she is obeyed by Evelina and, significantly, by Mr. Villars, an adult male.[29] Madame Duval is singularly incompetent at looking after young dependents: first she devastates her daughter, then her granddaughter. She consistently insists on self-gratification and just as consistently threatens others, especially daughters and daughter figures.

Nor is novelistic anxiety limited to the commodification of women. As Sterne suggests by equating Toby Shandy with Widow Wadman's furniture in *Tristram Shandy*, for a woman who owns other forms of property, remarriage is simply an extension of ownership. "A daughter of Eve, for such was widow Wadman," the narrator warns,

> had better be fifty leagues off—or in her warm bed—or playing with a case-knife—or any thing you please—than make a man the object of her attention, when the house and all the furniture is her own.
>
> There is nothing in it out of doors and in broad day-light, where a woman has a power, physically speaking, of viewing a man in more lights than one—but here, for her soul, she can see him in no light without mixing something of her own goods and chattels along with him—till by reiterated acts of such combinations, he gets foisted into her inventory—
>
> —And then good night. (455–56)

Let us remember that she does not pursue him until she has thoroughly read over her marriage settlement, presumably to find out what happens to her other property if she takes a second husband (457). Henry Fielding's Lady Booby also uses her wealth and position to buy the compliance of men further down the social scale (*Joseph Andrews*, 252–56). Lady Bellaston's efforts to give or betray Sophia to Lord Fellamar are based on the desire to possess something that Sophia already "owns," which is Tom Jones (H. Fielding, *Tom Jones*, 648). Tom is not quite the same object as a country estate, but he is certainly regarded and treated as property by Lady Bellaston. In *The Widow*, Mr. Howard observes that Mrs. Vernon "aims at an eternal bondage" for her fiancé, Lord Woodley (Robinson, 1:28). This use of young men by widows overturns the gender hierarchy, the age hierarchy (youth is superior to age, at least in the novel), and the sentimental hierarchy—the sentimental protagonist, especially the Man of Feeling, is superior to everyone except, perhaps, his or her counterpart.

The commodification first of goods and property and then of people is not just capitalist but also, one might argue, imperialist. Fenwick's *Secresy*, which bases Mrs. Ashburn's wealth in the British exploitation of India, makes such a connection explicit. As Caroline Ashburn exclaims, "my mother can look on this existing fact with indifference, while I shudder. Those enormous sums of wealth she lavishes away, that cluster of pearls she triumphantly places in her hair, those diamonds heaped into different ornaments, how were they obtained?" (67). Women like Widow Wadman or Lady Bellaston not only commodify Toby and Tom, but also colonize them by claiming otherwise independent entities as their own. Women as consumers might justify the imperialist effort, according to Laura Brown in *Ends of Empire*, but women as the procurers of what they desire to consume expose imperialism for what it really is, undermining efforts such as the women-as-consumers theory to render it acceptable.[30] To restore or maintain their passive role as mere (but essential) catalysts in the imperialist system, women who conduct trade for their own profit, enjoyment, or both are depicted as monstrous on their own, rather than as illustrations of the monstrosity in the system.

This is not to suggest that these novels are anti-imperialist or abolitionist as a whole, although Fenwick's *Secresy* is loudly critical of the empire. As scholars such as George Boulukos and Gary Gautier point out, sentimental novels as a group did not tend to attack exploitative systems like slavery, but rather to use them to reaffirm a stable hierarchy. "As the concept of 'sensibility' grew into a form that could offer ideological support to a hierarchy that was otherwise losing its ideological viability," Gautier explains, "so the concept of 'race' came to give 'slavery' a new kind of ideological support." It is only problematic to treat certain types of characters, like white English virgins, as property. It is still more problematic if the person trading in the flesh of the sentimental hero or heroine is a woman, and even worse if she is a widow.[31]

As might be expected, then, virtuous widows do not participate in imperialistic or commodifying forms of exchange. They do not desire anything but good for others, and sexual desire is particularly unimaginable. Thus, when virtuous widows receive freedom, they do not embrace it; rather, they embrace the limitations placed upon that freedom. They do not convert anything, and certainly not people, into objects to be used or exchanged for their own gratification. In *Millenium Hall*, when Mrs. Alworth's second granddaughter wishes to marry a man who will not marry her unless her grandmother contributes another two thousand pounds to her dowry, twice-widowed Mrs. Alworth "saw no temptation to purchase so mercenary a man," refusing, in effect, to commodify her granddaughter even though the young lady is perfectly willing to be sold in that manner (Scott, 191). Even if widows are permitted to act in a businesslike manner as the guardians of an estate, they are not permitted to do so with businesslike motives. Reeve's Mr. Strictland's will leaves Mrs. Strictland executrix of the estate with two men, and "residuary legatee," entitling her to the "whole rents and income of his fortune during the minority of his children" to be used to look after them, but only so long as she does not remarry. If she remarries, "the children are to be taken from her, and put under the care of the other guardians, who are to be accountable for the rents till his son comes of age." *School for Widows* heartily approves of this kind of will and even encourages the "Legislature" to dictate how long widowhood should last and to impose an upper age limit for remarriage, preventing "widows from squandering their fortunes, and buying themselves husbands."[32] "The moral experience of the domestic woman," Stewart observes, "is constructed out of a limitation of desire and out of an acceptance, even a celebration, of a restricted life," and Reeve's virtuous affluent widow certainly fits this formulation.[33] While her late husband's will confers certain powers on Mrs. Strictland, for example, it restricts others, but because Mrs. Strictland is a virtuous widow, she gratefully accepts the strictures her late husband's will places upon her, and voices the philosophy that such practices are good for women, families, and England.

Another version of this lack of desire appears as a refusal to remarry. Ideal widows do not even want to live without their first husbands. Ophelia Lenox's unnamed mother in Sarah Fielding's *History of Ophelia* delivers her daughter and then expires of grief for the loss of her husband (2–3). An unnamed Spanish widow in Sarah Scott's *History of Cornelia* survives her husband only a fortnight (231), and "the virtuous Estifania" in *Ferdinand Count Fathom* "did not long survive" her husband's death (Smollett, 115). In *The Widow,* Julia St. Lawrence feels death approaching upon receiving supposed confirmation that her husband is dead (M. Robinson, 2:33).

If they absolutely must live, however, virtuous widows often do so out of dedication to others, particularly their children. Eliza Haywood's Cleomira from *The British Recluse* (1722) reports that her widowed mother converted conjugal love into maternal love: "Instead of entertaining any Thoughts of a second Marriage, she transplanted all the Tenderness she had born my Father on me." When Mr. Somerive dies in Smith's *The Old Manor House*, his widow's "distraction" was "not to be described," but she "reflected on the necessity of her living for [her children], unprotected and helpless," and became "more tranquil."[34] Rather than a wide-ranging, one might almost say imperialistic, self-interested lasciviousness, virtuous widows possess a domestic, asexual outlook.

Sensibility strengthened eighteenth-century society's initial discomfort with remarriage into a rejection of the idea altogether. Before sensibility was at its cultural height, authors like Smollett, Penelope Aubin, and Eliza Haywood conditionally allowed their widowed characters to marry willingly a second time, and ultimately to find happiness in those unions. In *Ferdinand Count Fathom,* two virtuous widows—the Countess de Melvile and Madam Clement—remarry, although not entirely happily. The Countess de Melvile chooses badly and must suffer several years of tyranny from her second husband, who steals her son's estates, imprisons her daughter in a convent, and locks up his wife in a tower until the fear of death causes him to see the error of his ways. Madam Clement also remarries, although her sinner is reformed before they wed, but at no point does anything more than companionship enter into the discussion. The terms of their relationship are really set by her second husband, who desires company when he returns to the site and memories of his first marriage (Smollett, 355–56). While these second marriages are either tempered with suffering or emptied of the romantic love that other marriages in the novel are granted, they also ultimately win narrative approval. By century's end, however, sensibility had precluded even the possibility of virtuous, satisfying second marriages. Ann Radcliffe's Olivia in *The Italian* (1797) marries her brother-in-law, the man who murdered her beloved husband. As punishment, Olivia is yoked to her husband's murderer, secluded in a hypocritical and tyrannical convent until nearly the end of the story, and emotionally tortured during her life by the existence of her second husband and the loss of her children.[35] The very idea of remarriage is often rejected at century's end. When she is offered the chance of conjugal happiness with James Balderson, Reeve's Mrs. Strictland rejects it in order to continue caring for her family and her tenants (*School for Widows*, 2:276–77), and Sheridan's Sidney Bidulph is not allowed to marry her first and truest love even after a difficult marriage and roller-coaster widowhood.

A comparison of two novels with the same dilemma, Penelope Aubin's *Count de Vinevil* (1721) and Charlotte Smith's *Emmeline,* and two with the same plot, Eliza Haywood's *The History of Miss Betsy Thoughtless* (1751) and Margaret Lee's *Clara Lennox* (1797), high-

lights sensibility's impact on definitions of virtuous sexuality in independent women.[36] In both *Count de Vinevil* and *Emmeline*, side narratives involve a long-suffering woman who has the opportunity to
marry a good man who loves her. Aubin's Violetta, although not
technically married to the Turk who kidnapped and raped her, hesitates to marry the French captain who loves her despite her life and
illegitimate children with the Turk. Similarly, Smith's Lady Adeline
Trelawney refuses to marry George Fitz-Edward, her lover during
her marriage and her suitor during her widowhood. These women
reject the opportunity to replace their abusive husbands even in
memory, thereby emphasizing fidelity as part of virtuous female love.

They also regard themselves as goods whose value is connected to
emotional torment and social exile. Lady Adeline explains, "what
would [he] receive in the widow of Trelawney? A mind unsettled by
guilt and sorrow; spirits which have lost all relish for felicity; a blem-
ished, if not a ruined reputation, a faded person, and an exhausted
heart" (Smith, *Emmeline*, 4:346). In 1721, Aubin solves the problem
of virtuous remarriage by elevating the French captain to a marquis
and making him a European Christian; furthermore, Ardelisa, the
heroine of the story and a married woman, puts her stamp of approval on the match. Violetta and her captain are married. Later in
the century and under the influence of sensibility, Smith also grants
the remarriage the approval of the virtuous and married heroine,
Emmeline, but Smith never allows the marriage to take place. It is an
uncertain event, indefinitely postponed so the widow can suffer infinitely.

A more dramatic and central contrast appears in Haywood's *Betsy
Thoughtless* and Lee's *Clara Lennox*. In both novels, the young heroine is manipulated into marrying the wrong man. Both husbands
maltreat their perfectly nice wives and then die, obligingly removing
themselves as obstacles to the true union endorsed by the novel. The
heroines arrange to remarry, this time to the men they should have
married in the beginning. The endings, however, are considerably
different. In 1751, Betsy Thoughtless performs all the rites of widowhood but admits that she does not really miss her departed cruel
spouse. When her friend Lady Loveit wonders at Betsy's observing
all the proper forms of mourning, considering how glad she must be
to be rid of Mr. Munden, "'Mistake me not, dear Lady Loveit,' answered [Betsy], 'I do not pretend to lament the death of Mr.
Munden as it deprives me of his society, or as that of a person with

whom I could ever have enjoyed any great share of felicity, even though his life had made good the professions of his last moments;—but I lament him as one who was my husband, whom duty forbids me to hate while living, and whom decency requires me to mourn for when dead'" (617). Nevertheless, Lady Loveit responds, while "decency obliges you to wear black, forbids you to appear abroad for a whole month, and at any public place of diversion for a much longer time; . . . it does not restrain you from being easy in yourself, and chearful with your friends" (618). The novel achieves closure when Betsy marries the right man, Trueworth, much to everyone's satisfaction.

Almost fifty years later Clara Lennox, on the other hand, "from the agitations of her mind, with a deep sigh fell to the ground, lost in anguish, and insensibility" upon the death of her despicable husband (Lee, 1:170). Everyone, herself included, calls her an "unfortunate widow" throughout the rest of the novel, and while Betsy Thoughtless endures one decorous year of widowhood in genteel retirement, Clara Lennox must spend a good long time working in urban misery for her subsistence. In the end, while Betsy and Trueworth marry and Betsy is "at length rewarded with a happiness, retarded only until she had render'd herself wholly worthy of receiving it" (Haywood, *Betsy Thoughtless,* 634), Clara is prevented from remarrying and achieving wedded satisfaction by the sudden death of her fiancé on their wedding day (Lee, 2:228).

Betsy Thoughtless is not interesting simply because she suffers. She also matures and is rewarded, as the novel explicitly puts it, with happiness. Clara's suffering rather than maturing, however, is the focus of Lee's novel, just as Lady Adeline's infinite anguish is her final raison d'être. Clara's virtue lies in being miserable and in not remarrying, two conditions which are linked but are also significant on their own. Earlier in the century, sensibility was still interested in development, and so Betsy endures anguish in order to "render herself worthy of receiving happiness," as she should, and is allowed to remarry. By century's end, sensibility's emphasis on suffering as both virtue and purpose meant that remarriage was unacceptable because it would end the anguish. By replacing remarried happiness with misery, sentimental novels reject remarriage for widows because they would stop suffering and find happiness, and with another man.

The role of suffering in the portrayal of remarriage changes, then, as the notion of the function of character in a sentimental

novel changes. The concept of static virtue brought sentiment's didactic agenda of awarding virtuous marital suffering with marital felicity into increasing conflict with its aversion to second marriage
and female desire. The shift to an emphasis on suffering, undesiring
women, and therefore perpetual widowhood appears clearly in
Sarah Scott's *Sir George Ellison* (1766), which can be read as a turning
point. In *Sir George Ellison*, Scott performs some exceedingly delicate
footwork to render second marriage virtuous. Mrs. Tunstall and Mrs.
Blackburn, the two widows who remarry, do not develop as characters: they are static personalities. Nor does the love that they felt for
their first husbands develop. Instead, their rigid virtue and fixed affection endure and are rewarded with a second, loving husband.
Neither woman thinks about remarrying; both are surprised by the
professions of their second lovers despite ample evidence of each
man's attraction.[37] When Mrs. Tunstall receives Mr. Ellison's first visit
six months after her husband has died,

> She did not imagine, whatever remaining partiality he might have
> for her, that he could entertain the least design of renewing his ad-
> dresses to a woman, who, by a refusal of his hand, had shewn she did
> not deserve it, and one who was now too encumbered with children;
> and, she supposed, much altered, by the years of care and vexation
> which she had passed since he had seen her. (173)

As for Mrs. Blackburn, "A stranger to coquetry even in youth, she
had for some years ceased to imagine a possibility of any man's being
in love with her" (209). Each woman's genuine affection for her second husband is tempered narratively, as well. Mrs. Blackburn was
"well disposed towards Lamont; she thought him agreeable and deserving; his fortune afforded her some temptation, and his attach-
ment to her was too flattering not to prejudice her a good deal in his
favour," a nice endorsement but hardly passion (208). Mrs. Tunstall
must first disengage her heart from her first husband, then may not
be deeply in love until George Ellison has courted her for six
months and narrowly escaped death (176, 180–85). Scott constructs
this delay as a virtue: "Mr. Ellison was rather pleased to see that Mrs.
Tunstall was not insensible to the loss of a man, whom she had once
loved to excess, though his conduct had rendered him unworthy of
her. He did not think the affections of a heart he wished to gain
could be too tender" (173).

Furthermore, since society would condemn desire, neither woman appears to wish to marry even when her acceptance is a foregone conclusion. Mrs. Blackburn "appeared to yield to his reasons and importunity, rather than to her own inclinations," while Mrs. Tunstall, although deeply in love with Mr. Ellison, capitulates to his entreaties only when her father threatens to ruin her reputation if she does not marry Mr. Ellison immediately (209, 177–78). Nor does either woman marry for money although Mrs. Tunstall, who is penniless and the mother of three very small children, is surely entitled (176). Mrs. Tunstall, the novel's paragon of female virtue, articulates and resolves sensibility's conflict between remarriage and virtue. Like Scott's readers, Mrs. Tunstall's

> delicacy had always led her to dislike second marriages; to love twice, or to marry where a woman does not love, had appeared to her inconsistent with true delicacy; and though she was now obliged either to acknowledge she had refined too much, or to be the object of her own censure, yet she was desirous of fulfilling all that the forms of the world could require of her. (177)

In this way, Scott manages to avoid suggesting that virtuous widows wish to remarry, even if they are still young or in financial need, while acknowledging genuine, sentimental love for second husbands. Scott thus balances the claims of didacticism (rewarding suffering and virtue) and of the undesiring female. After Scott, the balance tipped in favor of the undesiring female and, for one branch of sensibility exemplified by novels such as Lee's *Clara Lennox*, the sensationalism of perpetual suffering.

Scott's phrase, "to love twice," suggests how the relationship with the departed husband is central to depicting a widow's virtue. Eighteenth-century novels, particularly those written under the influence of sensibility, often depict the choice not to remarry as a question of emotional fidelity to a departed spouse. Until late in the century, virtuous widows could remarry provided the virtue of the living husband outstripped that of the dead one. Ardelisa, Betsy Thoughtless, Mrs. Tunstall, and Mrs. Blackburn, for example, are offered second husbands far superior to their first. Once it is remarriage, rather than remarriage to someone in particular, that sensibility censures, the character of the first husband is less important than fidelity to his memory and second suitors are more often wicked, if only be-

cause they wish to marry the widow. Virtuous widows withstand the
blandishments even of powerful men to remarry by appeals to a vi-
sion, either literal or delusional, of a late husband. Lady Lovel in
Clara Reeve's *Old English Baron* (1777) maintains an admirable resignation upon hearing of the death of her husband, but only until his
ghost appears to her to tell her that he has been murdered.[38] In
Reeve's later novel, *School for Widows*, the bereaved Donna Isabella
loses her mind with grief and constructs a fetish of her departed
spouse. When her persecutor Captain Maurice enters her bedroom
after arranging a sham marriage, Donna Isabella runs

> to a corner of the room, as if for safety. There stood an old-fashioned
> high-backed chair: she had hung upon it a shoot of clothes of Anto-
> nio's, and buttoned it over the chair; and her disturbed imagination
> represented to her the idea of Antonio's being present there. She
> threw herself into the chair; she threw the sleeves of the coat over
> her, and then composed herself.
> "There! there! Now I am safe!—He dares not take me out of your
> arms!" (2:203–4)

As Isabella assures the suit, "I do not mind his foolish talking—no,
my love, I am yours only. Do not be uneasy; I promise you, I will
never marry any other man" (2:204). Even Robinson's Julia St.
Lawrence, who is not really a widow but who models ideal widowhood, claims to see the "form of [her] adored husband, which fancy,
unceasingly presents to [her] agonized gaze; [and it] shall never be
forgotten, till [she] freeze, in the gloom of a sepulchre" (*Widow*,
2:32). When attacked by Lord Woodley after he mendaciously assures her that her husband is dead, she cries, "Oh! shade of my departed husband, sustain me, or I perish!" (2:40). In virtuous women,
the apparition of the dead man serves as a reminder of the proper
course of action. By keeping, literally, the image of their late husbands before them, virtuous late-century widows avoid remarriage
and what the late sentimental novel therefore identifies as sexual
transgression.[39]

Sensibility's rejection of remarriage may be depicted primarily as
a question of emotion, but that emotion also screens the very real
property issues involved when widows remarry. Tobias Smollett's
Mrs. Trunnion from *The Adventures of Peregrine Pickle* (1751) is placed
in a second marriage by her husband on his deathbed, when he dis-
poses of her as part of the estate (392). The conveyance of the family

home is overtly tied to this conveyance of the widow: Jack Hatchway, the second husband selected by the first husband, will receive "possession" of the house "as soon as he should be able to accomplish this matrimonial scheme" (396). Reeve's Lady Lovel suffers the loss of her husband, her freedom, and eventually her life because of her kinsman's passion for her and the property attached to her in her widowed state. Sir Walter desires her because of what she would be were she a widow, and the actuality of that widowhood confirms her desirability. Donna Isabella also becomes the object for the passion of another man, Captain Maurice, while she is married. Captain Maurice accidentally kills her husband, then immediately pursues the lady, driving her to distraction. She too loses her freedom as well as her mind when she refuses to remarry, and control of her possessions becomes a metaphor for control of her person and affections. Radcliffe's Louisa, Baroness of Dunbayne from *The Castles of Athlin and Dunbayne* is imprisoned by her late husband's brother when she wishes to go to Switzerland to take possession of the properties left to her by her own father and not covered by the Malcolm entail, because he wants that property as well (153–54).

The remarriage of affluent widows is tied to the disposal of the estate that comes into their possession. Virtuous widows refuse to derail primogeniture, and they accept a man's will in the disposal of the estate and of themselves. They accept and reaffirm their role as a conveyor of property, not as an owner of it. In so doing, they reject desire—being desirable and feeling desire. Virtuous widows thus do not accept ownership of the dead man's property: of an estate, her affections, or even her person. Consequently, the violence that threatens many of these women when they refuse remarriage underscores the virtue, and therefore the importance, of their refusal. It also underscores the wickedness of those trying to get them to remarry, particularly if the motive is to derail property transmission.

In approving widows who do not remarry, the eighteenth-century novel links positive, maternal instinct to selflessness and benevolence, especially as they relate to the preservation of property and its continued transmission through traditional means—inheritance, family arrangements—rather than through autonomous, self-interested contracts. At the beginning of the century Daniel Defoe linked the city and widowhood with commerce in *Robinson Crusoe* (1719), which features a positive, urban, capitalistic widow: the "good ancient widow" who preserves Crusoe's capital for him while he is a slave with the Moors and who becomes his steward at the end of the novel.[40] Later in the century, and in the hands of authors less sanguine about trade, the relationship between money and widowhood takes a negative turn. Kate Ferguson Ellis points out that Radcliffe's villains "see the possibility of capitalism for making money out of money, and chafe at the 'slow diligence' that smacks of the old order of agricultural accumulation, with its dependence on nature." For Radcliffe, "What matters is not how much wealth you have, but whether or not you want more, and what you do to get it."[41]

Perhaps the tidiest embodiment of these principles is the first Mrs. Ellison from Scott's *Sir George Ellison.* Initially introduced to the reader more as she would have appeared to Mr. Ellison than as her true self so the reader can understand why he marries her, Mrs. Ellison turns out to possess almost all of the qualities rejected in widows. Admittedly, her seven years' seniority should have been a sign of things to come, since it is a mark of the desiring widow (9). She also has significant character flaws, however. She is unaccustomed to overruling her heart with her head, for example, and later the narrator admits that she had "never reasoned in her life" and was "too perverse to attend, and too weak to be convinced" by her husband's good sense (17, 29). She is manipulative and tyrannical, using her cunning to find and exploit Mr. Ellison's weaknesses for her own gain. In particular, she draws on her experience by comparing her first husband—"poor Mr. Tomkins"—with her second to get what she wants, demonstrating one of the reasons why remarriage was depicted negatively. "By these arts she soon made her husband that slave which he would suffer no one to be to him," the narrator reports (22); bad enough to do to any nice person in a sentimental novel but worse here because she upends the traditional hierarchy in marriage. When they disagree about managing the plantation, she "recompenced herself" with an "inward exultation on reflecting, that however it might be in other families, in their's woman was certainly not the weaker vessel, since she was above those soft timorous whims which so much affected him" (12).

Her willingness to do what it takes to get what she wants, particularly to exploit whatever resources are available, such as her husband, is an aspect of a larger problem: her commercial nature. After their argument about managing the plantation, she "recompenced herself," a monetary phrase, rather than "consoled" or "flattered" herself. Although her desire to remarry would have been a mark against her in any sentimental novel, it is couched in commercial terms: George Ellison "formed no designs on her, or her fortune. The widow was not equally insensible" (9). Furthermore, since her wealth derives from a plantation and the slaves that work it, her commercial values are associated with imperialism (9). Significantly, as a widow, Mrs. Ellison (then Mrs. Tomkins) "had always kept her slaves in as good order as any man in the island, and never flinched at any punishment her steward saw fit to inflict upon them" (12). She can exploit for personal gain as well as a man. Just like a man and therefore not like a woman, in fact.

Mrs. Ellison's self-interest, based in greed and associated with mercantile capitalism, allows her to reject sensibility and all its virtues, including social order. She has no compassion for her slaves and refuses to acknowledge their humanity, in direct contrast to her exemplary husband (10–13). When he wants to treat their slaves like "fellow creatures," she "fears . . . lest their fortune should suffer through his simplicity" (12). Although George Boulukos has pointed out that Scott, like other sentimental novelists, did not aim at abolition, Scott does use the first Mrs. Ellison to associate the worst of the emerging economy with slavery.[42] In contrast, George Ellison himself supports and even expands the free labor market whenever possible, embodying the possibilities and celebration of ethical (that is, sentimental) commerce.

Mrs. Ellison's sins converge in her function as a mother. Her manipulative nature, her selfishness, her rejection of benevolence and patriarchal hierarchy, and her ultimate dishonesty in pursuit of personal gratification all manifest themselves in her handling of her son. Instead of seeing his character clearly and acting for his good as a member of society, someone who must interact with and be responsible to and for others, she chooses to indulge his whims and exaggerate his importance. In particular, she is "pleased" when he acts cruelly to the slaves. "[S]o successful were her endeavours," the narrator reports, "that by the time he arrived at the age of five years, he was a little fury, bursting with pride, passion, insolence, and obstinacy" (29). George Ellison, a man, is a far superior parent: "He endeavoured to teach her the duty of a parent, and to convince her that her indulgence rendered her the child's most pernicious enemy," things she should already know (29). When he forces her to agree to his method of child rearing, she undermines his authority with their son; teaches the boy to act one way with his father and the way he wished the rest of the time; and encourages him to love her more than his father (30). Not only then has she enabled their son to acquire "a degree of deceit and hypocrisy, beyond what [Mr. Ellison] imagined possible at so early an age," but also she has damaged the English family by pitting the parents against each other and pushing the son to choose between them. Lastly, in corrupting the son in this way, she threatens the future of the empire. Her son will be unfit to take his place and act for the good of trade and the nation; in fact he is averse, like her, to England itself (30–31). All because "To be superiorly beloved, was so great a gratification to Mrs. Ellison's narrow and ungenerous mind" (31). Scott thus condemns not trade, but ways of pursuing trade and women in trade in particular, through the first Mrs. Ellison, for whom love and power are commodities to be acquired without scruples, even within the family, for her own benefit and profit, regardless of the cost to others.

Eighteenth-century novels often present delight in the worldly, visible pursuit and possession of material goods, rather than the benevolent application of wealth for the good of others, as a contribution to social fluidity. It often appears as conspicuous consumption and lavish display such as garish, inappropriate dress. Consider, for example, Madame Duval's wardrobe, which signals her refusal to acknowledge who she really is and her class change, as opposed to Evelina's effort to blend in sartorially when she first arrives in London with the Mirvans, or her humiliation at wearing dress appropriate to the pit in the gallery at the opera (Burney, *Evelina*, 15, 77, 78, 81). As Miss Trentham of *Millenium Hall* puts it, the world's greatest evil is its social mixing, where members of different classes overstep their bounds by trying to emulate their betters (Scott, 61, 116). Miss Trentham articulates philosophically what the Hardwicke Act of 1753 articulates legislatively: that social instability, which arises from the mixing of classes, is also social evil. This mixing takes place, as Miss Trentham points out, in the city, where the classes have easiest access to each other. As the site of both social mixing and economic opportunity, the city is the heart of social and economic instability.[43]

Scholars such as Raymond Williams, Gerald MacLean, Donna Landry, and Joseph P. Ward show that, certainly by the late eighteenth century, the city was firmly associated with trade. This association triggered others, particularly the notion that cities, especially London, were really dens of iniquity.[44] For Radcliffe, neither the city itself nor urbanity has anything to recommend it; city dwellers are neither accomplished nor knowledgeable, merely adept at pretending to be so, and their "immoderate and feverish animation, usually exhibited in large parties, results partly from an insensibility to the cares, which benevolence must sometimes derive from the sufferings of others, and partly from a desire to display the appearance of that prosperity, which they know will command submission and attention to themselves" (*Mysteries of Udolpho*, 122–23). Big cities, of course, are the worst: Griffith's marchioness initially seduces Lord Woodville in Paris and reseduces him in York, Paris ruins Radcliffe's Valancourt, and according to Reeve, London is the "place, of all others, most likely to spoil young people; to pervert their good principles, and give them bad ones instead of them" (Griffith, *Delicate Distress*; Radcliffe, *Mysteries of Udolpho*, 505–7, 585; Reeve, *School for Widows*, 2:99). Certainly in *Evelina, Camilla*, and *The Mysteries of Udolpho*, for example, the heroine's most difficult times begin when she enters a city.

Novelists critical of autonomous female economic activity, regardless of their position on the developing economy, used the city and commercially minded affluent widows to criticize both. The association could be direct: the character who behaves badly lives in the place that epitomizes her brand of bad behavior. In *Ferdinand Count Fathom* an unnamed but ridiculous widow who wants to marry Ferdinand first encounters him at a fashionable spa, and she lives in London (Smollett, 248). Lady Sheerness of London means well but only teaches her young charge about the pleasure and material things to be had in London, and she encourages Lady Mary Jones to live according to popular opinion rather than religion and morality (Scott, *Millenium Hall*, 126–27). Even Lady Bidulph in Sheridan's *Memoirs of Miss Sidney Bidulph* ranks among the city-oriented, affluent widows who damage the sentimental heroine through their inability to get beyond their own interests.

The criticism of female economic behavior and often also of the city and trade appears most clearly when wicked widows actually engage in trade.[45] Henry Fielding's Lady Bellaston, Sarah Fielding's Lady Palestine, Smollett's Lady Griskin, and Burney's Madame Duval exemplify some of the worst of London life as they exploit their novels' protagonists. Although Madame Duval's efforts are hardly unusual, Burney strips them of their class and therefore their veneer by bringing together Madame Duval's efforts, her relatives the Branghtons, a family that epitomizes the grasping crassness of commerce, and London. According to Reeve, London is the "place, of all oth-

ers, most likely to spoil young people; to pervert their good principles, and give them bad ones instead of them" (*School for Widows*,
2:99). It doesn't have to be London, however. Elvira in *The Monk*
lives in Madrid, Paris ruins Radcliffe's Valancourt, and Emily St.
Aubert's urban guardians offer her on the marriage market, "not because [they] desired to see her in possession of the happiness, which
rank and wealth are usually believed to bestow, but because [they]
desired to partake of the importance, which such an alliance would
give" (Radcliffe, *Mysteries of Udolpho*, 139). In connecting wicked widows with the city, novelists used characterizations of person and of
space to reinforce negative images of one and sometimes of both.

The converse, the association between benevolent widows and
the country underscores the withdrawal of goodness from the urban
and the commercial to the rural and agrarian. While not all novelists
celebrated the country over the city, representations of widows usually drew on the association of the country as the opposite of the
chaotic, iniquitous city to demonstrate a widow's virtue. Mrs.
Somerive from *The Old Manor House* moves to London upon being
widowed in order to keep an eye on her profligate older son, but her
health suffers from this remove (C. Smith, 415). *Camilla*'s Mrs. Arlbery is a somewhat ambivalent figure as long as she resides in the
country; once she arrives in Tunbridge, she becomes damaging to
the heroine. In contrast, *Evelina*'s kind and elegant Lady Howard
lives in the country; Cleomira's virtuous mother in *The British Recluse*
hastens to a rural retreat upon her widowhood (Haywood, *British
Recluse*, 162); and after the death of her husband, affectionate and
generous Lady V—— goes to a "distant part of Lancashire, in order
to spend the rest of her days with her eldest sister, a widow lady, of
whom she is very fond" (Sheridan, *Sidney Bidulph*, 267). The good
widow who gives Sidney Bidulph's papers to the male editor also
lives "altogether in the country, in a good old fashioned house,
which was part of her jointure" and Sidney herself gives up a fashionable, expensive, and elegant London residence for "an estate in
Buckinghamshire," which her friend Cecilia calls "her retirement,"
to look after her family (3, 428, 429). Even Betsy Thoughtless, upon
becoming both thoughtful and a widow, retires to the country for
her widowhood (Haywood, *Betsy Thoughtless*, 620). This association
of female, domestic virtue with the country, specifically the country
house, thus reinforces the opposition of landed and commercial values, and the association of femininity with the former.

As might be imagined, the economic activity performed by virtuous affluent widows in such places is Goldsmithian, a landowner's activity, not a tradesman's. Sidney's retreat involves pious meditation,
educating Orlando Faulkland's illegitimate son and her own daughters, and marrying Patty Main, her faithful maid, "to a gentleman of
a large estate" (Sheridan, *Sidney Bidulph*, 429). Reeve's Mrs. Strictland might go to London when she is widowed, but she always comes
home to the country and her estate, servants, and tenants. Scott's
Mrs. Morgan uses her estate to establish a community that nurtures
men and women of all classes and ages to preserve their character,
dignity, and self-sufficiency. It is not just a question of country-good,
city-bad, however, but also a question of how the country is managed. The aristocracy produces its share of selfish, wasteful, cruel
people, such as the young gentlemen of *Evelina* and *The History of
Ophelia*. Burney's Lord Merton is as selfish and cruel as Mr. Lovel,
the city fop, and Sarah Fielding's Lord Dorchester is manipulative
and selfish despite his large holdings in the country. The specific
issue for widows who inherit estates is whether they manage the estates and their own families in a nurturing way. Anna Howe's widowed mother in Samuel Richardson's *Clarissa* (1747) lives in the
country, but her failure through much of the novel to reconcile the
claims of her position in society with the claims of motherhood render her at best an equivocal character for much of the novel. Only
when she rejects remarriage because it conflicts with her connection
to her daughter is she able to redeem herself.[46]

Managing property for communal rather than personal gain is in
direct opposition to what Raymond Williams in *The Country and the
City* calls the rise of agrarian capitalism and what Beth Fowkes Tobin
calls the "New Economic Man," a figure defined by the "discourse
on agriculture" that arose midcentury.[47] The New Economic Man
was a professional farmer, a man who managed the estate to maximize profit, not the man whose family had owned the estate for gen-
erations. This figure emerged from the middle-class values of profit
making and efficient management, and he emphasized rational and
methodical business practices rather than the paternalism of the
aristocratic code. The New Economic Man contrasts with the young
men of *Evelina*, who are self-indulgent and entirely appetitive (ex-
cepting, of course, Lord Orville). Enclosure, which had been on the
rise from midcentury, really took off as tracts and treatises argued
that the "engrossment of small farms, and the consolidation of scat-

tered holdings" would centralize power and therefore increase efficiency and profits.[48] New systems for land distribution and land management brought new relationships among participants in those systems, including a redefinition of who got to participate at all. With the arrival of this "discourse on agriculture," then, came a new network of people involved in agriculture and the erasure of the old network involved in the traditional agricultural system.

For the novel's positive, landed widows, especially if they are sentimental widows, the behavior and attitudes that underlie this new discourse on agriculture and the New Economic Man are unthinkable. Although Reeve's Mrs. Strictland consolidates several parcels of land and asserts her opposition to breaking up estates, for example, she is trying to protect her tenants and to reward loyal, lifelong servants. When she takes control of the family estate, she maintains that "consolidating farms, and destroying cottages, was a cruel and wicked policy, and had a tendency to depopulate the villages, and destroy the peasantry of the land. I therefore declared myself the protector and patroness of this most useful order of men" (*School for Widows*, 2:92). Her speech sounds not unlike Goldsmith's "Deserted Village," which complains that "The man of wealth and pride / Takes up a space that many poor supplied" (275–76). His "seat, where solitary sports are seen, / Indignant spurns the cottage from the green" while the "sounds of population fail" (281–82, 125). In the hands of virtuous, novelistic widows land, people, their labor, and the attributes of farming such as cattle or equipment are not commodities to be manipulated but aspects of a community with its mores, responsibilities, and culture, all of which are to be preserved.

Hence, while opposition to the new discourses on agriculture and around commercialism can be seen as a female response to a male discourse that expressed and was responsible for the decline of women's fortunes in the emerging economy, it is also more than that. Resistance to such discourse is not only about gender, but also about landed conservatism and a sort of socioeconomic nostalgia. By century's end, the concept of the "land economy and the power relations that derive from land emphasize continuity, legitimacy, custom, privilege, and autonomy. The use of land is determined by customary social relations rather than by economic forces. This discourse of wealth sharply opposes the discourses emerging from the market economy, in which all social relations tend to be subsumed within a self-regulating economic system."[49] Ultimately, it is not enough to live in the country if one lives selfishly. That would be tantamount to city living. Lady Galliard, for example, is debauched, selfish, and ignorant, all on her extensive country estate; Mrs. Arlbery indulges herself at the expense of genuine friendship and respect; and Mrs. Ellison brutalizes slaves and tyrannizes her family. Virtuous women who have the means and the right to engage in autonomous, economic activity are virtuous because their activity, if they act at all, is associated with the country and occurs within a framework of nurturing, of dispersal, and of benevolence.

Land-based wealth was not the only form of wealth obtruding itself upon the notice of eighteenth-century English society, however, and affluent widows consequently were not the only ones to provoke anxiety among readers and writers. One group, working widows, bears a close affinity to affluent, upper-class widows. These widows inherited their own forms of wealth and capital, and therefore triggered considerable and related anxieties of their own. The novel contained the working widow in models similar to those used on the affluent widow, only applied to the power of her labor as well as to the power of her resources.

3

Diligent and Sentimental Labor: Work and the Widow

Consider the life of Frances Darnford, one of the protagonists of *The School for Widows* (1791) by Clara Reeve. At the beginning of her bereavement, Mrs. Darnford appears to be a study in tragic widowhood, reduced from landed gentility to near poverty in a matter of days. By novel's end, however, she has returned to a life of leisure, and done so through constant and disciplined work. Mrs. Darnford embodies, in fact, the very potential of widowhood so frightening to the period. Here is a woman who, when left to her own devices, proves highly successful at not simply taking care of herself, but also achieving considerable social and economic success, enough for her to move among different social classes. She uses all the rights and privileges available to a widow to pursue an independent course, and she experiences and takes advantage of the social fluidity that economic opportunity provides.

At first glance Mrs. Darnford would seem a most remarkable creation. After all, she appears at the end of a century grappling with the social volatility produced by emerging mercantile capitalism, and with the effects of that volatility and expanding economy on gender. Given her career and the approving way the novel presents it, one might conclude that whatever discomfort eighteenth-century novelists expressed with affluence and widows, they did not suffer it when it came to work and widows. A second look, of course, suggests a very different and a far more complex story. Placing Mrs. Darnford within her context—at the end of the century and at the end of an arc of social thought and economic change, for example, or as a creation of Clara Reeve or one of a number of working widows represented in eighteenth-century novels—reveals that the eighteenth-century novel made the same efforts to limit autonomous working women that it made to limit autonomous affluent women.

The novel's approach to widows who work indicates that it is not simply the possession of wealth that rendered widows worrisome to eighteenth-century society. Their other inheritance, the right to act independently, offered them the chance to change their economic status and to compete with, or at least not depend on, men. Such an entitlement was not merely theoretical: the historical record bears witness to such womens' willingness to embrace this opportunity, especially when widowhood made the need to work pressing. The novel responded to the possibilities that work provided women by depicting widows, the women most entitled to and often most desperate for work, as not working. In the hands of eighteenth-century novelists, work as independent economic activity, and even work as work per se, transmuted into natural female behavior, a legacy women and especially mothers continue to live with in the twenty-first century.

As chapter 1 discusses at greater length, the eighteenth century witnessed the contraction of economic opportunities for women in a wide variety of ways. While industrialization was not generally good for the working class, it was especially bad for women who had to work for their living. In addition to their growing exclusion from trades that traditionally had included women, women faced a devaluation of the work they were still allowed to do. Beginning in the 1750s, wages steadily fell for women. This erosion of earning power included cottage industries like spinning, which women continued to pursue simply because it brought some small cash into the family. It was related to the exclusion of women from skilled trades as well, since skill was increasingly associated with masculinity. Apprenticeship records from The Society for the Relief of Necessitous Widows and Children of Poor Dissenting Ministers demonstrate that sons could become sailors or goldsmiths, watchmakers or grocers, but daughters almost invariably became mantua makers or servants.[1] These trades in turn became particularly associated with women, and as the range of occupations open to women narrowed, the market for their labor eventually became saturated.[2] Overall, women lost out economically in the eighteenth century, and would not begin to gain back their losses until well into the nineteenth century.

This contraction was particularly ironic for widows, since these were women who would seem to be well-situated to survive in a commercial economy. Historically, the widow of an independent working man faced the world with important resources: experience, knowledge, and frequently, means. The wife of an artisan or tradesman often inherited work premises, stock, and tools. She was likely to have worked with her late husband, participating in the business of producing and selling. If not, she watched him conduct his business, and—sometimes for many years—would have listened to him discuss his work in the shop or over meals. She may or may not have known his suppliers, but in any case, she was known to them. If she chose to continue the business, she had an established clientele and work force. The widow of a farmer often inherited fields, livestock, and the family cottage. If she had not been selling produce and perhaps livestock at local markets, she was likely to know where they were sold, and whom to ask for information and advice. These widows may not have had riches, but they had means, know-how, and options, and many were quite successful.[3]

At the same time, a widow's ability to use such resources, including the amount of social acceptance she might enjoy if she used them, shrank as the working world closed to women. The changing economy put a premium on marriage for working men and on the married pair as an effective unit. From the late eighteenth century on, employers preferred to hire married men since they were easier to control, and so men married in order to find and keep work. Widows were especially prized in such communities because they had experience running a home, they might bring money or goods into the marriage, and they were often proven childbearers.[4] The pressure on a widow to remarry in these circumstances was considerable because of her usefulness to men. Other working widows, such as those who inherited a business, might face pressure to remarry so the business could fall within male control again. This pressure to remarry was at odds with the idea that women should not possess desire, such as sexual desire or the desire to replace their late husbands. It was also contrary to the pressure not to remarry that affluent, land-based widows faced, since the latter's remarriage could derail the transmission of estates through primogeniture. Pressure on working widows to remarry was consistent, however, with the overarching idea that property and its transmission should be controlled by men, since remarriage would return an estate not regulated by primogeniture, such as a business, to a man.

Nor did inheriting resources such as a business ensure even subsistence. As work shifted outside the home, children became an obstacle; some positions open to widows specifically stipulated "no dependents."[5] Calamities like enclosure could strip a widow of her property rights, and she usually lost her ability to feed her family as a result. A widow who inherited a business might be forced to marry an apprentice to keep the business going, or she might have to advertise that she planned to keep the business open.[6] She might not be able to save the business from overwhelming debt and ruinous mismanagement. Some businesses were considered unsuitable for women—too public or unfeminine—and guild rules often prohibited a widow from continuing.[7] Even widows in this group could easily fall into poverty, a subject addressed in the next chapter.

Mrs. Darnford and her working peers in the eighteenth-century novel show how the novel reflects and encourages this reluctance to accept women working. Generally, the novel represented virtuous working widows as women detached from business. Removed from the realities of economic exchange like actually laboring, managing employees, handling money, and acting in a professional, businesslike manner, the work that such widows do is converted into aspects of service to family and to community. Like the representation of the virtuous use of affluence by widows, the representation of the virtuous use of work by widows separates such women from the commercial sphere and situates them firmly within the maternal and the domestic.

Very few if any working widows in eighteenth-century fiction bear much resemblance to working widows in real life. Throughout the century, novels used a variety of strategies for representing working widows as anything but members of a commercial society. For example, although widows in novels do work, readers never see them exchanging their products or services for payment. In fact, money itself is noticeably and significantly absent from depictions of widows working. The nameless elderly spinners in Sarah Scott's *Millenium Hall* (1762) work in a self-sufficient, entirely closed and cashless barter economy. Sidney Bidulph in Frances Sheridan's *Memoirs of Miss Sidney Bidulph* (1769) plans to ease her poverty by starting a needlework business with her faithful maid, Patty. Although Patty sells a piece of her work, Sheridan does not show the transaction,

Sidney is almost ashamed of it, and the women put off their business until the spring. Had they proceeded according to their original plan, Sidney's landlady would have handled the actual sale of their handiwork. Sidney is ultimately rescued from having to work at all by the arrival of her wealthy cousin, Mr. Warner. Similarly, in *Clara Lennox* (1797) by Margaret Lee, while Clara describes herself "busily engaged with my needle and pencil" to support herself and her maid, at no point does the novel tell how her "painting and embroidering" are actually exchanged for money.[8]

Fictional widows also shy away from meaningful profit. They might start a business to insulate themselves from hardship, but they never "aspire beyond self-support" as Leonore Davidoff and Catherine Hall put it. Mrs. Darnford in Clara Reeve's *School for Widows* establishes a school, but when it becomes profitable, she gives it to a friend. In *The Governess* (1749), Sarah Fielding's schoolmistress Mrs. Teachum "was moderate in her desires, and did not seek to raise a great fortune, [so] she was resolved to take no more scholars than she could have an eye to herself without the help of other teachers."[9] Novels like *Sidney Bidulph* and *Clara Lennox* carefully distance the virtuous working woman from the actuality of commerce. None of the widows who work, from nameless nurses to sentimental protagonists, visibly exchanges the product of her labor for money, nor aims at more than a modest existence. Hiding this exchange emphasizes the behavior and feelings involved in the widow's situation and de-emphasizes its commercial aspects, a strategy particularly crucial in sentimental novels.

This limiting of ambition appears in the issue of social status, as well. Narrative's virtuous working widows accept their reduced circumstances. One of the most useful representations of widows working as subordinate to others, whether to men or to women of more exalted rank, is the virtuous widowed servant. Service was one of the common outlets for widows who needed to work, although widows with dependent children usually could not become live-in help.[10] When in Sarah Scott's *Sir George Ellison* (1766) the title character requests a housekeeper from his cousin, Mrs. Maynard of Millenium Hall, she tests his benevolence by offering a candidate with a twelve-year-old daughter whom she will not leave, and he passes the test by agreeing to hire her. As the narrator explains, "Mr. Ellison's fortune not obliging him to confine his expences within narrow bounds, he had no objection to his housekeeper's bringing a daughter with her;

and thought it a sort of duty, arising from the affluence of his circumstances, to take one who was by that particular excluded from most services."[11] His benevolence is first presented in economic terms—his "fortune not obliging him to confine his expences within narrow bounds"—and then in moral terms—he "thought it a sort of duty." The widow will cost extra, a practical consideration whose primacy in the discussion indicates its significance. As for the women who might have had their own home and a small business before bereavement, going into service, with all the dependence and lack of control such a situation entails, could not have been easy. Eighteenth-century novels tend to obscure any conflict such a decision might have entailed, however. Mrs. Gilson from *School for Widows*, for example, is the widow of a small farmer who inherited a debt that forced her into service. Now the housekeeper at Woodlands and her son a "farmer's servant," her only ambition is for her son to be promoted to "upper servant" (Reeve, 1:296–98).

Accepting their reduced social status includes insisting on their own subordination. Servants like Reeve's Mrs. Gilson or Mrs. Jervis in Samuel Richardson's *Pamela* (1740) possess a significant degree of potential influence in their respective households: aside from being the housekeeper of considerable estates, each has in her care impressionable, younger protagonists. But this is power that they sedulously avoid not only using, but also even recognizing. *School for Widows*, for example, makes Mrs. Gilson inferior in mental and financial self-sufficiency to her employer, and highly aware and accepting of these differences. Upon Mrs. Strictland's return from a long stay in London during her widowhood, she writes that Mrs. Gilson says "that I had spoiled her by my kindness and indulgence, and she could hardly endure my absence" (Reeve, 2:105). Evidently Mrs. Gilson cannot bear to be sole commander of Woodlands, but instead must be emotionally as well as financially dependent on a woman whose experience and knowledge of human nature as well as country life is inferior to her own. Similarly, Mrs. Jervis from *Pamela* takes such good care of Pamela that the girl repeatedly refers to the housekeeper in maternal terms, even calling her "my other mother!" Mrs. Jervis gets into trouble when she gets above herself: she is "turned away" for defending Pamela too assiduously and undermining the authority of her male employer. She stands as a warning to housekeepers, even those who are "poor gentlewom[e]n," not to overstep the bounds of their rank.[12]

As with the use of affluence discussed in chapter 2, virtuous widows use work either to restore or preserve class stability. When a virtuous working widow does change her social and financial situation, it is to return to the class from which she has fallen by loss or by marrying badly. Mrs. Darnford's work reinstates her in the independence to which she is entitled by birth and marriage. She becomes Donna Isabella's friend and "sister," not her nurse or housekeeper, and her employers or patrons reassert their dependence on her, rather than her dependence on them. Even when children are involved, widows act on their own behalf to restore the family's class position, but not to augment it. It is acceptable for a widow to maintain her class standing or to improve it in order to provide for her children, but rising beyond her original station is not. Reeve's Mrs. Martin achieves much, for example, but only with help and for the purpose of launching her son and marrying off her daughters. "I had four children to maintain," she says, "and wanted to fix uppon some way of business to help them and myself, till my son should be out of his time, and succeed to his father's business" (*School for Widows*, 1:13). Mrs. Teachum achieves sufficient success with her school that she need never seek pupils again, and the work that she does with her students is the same work that she performed with her own late daughters. She, too, returns to the situation from which death and bankruptcy dislodged her.

This restoration of class involves the restoration of their social milieu to its proper order as well. In *The Governess*, Mrs. Teachum's star pupil, Jenny Peace, returns to her family and to her surrogate mother, thereby repairing her birth family (S. Fielding, 103). Reeve's Mrs. Darnford recalls Donna Isabella to her senses by reestablishing order in Donna Isabella's house. First she reinstates appropriate relationships: her first effort is to create hierarchy in the household by "throw[ing]" servants such as Susan Dobbins to their "proper distance" (*School for Widows*, 2:239). Then she restores the physical manifestation of that proper order, reversing renovations in furniture and architecture. "I have ordered the double door to be opened during our absence," she reports. "The room is to be new white-washed and painted. The old escritoire and bureau are to be sent up another pair of stairs, and the room furnished as a dressing-room" (2:289). She teaches Donna Isabella how to run the house and begins to lead her into religious tolerance (2:249, 2:245–46). Captain Maurice, whose persecutions initially deranged Donna Isabella, also remains in his proper place: in the exile to which he has retreated from this well-ordered and distinctively female, domestic space.

Related to this limited ambition, particularly in the matter of servants, is the eighteenth-century novel's remarkable reconfiguration of work into its opposite, dependence. Clara Lennox, though earning money, articulates this conversion most overtly when she considers herself to be in a "dependent state" rather than in a commercial one (Lee, *Clara Lennox*, 2:115). Women making their own financial way consistently appear in narrative as unable to go it alone. Mrs. Darnford, for example, never loses her dependence on men. When she is menaced by the heir to Darnford Hall and by the wicked Lord A——, she seeks the help of a male protector, Mr. M——. "I should have been terrified by this letter, but my reliance upon my friend gave me courage: I depended that he would not suffer me to be arrested or insulted, and I despised these threatenings. I sent this letter also to him, and begged his advice and direction," she explains (Reeve, *School for Widows*, 1:176). With his help, she achieves emotional, personal, and economic security. She consults him again when she wants to start a school in the country, another critical point in her journey to financial independence (1:164–65, 1:230).

Henry Fielding's Mrs. Miller in *Tom Jones* (1747) also has achieved self-sufficiency through the benevolence of a male protector, and she repeatedly undercuts her autonomy with demonstrations of dependence. She has attained financial stability through Mr. Allworthy, who installed her in a house, gave her the money to furnish it, and endowed her with an annuity of fifty pounds per annum simply because he respected her husband.[13] She now lets rooms except when Mr. Allworthy wants them for himself. She feels perpetually and permanently indebted to him in a way that prevents her from feeling, and certainly appearing, assertive and entrepreneurial. The novel emphasizes her dependence, and at the same time reestablishes a hierarchical—and patriarchal— relationship where death—the advent of widowhood—would be understood to have eliminated it.

If a widow can't rely on a male savior, she usually can rely on a female one, sometimes even another widow. Although Mrs. Martin learns how to establish and run a business, ostensibly becoming independent, her endeavor is limited by her dependence. She inherited a shop, but it remains for Mrs. Darnford to supply the knowledge and determination to create a business, all the while educating

Mrs. Martin and her daughters. Mrs. Darnford provides the idea, training, and capital for Mrs. Martin to begin a local business in haberdashery (1:19). She offers, furthermore, to

> write, in your name, to an eminent haberdasher in London. I will desire him to send the best goods of every kind. I will write your letters, and shew you how to keep your book. One day-book will be sufficient for you, for you must sell for ready money only. You must be very punctual in your remittances of payment, which will induce your dealer to serve you well for your own sake. I shall be a customer to you, so will my scholars; and if your goods are of the best kinds, there is little doubt, that many people will come to the shop of a person so well known and respected as you are in this place. (1:20)

Mrs. Darnford even risks her own reputation and credit by placing all the orders under her own name. Furthermore, despite possessing two successful businesses and an excellent education, Mrs. Martin suffers without her mentor's presence: "I shall never for get the blessing I had in her society, nor ever cease to regret the loss of it, though it is for the good of her health, and for her worldly advantage," she announces, and "burst into tears" (Reeve, *School for Widows*, 1:18). Even the amazing Mrs. Darnford, the patroness of other women, seeks the advice of a female social superior about finding governess positions and opening her school (1:230).

Like Mrs. Martin in *School for Widows*, Madame Miteau in Sarah Scott's *The History of Cornelia* (1750) inherits a business from her husband but has no idea what to do with it. She is so overwhelmed by the responsibilities of the business and the debts that come with it, although presumably she has lived with the business during her marriage, that she sinks into depression. She has to be first restored to her proper senses and then introduced to the principles of running a business before she can take command of the millinery shop, and even then her potential authority as a self-sufficient businesswoman is undercut by being taught the business by her children and by the aristocratic, unmarried heroine, Cornelia. What Cornelia is allowed to figure out on her own from studying the books and watching other shops, the widow who has lived with the business is not allowed even to contemplate with equanimity.[14]

In reality, the working widow very probably knew the business well, especially if it had been conducted out of her own house, since at the least she would have been responsible for caring for apprentices and other workers. Consequently, she very probably understood how it worked. Paula McDowell points out that "For all but the wealthiest families, home and workshop were the same location, and businesses were passed down through families by intermarriage." When possible, widows frequently took over their husbands' business, and often apprenticed their own children to them to ensure their help in continuing it.[15] This is not the reality of the novel, however; instead, working widows serve at the pleasure of social superiors who grant them permission to know and to do. Equally important, while it is permissible for a good woman such as Mrs. Darnford or Cornelia to know the principles of business, it is less permissible for the woman who has been living in the house her whole married life to know the details of it. One explanation might be, as Peter Earle points out, that the practice of training a tradesman's wife to help in the business was dying out by the 1720s and 1730s in favor of female leisure.[16] Under those circumstances, one might argue that widows of tradesmen such as Mrs. Martin or Madame Miteau are ignorant because their husbands have kept them so, to follow the higher classes in their demonstration of wealth by keeping their women leisured. In this way, the eighteenth-century novel reflects the notion that the wife of the small-businessman should not be a participant in the business.

But the novel also goes further, suggesting that the widow of a working man should be given this knowledge and agency only by the correct authorities—higher class, often unthreateningly female—in order to save her family when the time comes. These authorities, although possessed of commercial knowledge, do not want it for themselves. Business knowledge thus is transformed from commodity to charity, the gift of a superior to an inferior. In this sense, the eighteenth-century novel places the transmission of economic knowledge within a sentimental framework. Widows of working men must acknowledge a stable class hierarchy to be eligible for the benevolence that grants them business knowledge. Business knowhow handed down in this fashion has as little connection to commerce as gifts of money have to commercial exchange. Removing this kind of knowledge from its commercial framework also obscures the idea that knowledge is a commodity. Living with a business, perhaps being part of its management, offers a wealth of experience and knowledge. By rendering women like Madame Miteau ignorant, the novel strips the widow of that dangerous asset, her experience, which all too directly connects widowhood and her life with the economy.

While ignorance of the commercial world is valuable, however, ignorance of the difference between the social and commercial worlds is not. When Clara Lennox tries to support herself by selling art and fancy embroidery, she reports that one possible customer responds, "There is bread for every person that will work, (said this once dear kind friend, as she presented me the guinea,) you should take in plain work; but you must draw and paint, and be a fine lady, and live on the public; be assured this is the last you will ever receive from me" (Lee, *Clara Lennox*, 2:38). As the former friend sees it, by selling her drawing and painting rather than plain work, Clara is insisting on maintaining as much as possible her status in the leisured classes. If she accepted her economic situation and its consequent translation in social terms, she would realize that she is no longer a "fine lady," stop depending on the charity of her friends to buy her work and therefore to support her, and start generating a client base by doing unglamorous, menial plain work. To the "once dear kind friend," Clara is a fraud, disguising dependence as self-support. The friend gives Clara too much credit: Clara has not thought through her business plan this carefully, which is a virtue in the sense that she is not commercial by nature. On the other hand, Clara transgresses by not distinguishing between the social and the commercial realms, as when she inappropriately asks a good friend for a post as governess in the woman's house (2:59). An employer and a friend are not the same. Unlike Mrs. Darnford, who has her jobs and her friends, Clara cannot separate personal from commercial, benevolence from commerce. Clara thus treats social relationships like commercial relationships, and social accomplishments like commodities. This doesn't bother Daniel Defoe earlier in the century; his *Moll Flanders* (1722) explores the way social and commercial markets overlap in principle and practice. It does bother Lee at the end of a century promoting a separation of women and the domestic from commercial endeavor.

As the example of Clara Lennox suggests, although sensibility offered a framework for women's economic behavior that allowed working women to be seen as moral rather than as depraved, that framework was more useful as a philosophy than a practice. Within sensibility, women's work had to be part of what Gillian Skinner calls a "virtuous display" intended to reveal a "virtuous femininity." Sensibility never fully reconciled work's association with the world and with knowledge, however. In certain cases economic understanding in women became virtually synonymous with sexual understanding, and therefore "To have prudence . . . implies sexual knowledge which a virtuous, innocent woman was not supposed to possess."[17] Commercial experience was equated with sexual experience, bad enough in married women but terrifying in unmarried women, especially widows. The "Jew's Widow" from Laurence Sterne's *Tristram Shandy* (1760–67), for example, is hotly pursued by Trim's brother Tom because she is the sole possessor of a successful sausage shop. Sterne constrains her autonomy by having her conform to stereotype: she remarries almost immediately, she chooses a much younger man, and she chooses a man who is marrying her for her money. She is both desirable and rendered inferior by desire because she is a self-sufficient widow.[18]

The concept of the domestic sphere solves the problem of public exposure for working women because the domestic was increasingly defined as a woman's proper place. The work that a woman did there was private; better still, if it was maternal in nature, it was increasingly defined not as work, but rather as normal female behavior. Work thus becomes mothering and stops being work. Even when the work takes place in what would seem like the public, commercial arena, as long as it is really or ultimately motherly behavior, it is not really work.[19] A plethora of minor characters demonstrate how work can be rewritten as maternal behavior and therefore dismissed. Often such women barely appear in the story, although they can serve important roles for the characters who encounter them. Caleb Williams (1794) is cheered by the "buxom, bluff, good-humoured widow" who runs an inn at which he briefly takes refuge. Her support for "Kit Williams" is based in both the maternal and the folk traditions of embracing the underdog, but she is excused from active service in Caleb's behalf by her ignorance that the young man to whom she speaks is the "handsome, likely a lad, as any in four counties round" whom she "loves" for outwitting his captors and pursuers. The nameless housekeeper in *Sir George Ellison* appears in the novel almost exclusively to nurse her employer, and widowed Mrs. Maningham in the same novel, managing the domestic aspects of her son's school in Jamaica, is never considered an employee of the school. Her work is presented as an excuse to remain with her son, not as employment. As James Balderson explains in *School for Widows*, when he fell ill, his daughter, Hannah, "advised me to send for a poor widow, that nursed us in our past illness, and did the last offices for my poor wife," and who helps Mr. Balderson find a buyer for his business.[20] These are the women who tend the hungry and the lonely, the ill and the pregnant, the newborn and the aged. Significantly, while the recipients of their nurturing are always grateful, those recipients and their authors often quickly move past the work such nurturing entails or past the person doing that nurturing; their narrative moments are brief. In this way the novel, especially the sentimental novel, minimizes their importance in society, even though in fact they are an important part of the fabric of life.

Widows who go into service also recast work as maternal behavior. *Pamela*'s Mrs. Jervis needs money to pay "old debts," but they are "old debts for her children" (Richardson, *Pamela*, 478). While such characters may have started in their position from financial need, they serve others as part of their natural, maternal impulses. They don't need the money; they just like taking care of people. When Mrs. Strictland comes to Woodlands as a bride, she has very little idea of how to be a wife, especially a squire's wife. Mrs. Gilson mothers her, teaching her how to run the house, curb her imagination, establish a relationship with her husband, and arrange to get as much as possible of what she wants from a temperamental and tyrannical spouse. Although her service is invaluable, Mrs. Gilson never escapes her servant status for a moment. These women also reinforce the depiction of working widows as comfortable with their subordination, because they are not simply content, but acting naturally when they subordinate their desires to take care of others. In this way a class hierarchy is simultaneously reinforced and obscured by depicting service as mothering.

The depiction of work as service to others, especially as mothering, appears in novels published throughout the century and includes protagonists. Mrs. Teachum considers her role as a "trust [which] she endeavoured faithfully to discharge" and considers her students "committed to her care" (S. Fielding, *Governess*, 1). Clara Lennox first seeks employment as a governess. Mrs. Darnford takes several governess positions in London and at each, exposes flaws in the parents and offers solutions. After her last place, one of the girls whose mother encouraged disrespect, ignorance, and ingratitude pursues Mrs. Darnford by letter, soliciting her help despite the girl's mother's opinions (Reeve, *School for Widows*, 2:215–17). Even when she seems to fail, in the end Mrs. Darnford succeeds—she replaces the improper mother of the family—because her impulse is genuinely maternal. When she moves to the country, she does so to become a schoolmistress, taking up the education of girls exactly as Sarah Fielding's Mrs. Teachum does. Such an undertaking conforms to constructions of maternity gaining currency throughout the period and Mrs. Darnford, for one, applies it everywhere, as a code of life rather than as an occupation. She mothers her landlady into opening a shop, mothers Mrs. Martin's daughters into being assistants at the school, and finally mothers Donna Isabella into sanity.

These efforts are novelistic versions of the Hardwicke Act's attempt to promote families that would produce self-sufficient, contributing members of the empire, and they are most explicitly spelled out by Daniel Defoe's *Moll Flanders*. Moll's first nurse takes in orphans of the parish, educates them, teaches them proper deportment, and trains them to "go to Service, or get their own Bread." By training Moll with the needle, Moll's first Nurse helps her avoid service and begin to establish her own business in needlework.[21] Her death deprives Moll not only of a "good Motherly Creature" but also of her bank, since Moll loses all the money that has been set aside for her by her Nurse. Defoe's connection between a surrogate mother and a bank spells out in fairly unambiguous terms the period's recognition of the connection between mothering and economics, preparing one's children for adulthood and training them to be economically productive without being productive (unless reproductive) oneself.[22]

Narrative's virtuous widows more obviously in business—entrepreneurial widows, one might call them—still base their endeavor on maternal behavior and values. Because Mrs. Darnford and Mrs. Teachum worry about the children in their care, they achieve tremendous economic success and the adulation of everyone who knows them. Similarly Mrs. Miller from *Tom Jones*, while running a business, is really first and foremost a virtuous maternal widow. "In short," the narrator reports, "though her power was very small, she was in her heart one of the warmest friends. She had been a most affectionate wife, and was a most fond and tender mother" (H. Fielding, 579–80). These are character recommendations, but not the hallmarks of strong business sense in a vicious, unregulated, commercial economy. Her efforts to maintain the good reputation of

her lodgings, something requisite for attracting respectable and sol-
vent lodgers, are based on her widowhood and connected overtly to
her skills as a mother. When Tom's visits with assorted women in the
middle of the night become obtrusive, Mrs. Miller asks him to either
stop or take up residence elsewhere. She does not do so for the ab-
stract claims of respectability that accompany the protestations of
innkeeper's wives along the road to London in *Tom Jones*, but for the
particular claims of her family. "I hope you will consider the ill consequence which it must be to the reputations of my poor girls, if my
house should once be talked of as a house of ill fame," she explains
to Tom, "but if you are resolved to [intrigue], I must beg you to take
another lodging; for I do not myself like to have such things carried
on under my roof; but more especially upon the account of my girls,
who have little, Heaven knows, besides their characters to recommend them" (617, 618). Her concern is well-founded: when Tobias
Smollett's Peregrine Pickle interrupts a tryst between a lecherous religious man and the young woman procured for him, it turns out
that the young woman has become a prostitute after one of her widowed mother's boarders seduced her.[23]

Furthermore, Mrs. Miller generously takes a parental interest in
other families and in Tom himself, fretting that "if my daughters and
my own reputation were out of the case, I should, for your own sake,
be sorry that so pretty a young gentleman should converse with
these women" (618). In explaining that Tom's behavior cannot continue under her roof, Mrs. Miller does the correct business thing to
do but, like Mrs. Teachum, justifies it as the correct maternal thing
to do. In so doing, these women make good business, good mothering, and good morals all the same thing. Business under these circumstances, although (or perhaps because) it is conducted by a
woman, is acceptable in spite (or perhaps because) of her gender.
Since certain kinds of maternal behavior are presented during this
period as natural, these kinds of work stop being part of commercial
enterprise and instead are manifestations of woman's nature.

So far, the widows examined here succeed precisely because they
integrate maternal behavior or instincts with their work. In taking
care of individuals' well-being, however, widows whose work is recast
as mothering are also taking care of society's well-being; they are
maintaining the social structure. Women who work know their
place, as demonstrated by their willing service to others, and that
service in turn teaches its recipients what their own place is. Moll

Flanders's first Nurse does not just teach Moll how to get started in business; she also teaches her a great deal about financial stability and class. George Ellison's housekeeper teaches the Grantham girls to read, thereby helping them acquire accomplishments suitable to their future as daughters of a duke (Scott, *Sir George Ellison*, 75). Mrs. Teachum's educational aims—to give students "all useful knowledge; to render them obedient to their superiors, and gentle, kind, and affectionate to each other" (S. Fielding, *Governess*, 1)—reflect a communal orientation and acceptance of female subordination. Running a dairy, a traditionally female and independent occupation, becomes a business designed to mother girls, and girls of higher rank. For *Pamela*'s dairy woman Mrs. Dobson to establish an "elegancy" in "every thing, persons as well as furniture," her primary business seems really to be supplying the Brandons and the local school girls with amusement and refreshment (Richardson, *Pamela*, 495). The dairy woman in Sarah Fielding's *The Governess* also runs her own dairy farm, but Fielding strips her of her name as well as of her independence by making her serve Mrs. Teachum, formerly married to a clergyman and therefore married to better things, and her pupils, "our little gentry" (49). Although "rewarded" for twice allowing the students to "eat plentifully" of the dairy's products and pick her "finest roses and pinks," the "good old woman" explains then and again on a later visit that her real pleasure is in the company of young people and in making them happy, even giving them "three baskets of very fine" strawberries picked by her daughter (49–50, 92). Technically she is in business selling milk and dairy products, but she succeeds because her real interest lies in nourishing and delighting her social superiors.

Using relationships to legitimate and also to limit the connection between work and widows specifically, and women more broadly, shifts the emphasis on work from a solo enterprise for the benefit of the person working to an enterprise for the benefit of others, namely a community. As participants in a highly competitive, increasingly commercial economy, such figures are expected to contend with others. Recasting their work as service to a community, however, prevents working widows from vying with others, which as businesswomen they are entitled to do. In her reading of *School for Widows*, for example, April London argues that the novel endorses a middle-class set of values, but orients those values toward community rather than "the competitive behavior often seen as characteristic of the new economic order." Similarly, Sara Gadeken points out that novels of female community consistently

> suppose instead that an individual is produced by and embedded in her community, and that her capacities develop within a context of nonconsensual relations, namely a society and a family, which she does not choose. The values that these communities hold to be of paramount importance, which the members must not learn but internalize, include self-control, trust, compassion, and respect for truth.

These novels reject competition for community, but accept the virtue of hard work and so forth. I also would argue that this community orientation and rejection of economic competition characterizes the treatment of working widows, and that it is one aspect of a larger collection of values emerging during the period to conceptualize women, work, and commercial society.[24]

This problem with competition and the appropriation of work, even traditionally female work, by the commercial economy as "man's work" appears perhaps most famously in the conflict between wife and husband, and especially between midwife and man-midwife, in Laurence Sterne's *Tristram Shandy*. Sterne's depiction of the contest between male and female control of childbirth provides a microview of a very real development, physicians' self-organization into the medical profession and their move to take the lucrative and consistent market in childbirth away from midwives, who were always women. One casualty of medicine's professionalization was midwifery, a traditionally female province, which increasingly gave way to doctors, medical schools, and instruments such as forceps starting in the early eighteenth century.[25] Sterne's depiction of the battle in the Shandy household for control of the birth process and for respect, then, is a narrative depiction of a larger historical trend occurring throughout England, although hopefully not taking place in scenes like this.

Sterne's Midwife is historically exact. She has been rescued from an inappropriate poverty by training her for a profession, but that profession is designed to support the community rather than to profit her. In *Tristram Shandy*, the midwife

> had been left, it seems, a widow in great distress, with three or four small children, in her forty-seventh year, and as she was at that time a

person of decent carriage,—grave deportment,—a woman moreover of few words, and withall an object of compassion, whose distress and silence under it call'd out the louder for a friendly life: the wife of the parson of the parish was touch'd with pity; and having often lamented an inconvenience, to which her husband's flock had for many years been exposed, inasmuch, as there was no such thing as a midwife, of any kind or degree to be got at, let the case have been ever so urgent, within less than six or seven long miles riding; which said seven long miles in dark nights and dismal roads, the country thereabouts being nothing but a deep clay, was almost equal to fourteen; and that in effect was sometimes next to having no midwife at all; it came into her head, that it would be doing a seasonable kindness to the whole parish, as to the poor creature herself, to get her a little instructed in some of the plain principles of her business, in order to set her up in it. (12)

Evidently the rescue of poor women to train them for midwifing service to the community was not unheard of. Jean Donnison reports that the squire or parson in country parishes might sponsor a midwife to attend the poor, either by paying her salary or funding her training. In the records from Society for Bettering the Condition and Increasing the Comforts of the Poor (1798), the Reverend Mr. Dolling, late Vicar of Aldenham, reports that he

selected a poor widow, who had three children supported by the parish, and sent her up, for instruction, to the Lying-in Hospital, in Store-street, near Tottenham-Court Road; where Dr. Osborn permitted her to continue for three months, at a very small expence. Tho without any preparatory education, she returned so well instructed, as to exercise her calling in the parish ever since, without a single accident, or ever having occasion to call in medical assistance. She has been enabled thereby to support herself and her children comfortably; and is now living, and in the enjoyment of the confidence due to her skill. She attends all the day-labourers' wives, at the stipulated sum of half-a-crown.[26]

Sterne and Dolling's midwives have crucial similarities: they are not young women, they have dependents, and, like Madame Miteau, Mrs. Miller, and Mrs. Martin, they have been established in business by a social superior who intends them to serve the neighborhood, as they do. Considering such women servants of the community rather than professionals establishes a conceptual framework that permits their work because it serves others, not just—or primarily—themselves. Working widows must work for a greater good, and they must do that work through the developing and narrowing female sphere.

Sterne's interpretation of the shift from midwife to medical man favors the midwives. Although the midwife "had really some little claim to be depended upon,—as much, at least, as success could give her; having, in the course of her practice of near twenty years in the parish, brought every mother's son of them into the world without any one slip or accident which could fairly be laid to her account" (Sterne, *Tristram Shandy*, 39), the majority of men in the novel have no respect for her or her record, even when faced with the questionable competence of Dr. Slop. He and the other men insist that the midwife indicate her subordination to him by leaving the birthing chamber to attend on him, and Walter Shandy insists that having an "old midwife" or a "lean old mother of a midwife" endangers his wife's life, the life of the baby, and the life of all future children (116, 81). The midwife's excellent record cannot withstand male society's misogyny, and Sterne makes it clear that this refusal to recognize female skill, at least in some areas, endangers society in others.[27] As the professionalization of medicine appropriated experience (women have babies) for expertise (doctors make it possible for women to have babies properly), what had been traditionally female (giving birth, midwifery) became gendered male (a disordered body, obstetrics). The attitudes that accompanied and enabled this shift, articulated by Mr. Shandy, show how in belief and practice the regendering of work could take place. Furthermore, scenes like this one in *Tristram Shandy* also show how virtuous women's work was presented as supportive of the community, rather than of the individual in his quest for money, power, and status through the commercial system.

This framework for representing the working widow reinforces the notion of a stable hierarchy even at the same moment that the commercial economy was coming to offer tremendous opportunity for socioeconomic mobility. As part of this framework, the eighteenth-century novel criticizes working widows who reject the notion of a stable hierarchy and often zestfully participate in the commercial world. These women have an eye for the main chance, frequently see their own gain deriving from the exploitation of others, and therefore do not have a good sense of their place. Susan Dobbins, Mrs. Gilson's counterpart in *School for Widows*, is "a young widow, who had lately buried her husband and child: they died of the small pox." She recovered, however, and "Finding she could not support herself, she resolved to go into service" (Reeve, 2:191–92). While Mrs. Gilson speaks beautifully and has a responsible and hearty son, Susan Dobbins has neither the correct speech nor the children to prove her worth. Although the novel allows her to be "an honest and tidy woman," she is always also "very vulgar and clownish; and Isabella was disgusted with her, and did not like her about her person" (2:191–92). She begins the novel badly by offending Isabella, helping Captain Maurice deceive her with a sham marriage, and tricking her into receiving him in the house after he has insulted her with his advances one time too many. Once she gives up her self-interested initiative, however, she becomes nurturing rather than exploiting. She warns Captain Maurice that Mrs. Barton, the nurse he has hired to cure Isabella of her insanity, is abusing Isabella; she stays in the house despite her firm belief that it is haunted and her knowledge that it shelters a crazy woman; and eventually, she takes up her proper place as a deferential servant to the real owner of the house, not its usurper.

Widows such as the unreformed Susan Dobbins work without the ameliorating effects of benevolence or other appropriately female-associated qualities; they are women interested primarily in the personal gain to be expected from working for money. Landladies comprise a particularly notable population of this group. Both the aptly named Mrs. Miser and Mrs. Savage from *Clara Lennox* threaten their female tenants with eviction or debtor's prison, and Mrs. Miser attempts to force Clara to accept depraved Colonel Elwood's immoral attentions. As the Colonel explains, he has

> engaged my landlady in my interest, and bribed her with that sweet charm gold, to stop all the letters to and from her, and comfort the poor girl, yet act as my friend. As soon as my charmer was able to sit up, Mrs. *Miser* introduced me, declaring I would pay her whatever debts Miss *Lennox* had contracted, if she would aid and assist in getting her for me, and would do something handsome for them both: this had the desired effect on this mercenary woman. (Lee, 1:22–23)

When Susan Dobbins reforms, she becomes a servant interested in someone else's welfare; these women never reform and never become interested in someone other than themselves.

This self-interest is not always associated with sexuality, as the case of another mercenary landlady, Mrs. Horton from Elizabeth Inchbald's *A Simple Story* (1791) demonstrates, but it clearly remains associated with financial avarice and the consummation of individual desires. Mrs. Horton took in lodgers before she was widowed, but she seems particularly unforgivably interested in the pecuniary advantage of this scheme now that she has lost her husband.[28] When she hears that Miss Milner is to join her house, "Mrs. Horton was delighted with the addition this acquisition to her family was likely to make to her annual income, and to the style of her living" (7). In addition to money, which she enjoys but does not need, Mrs. Horton seeks gratification in almost every other possible, nonsexual way. She "expected every thing to happen just as she wished, (for neither an excellent education, the best company, or long experience had been able to cultivate or brighten this good lady's understanding,)" and consistently acts hypocritically, equivocates, enjoys a good fight, approves her own actions, and relishes gossiping with other mean-spirited women (10, 17, 29, 31, 75). Mrs. Horton could be a motherly figure to Miss Milner and the other unmarried, younger woman of the house, Miss Woodley, but she chooses not to be. She is no Mrs. Miller from *Tom Jones*. Similarly, Betty Grant, the "beldam" from Charlotte Smith's *Old Manor House* (1793) who looks after Rayland Hall after it has been stolen from its proper heir, is more interested in her own situation than in the preservation of the house or in the sentimental protagonist, Orlando. She looks after herself to the neglect of justice, the proper transmission of property, and therefore of England. Her appearance raises associations with witches, underscoring how her work supports values rejected by the novel.[29]

Such women are the commercial spirit in an ugly incarnation, particularly since they convert domestic space into profitable space. In this transformation they reject the rules for women through their own behavior, and the rules for space through their commercial manipulation of it. By attempting to make the domestic the commercial, these landladies reject efforts to separate male and female activity, and male and female space. They are therefore vilified thoroughly. Other characters also serve as explorations of the problem when commercial and domestic space overlap, most notably Mrs. Martin and Madame Miteau, two widows who, in inheriting domestic space, also inherit business space. If the home and the business are to be separated according to which members of the family operate within them, then what happens when a widow must control the commercial space as well as the domestic space? What if those areas are not just under the one roof, as they are with the landladies and the artisans' widows, but embodied in one woman, a widow? In deplorable widows like Mrs. Horton or Mrs. Savage, this convergence of space, practice, and identity are willful, enjoyed, manipulated for greater profit and enjoyment. In virtuous widows like Mrs. Martin and Madame Miteau, the widows first refuse to accept this convergence (Mrs. Martin is stymied and Madame Miteau is catatonic) and only come to terms with it when granted permission by a benevolent, higher social authority.

In many ways, the epitome of how sensibility and its economic links created an acceptable framework for widows' work is the first working widow presented in this chapter, Mrs. Darnford from Clara Reeve's *School for Widows*. Reeve's portrayal of Mrs. Darnford's fall into poverty is detailed, protracted, and compassionate. Mrs. Darnford's husband, a landed gentleman, drank and gamed himself to bankruptcy and death, leaving Mrs. Darnford destitute and homeless. During her marriage, she nobly and obediently signed over her jointure to him to support his final efforts to salvage himself and the estate. Upon her widowhood, she needs money more than goods and therefore chooses to exchange dower for a lump sum, allowing her friend Mr. M—— to threaten James Darnford, the heir to the Darnford estate, with a lawsuit to claim Mrs. Darnford's one-third unless young Darnford settles one hundred and fifty pounds in cash on her immediately. She receives the money after relinquishing "the plate, linen, &c. the farming stock, and utensils; and the crops now upon the ground" (1:186–87). Homeless and without a husband, jointure, or trade, Mrs. Darnford appears on the brink of destitution.

Mrs. Darnford is not allowed to starve, however, nor is she allowed to wallow in misery the way a widow like Clara Lennox is. By the end of her correspondence and the novel, Mrs. Darnford is no longer working for her upkeep, but living as the guest and friend of her last client, Donna Isabella, and the occasional guest and constant friend of the affluent Mrs. Strictland. Simply removing her from the exchange of cash for services and rendering her dependent, useful strategies with other characters, cannot obscure the fact that Mrs. Darnford goes into business for herself several times, succeeds spectacularly, and, after moving up and down economically and socially, concludes the novel safely ensconced in the class in which by birth and marriage she ought to be.

Salvation for Mrs. Darnford is achieved through a middle-class work ethic that justifies and explains the economic and social movement that saves her from penury. Her eldest sister married a "woollen-draper and stuff-mercer in London," and the family goes there for the wedding (1:42), suggesting that Mrs. Darnford was born into a provincial tradesman's family. Exemplifying the economic possibilities of the period, Mrs. Darnford's father clearly has sufficient means to bring both his children to London, to provide well for them, and to marry Mrs. Darnford to a landed gentleman. Mrs. Darnford possesses all the values propounded by a group that would become the middle class: responsible handling of money, expending only part of one's income, retrenching when necessary, abjuring sensual pleasures for charitable deeds and domestic life, and living on the estate rather than idling in London. In fact, while she has married into leisure, Mrs. Darnford applies a working mentality to her marriage and new status, and then to her widowhood. Her tragedy is her husband's rejection of her attitudes in favor of a hedonistic, aristocratic existence, and her triumph is her ability to adhere to bourgeois values and behaviors in spite of him and the life he inflicts on her.

The events of Reeve's life partly explain Mrs. Darnford's career and beliefs. Reeve's values were resolutely middle class, which from what we know or conjecture about her life was consistent with her experience. Born into a family that worked for a living—there were clergymen, jewelers, and navy men among them—Reeve, like many other female novelists, experienced a fall from her birth class when her father died. She managed to return to her original station first by working as a domestic, then by combining income from writing with a small annuity from one of her employers. Reeve's life certainly confirms Mrs. Darnford's experience that honest work can sustain, redeem, and reward.[30]

Although Reeve's deployment of a form of practical, heavily moral sensibility may be consistent with the facts of her life, however, it is also part of larger developments at the end of the eighteenth century: the consolidation of middle-class power and the development of sensibility. Certainly Mrs. Darnford's work life conforms to the expectations for working women established by sensibility earlier in the century. For example, since virtuous employment by a widow must take place within a framework of giving, whether through benevolence or through maternalism, almost from the start of *School for Widows*, Mrs. Darnford is firmly situated within this system of benevolence. She does not depend on others, especially her friends, to pay her for her abilities, although she relies on them for advice and support, the exchangeable goods of friendship rather than of commerce. Nearly the first thing we learn about her, for example, is that although impoverished by her late husband, Mrs. Darnford has helped a still-poorer widow with four children to become self-sufficient. First, she takes Mrs. Martin's two daughters as assistants at Mrs. Darnford's school for girls (1:16–17), and then helps the other widow, Mrs. Martin, to go into business for herself. She then offers to give Mrs. Martin all the skills which she, Mrs. Darnford, already possesses and could use herself to make money. She even promises to spend money at the store that she has created to benefit someone else. Ultimately, she decides to make Mrs. Martin "full partner in school. . . . [And] If I like my situation, and if the school succeeds with you, I will quit it entirely to you" (1:30). Mrs. Darnford demonstrates economic disinterest rather than commercial self-interest. At no time, in fact, does she work for her own benefit or economic gain, but rather for other women. Even if a widow is struggling with poverty, to be virtuous as well as struggling, she must be trying to care for others. Whether a benefactress or benefactee, as Mrs. Darnford illustrates, the working widow is most virtuous when she is firmly situated within sensibility and seemingly removed from business.

While sensibility's general characteristics such as the emphasis on sympathy and benevolence may have remained somewhat constant during its rise and fall, however, Reeve's sentimental framework is not quite the same sentimental framework used in earlier works. Sensibility does appear throughout the century to be meant as a form of social glue, but its relationship to and valuing of different groups such as people in trade, working people, or the aristocracy changes over time. In novels such as Sheridan's *Memoirs of Miss Sidney Bidulph*, Frances Burney's *Evelina* (1778), or Scott's *History of Sir George Ellison*, sensibility remains strongly tied to traditional values, including the traditional ordering of society. Sheridan and the early Burney are critical of the aristocracy, for example, but not unrelievedly so. Sheridan's Lady Bidulph and her titled friends are certainly set on having their own way and therefore are damaging to Sidney, while the young male aristocrats in Burney's *Evelina* are almost to a man contemptible objects. On the other hand, Sheridan's titled ladies are well-intentioned, and her Lady V—— and Burney's Lady Howard are truly good women; both Sidney and Evelina, although not equally happy, end their novels in landed comfort. Evelina has even married a lord.

The career of Sir George Ellison most clearly illustrates how sensibility at this point reflects a need to defend mercantile capitalism and its practitioners against charges of selfishness and greed. When George Ellison leads his exemplary life in 1766, he does so first as a merchant, then as a landed gentleman, and last as a knight, having inherited title and (a second) estate. He has pursued trade brilliantly, but never simply to be rich. Consistently, the wealth he accrues is meant for doing good—for his family, his slaves, the local poor, and so forth—without changing the social and economic superiority it confers on him. In a speech to his cousin, Sir William, he emphatically "allow[s] the necessity of subordination." "I raise no one to the same affluence that I enjoy, though I endeavour to give them the blessing of plenty," he assures Sir William; "surely then I am far from destroying the subordination you think so necessary; an opinion I am not going to dispute" (78–79). Sarah Scott may have wished to reform society to be less selfish, to educate women, and to support the English worker, but in the 1760s, she also employs sensibility to confirm the class hierarchy, including its placement of landed aristocrats at the top. When Sir George has been able to retire from engaging in trade himself, succeeded to title and estate, and married to the partner appropriate to his extensive catalog of benevolent projects (a widow, by the way—Mrs. Tunstall), his life has reached the apex of virtue and success according to sensibility at this moment. This picture of society indicates that trade was still valued as inferior and that those engaged in it still needed to present their search for profits as designed to facilitate benevolence.

Late-century texts such as Reeve's *School for Widows*, however, reveal that the values used to justify and legitimate mercantile capitalism had moved considerably closer to the mainstream. That is not to suggest that those in business dominated Britain by the 1790s; novels like Robinson's sensational *The Widow* or even Smith's *The Old Manor House* show how criticism of the aristocracy based on ideas catalyzed by trade did not automatically entail the overturning of the traditional hierarchy. Nevertheless, that in Reeve's England the aristocracy is generally corrupt indicates how far those in trade had come. In *The School for Widows*, the newly landed Mr. Darnford is uncomfortable with his wife's commercial origins, and as she explains it to Mrs. Strictland, "desired me not to visit my sister or her husband often, but by degrees to break with them . . . for he had no relish for any *bourgeois* acquaintance; and besides, if it were known that he visited tradesmen, he might be excluded the higher circles" (1:44; Reeve's emphasis). When Mrs. Darnford exhorts him to "regularity and oeconomy," Mr. Darnford disdainfully rejects her "Paltry bourgeois qualities!" (1:49). He is repaid for this attitude with conjugal and economic failure and death. His friend Lord A—— chases Mr. Darnford's wife and even essentially buys her from him, and women like Lady Houghton treat Mrs. Darnford as a piece of furniture. Reeve's aristocrats are indolent, ungrateful people who abuse their wealth and the people who make it possible. Conversely, landowners like Mrs. Strictland who operate their estates for the benefit of their family and the community that depends on them are approved, and working people such as Mrs. Darnford and Mr. M—— are commonsensical, competent, and virtuous. When people choose to abandon their middle-class orientation, as Mr. Darnford does upon inheriting his uncle's estate and therefore a place among the upper echelons (1:42–43), disaster ensues.

The handling of commercial and domestic space in late century novels also demonstrates how much acceptance the changes wrought by mercantile capitalism had achieved. Admittedly, Mrs. Martin and her counterpart from 1750, Madame Miteau, experience similar problems—the overlap of domestic and business space, the inability to run a business without permission from a social superior—and other novels of the 1790s, such as *A Simple Story* or *Clara Lennox,* sound much like Henry Fielding's 1749 novel *Tom Jones* in their insistence that landladies be maternal and in their rejection of the home as a site of business. Nevertheless, while Reeve's strategies for handling commercial and domestic space are not so different from her predecessors, that she deploys them at the same time that she boldly endorses a set of values associated with mercantile capitalism indicates how far mercantile capitalism had moved toward acceptance. Furthermore, when Mrs. Darnford tries to get Mr. Darnford to apply what would later be called middle-class values to living his life, she is doing more than carrying domestic virtues into the workplace, thereby converting the workplace into a version of the home (as she does with Donna Isabella's house, for example). She is also carrying commercial virtues into the home. In other words,

Reeve's *School for Widows* illustrates that at the same time that work was becoming a public function undertaken in specific, public places, the values associated with work were becoming simply values, a sign of the proximity to the center—the political, social, and cultural center—that attitudes generated by commerce had achieved by century's end.

At the same time that sensibility was more overtly connected to the values and ideas of those working for a living, it was also dividing. Sentimental works emphasizing emotional response, such as Lee's *Clara Lennox*, were still a literary presence and influence, but as Anne K. Mellor demonstrates, starting in about 1780, women writers also developed an alternative tradition, which synthesized emotionality and rationality. For them, "sensibility must be joined with correct perception" as well as the "workings of the rational mind." This meant that in the novels of authors like Reeve, the "values of domesticity—the private virtues of sympathy, tolerance, generosity, affection, and a commitment to an ethic of care—should become the guiding program for all *public* or civic action," male or female, since these values unite reason and feeling, head and heart. Certainly the practical, didactic vein of sensibility appears in *The School for Widows* in Reeve's celebration of Mrs. Darnford, whose work ethic is impressive but also impressively community oriented. Reeve's *School for Widows* demonstrates the emerging ideology of a "subjectivity constructed in relation to other subjectivities," a self that "typically locates its identity in its connections with a larger human group, whether the family or a social community."[31]

School for Widows thus indicates the strengthening position of mercantile capitalism in the English social consciousness at this point in the century. In placing Mrs. Darnford, the embodiment of "bourgeois" values and behavior as one of the poles of the narrative, Reeve reveals how far those who work for a living, particularly those in trade have come culturally. That is not to suggest, however, that *School for Widows* advocates women in business. On the contrary, Reeve uses the "bourgeois sensibility" that Mr. Darnford mocks to pursue an agenda that characterizes sensibility throughout the eighteenth century: the limitation of women's economic activity. Both rational sensibility and emotional sensibility resist the idea of independent women's work: as this study shows, sensibility was a useful tool for stabilizing a society unbalanced by rising commercialism, particularly as it described proper female behavior as removed from economics. Reeve's Mrs. Darnford epitomizes these attitudes. She is not interested in personal gain, but in the welfare of others. Her business acumen may derive from her family background and gender, but never from any employment experience. She remembers her place, accepts the benevolence of others with appropriate gratitude, and uses sensible but equally benevolent and nurturing behavior to shape her work as a wife, governess, teacher, and nurse. She proves the claim that when good women work, they are only doing what comes naturally to them through their genetic makeup as females. Lastly, Mrs. Darnford's work eventually returns her to a life of leisure, a state that developing ideas about gender and work endorsed for women. Her life is "Bourgeoise's Progress," as it were, from work in the city to retired leisure in the country. The ideal situation was for a man to make enough money to keep the women in his family from having to work, and therefore the ideal situation for a woman was to not work. When Mrs. Darnford restores herself to a life of leisure, she is merely reinforcing the ideal trajectory sketched for anyone in mercantile capitalism, and especially for women: work so that women do not work.[32] In all these ways—redefining women's work, redefining the nature of work, and aiming virtuous work toward leisure—the eighteenth-century novel participates in the period's evolving ideas about the relationship between men, women, and their emerging commercial economy, a project well developed by the time *School for Widows* appeared in 1791.

Peter Earle notes that "despite the literary emphasis on the wealthy widow," real widows of the "middling sort" had a hard time making ends meet, even when they inherited a thriving business.[33] His remark about "literary emphasis" acknowledges another significant phenomenon of the working widow in the novel: the difficulty in finding one. Not so for working men. Male merchants, bankers, surgeons, laborers, peddlers, footmen, valets, guides, lawyers, farmers, innkeepers, gamekeepers, gaolers, bailiffs, sailors, soldiers, musicians, goldsmiths, blacksmiths, mercers, linen drapers, and so on riddle the novel from its inception to the end of the century. The relative invisibility of the working widow, and I would add, of the poor and criminal widow, is part of the relative invisibility of the nonaffluent woman. This chapter thus heralds the opening of an inquiry into aspects of the eighteenth century's commercial and industrial society that are usually not well illustrated or represented. The difficulty in finding such women is a symptom of a larger disease, a product of

and discomfort with the fact that the gendered justification and the-
orization of mercantile capitalism not only explains and produces
the tremendous wealth and wealth of opportunity available to men,
but also explains and produces the tremendous dearth and dearth
of opportunity available to women. These shortages resulted in
crushing poverty and hardship to the same female figures so determinedly sentimentalized in literature. The novel's representation of
working women is complex because of ambivalent or negative attitudes toward working women, but also because of the novel's struggle to negotiate the tension between preference and actuality. The
novel may or may not be realist; that argument is for others. But in
responding to its time, the eighteenth-century novel's depiction of
working widows suggests ways in which the endorsement of mercantile capitalism is also a very specific erasure of populations and the
issues that they represent.

4

Poor, Pathetic, and Positive:
Poverty and the Widow

> . . . it may be some poor Widow like me, that had pack'd up
> these Goods to go and sell them for a little Bread for herself
> and a poor Child, and are now starving and breaking their
> Hearts; for want of that little they would have fetch'd. . . .
> —Daniel Defoe, *Moll Flanders*

AT THE SAME TIME THAT OPPORTUNITIES FOR A WOMAN TRYING TO
work diminished, the system of charity for impoverished women was
also changing. Despite the tremendous increase in national wealth
and the rise of sensibility, resistance to systemic charity intensified
throughout the eighteenth century, making the poor increasingly
dependent on private institutions and individuals. Nor did the novel
provide a representation of impoverished widowhood designed to alleviate its very real misery. Although the historical record offers evidence that poor, nonworking widows—women who, for various reasons, did not turn to labor to mitigate their poverty—did their active
best to find help, the fictional record offers an opposite image of
these women. The eighteenth-century novel's poor widows consistently appear as passive, dependent, and grateful, a depiction that
underscores not the calamity of their poverty but the triumph of others' generosity. In portraying poor widows as submissive and dependent, novelists supported the idea that the proper response to gross
economic inequality was the display of individual benevolence by the
wealthy toward the less fortunate. Like the representation of work
discussed in chapter 3, the representation of poverty shifted the
focus from labor and commerce to emotion and hierarchy. As a re-

sult, the novel's representation of the poor widow offered another way to model the exclusion of women from the economy, simultaneously justifying and hiding the realities of emerging capitalism, and helping to establish the novel as a genre and sensibility as an ideology.

Perhaps the earliest appearance of a poor widow in an eighteenth-century novel is the "good ancient widow" from Daniel Defoe's *Robinson Crusoe* (1719).[1] This nameless woman is the widow of the Captain who introduced Crusoe to trade. She is a steadfast friend to Crusoe throughout his life. "I trusted her so entirely with every Thing," Crusoe reports, "that I was perfectly easy as to the Security of my Effects; and indeed, I was very happy from my beginning, and now to the End, in the unspotted Integrity of this good Gentlewoman" (218). She is not only his "old Friend," but also his "faithful Steward and Instructor," "principal Guide, and Privy Councellor" (206, 218). She is "just," "faithful," generous, caring, and a "true Friend" (14, 200, 206, 219). She has been, in fact, the caretaker of his finances for much of his life. When Crusoe left on his first independent trading voyage, he "lodg'd with my Friend's widow, who was very just to me" the two hundred pounds he earned by selling the gold dust that he brought from Guinea (14). Upon his return from captivity with the Moors, "she not only delivered the Money, but out of her own Pocket sent the *Portugal* Captain a very handsome Present for his Humanity and Charity" when rescuing him and Xury at sea (28).

Here then is the perfect bank: it returns money readily when asked and it takes a special interest in depositors' circumstances.[2] This widow combines financial probity with maternal benevolence. She still holds Crusoe's money even though he is gone some time and she is living husbandless in London, and she is so concerned with his welfare that she rewards out of her own pocket the man who returns Crusoe to her. In this gesture, she models the generous, charitable behavior that readers might expect from virtuous widows in later novels. In fact, the good woman is a mother figure to Crusoe, mothering both the man and his finances. She guards his fortune and she looks out for the welfare of his family. Her sound advice to Crusoe after his estates have been returned to his management is to look after his family by undertaking the necessary spending to prepare them for life (218). The caretaking that Defoe's "good widow" performs thus combines personal and financial nurturing of others, even though she has not been able to preserve her own financial well-being; when Crusoe finds her near the end of the narrative, she is in dire straits indeed (206).

Defoe's "good widow" in some ways provides a model for the poor widows who appear in later eighteenth-century novels: her own identity is less important than the relationship that she bears to more powerful characters; her poverty is never graphically described; and her financial situation and abilities are linked to emerging gender expectations for women. Her concern with money is not for herself but for her children or wards; she needs to be rescued; and she has a benevolent rescuer. And like many widows in future novels, her poverty is a transitory state.

There are also ways, however, in which Defoe's "good widow" is very different from others of her kind. However nameless, she is a woman of character and financial ability, a woman who has weathered adversity and managed success with equal fortitude. Her relationship with Crusoe is reciprocal: they take care of each other emotionally and financially. Crusoe may rescue her at the end of the novel, but she rescues Crusoe at the beginning, and Crusoe's rescue consists of making her his steward, a position of impressive power and influence. In these respects, she is not the model for later representations of poor widowhood.

Defoe's "good widow" stands at a fork in the road for the eighteenth-century novel, indicating a road not taken by later novelists. These authors emphasized and linked her dependence and nurturing, although in Defoe's "good widow" one does not follow from the other, and certainly not inevitably. At the same time, later novelists tended to neglect the self-sufficiency, agency, and financial acumen demonstrated by Defoe's widow, as well as the reciprocity of her relationship with Crusoe. In selecting for and against certain aspects of the widow and her relationship with others, these novelists chose the path of sentiment.

Eighteenth-century women were more precariously positioned than men in the economic and social changes taking place, since a woman easily could be driven into poverty by the death of a husband and might not be able to obtain work to alleviate her situation. As Toni Bowers points out, one explanation for the high infant mortality rate is the fact that poor mothers could not take care of their children and could not always find help, or sufficient help. More than 86 percent of single parents on relief in the eighteenth and early nineteenth centuries were female. In the cities, where people often went to find work, poor widows made up a disproportionate part of the indigent population. At a time when widows were not quite 13 percent of the population, a random sample in 1798 of ninety-nine women reduced to begging in London revealed that 50 percent of them were widows.[3]

There were some mechanisms in place to help these women. Poor widows might find aid from a variety of public and private charitable institutions. In addition to parish poor relief, a system made more difficult to negotiate during the eighteenth century, private charities grew in number over the period to serve a widespread population of poor people. Aid took many forms, such as lying-in clothes, soup, or a loan to buy a cow. Charities specifically designed to help widows, such as the London-based Society for the Relief of Necessitous Widows and Children of Poor Dissenting Ministers, or provincial organizations, such as the Yerbury Almshouses, might offer cash allowances, funds to help apprentice a child, or subsidized housing. As the appendix discusses in greater detail, such organizations were carefully limited in their missions by their governing boards, however. They distributed aid only to desperately poor widows and never to enable them to become self-supporting. The disbursement of aid was conservative, reinforcing the social hierarchy and gender expectations: recipients of such institutions' aid had to be dependent, grateful, and undemanding.

Such policies in private charities reveal how as the circulation of wealth changed, attitudes toward poor relief changed as well. While the state had been managing aid to the poor since the fourteenth century, the eighteenth century saw an unprecedented rise in resistance to this idea. Scholars such as Donna Andrew and Mona Scheuermann explain that this resistance appeared as an attitudinal shift from valuing systemic, tax-based poor relief to individual, benevolence-based poor relief.[4] Charity thus evolved over the eighteenth century to prioritize individuality: the individual giver, whose benevolence determined to whom and how much charity was given, and the individual recipient, whose deservingness determined whether and how much charity was given. The cult of sensibility can be seen as part of this resistance, since it emphasized personal responsibility for the poor through sympathy and benevolence, rather than state responsibility through poor laws. Sensibility, a direct outgrowth of the changing economic desire of people with means both to retain those means and to use them to regulate the poor, reinforced the idea of social inequality and justified inequities by claiming them as ways of inculcating morality in members of the different classes. "The relationship between the poor and their betters is necessary for both," Scheuermann observes, "for while the poor receive charity and can feel those 'amiable' affections of love and reverence and gratitude, the rich get to experience benevolence. Note that, again, this exchange rests entirely on the assumption that one group is subordinate to the other." Or as Paul Langford summarizes in *A Polite and Commercial People*, to people with property, people without property "were a continuing source of irritation, an implied rebuke and source of guilt, a cause for concern, a potential threat, and a stimulus to philanthropy. The story of politeness and commerce as it developed in the mid-eighteenth century is not least an account of the way in which the polite and commercial class dealt with its inferiors."[5]

Scholars such as Ann Jessie Van Sant, Markman Ellis, John Mullan, and Gillian Skinner have shown that sentimental novelists necessarily participated in this social engineering when they wrote novels that promoted these attitudes.[6] Representations of impoverished widows were one part of sentimental fiction's contribution to efforts to stabilize society through justifying as moral class inequality. While poor widows are not a numerous population in the eighteenth-century novel, it is no surprise that the vast majority of them turn up in sentimental fiction. Sentimental fiction focuses not on the alleviation of distress, but on the suffering engendered by that distress in the widow and in the observer of the widow. As Van Sant explains, "Watching the responses of a provoked sensibility may, then, satisfy an observer's curiosity and / or create pity for the object of observation. There is, however, a further complexity in this alliance of curiosity and pity: observers may be interested not only in the sensibility being displayed before their eyes but also in the responses raised in themselves" (57). The necessary distance between the observer and the observed in this dynamic allows the former to practice correct moral, i.e., sentimental behavior, although even in fiction composed before and after sensibility's heyday, poor widows were depicted in a tableau of sentimental suffering designed to arouse the compassion of the reader as well as of the characters who see them and respond. In the epigraph to this chapter, even Moll Flanders imagines to herself what the original owner of her stolen goods is enduring, and reveals herself a woman of feeling. By emphasizing the observer's response to the suffering rather than the cause of that suffering, sensibility deflected criticism of the system or situation that inflicted misery and focused on particular responses to individual crises. Portraits of women struggling with poverty thus helped eighteenth-century novelists to reiterate the notions of power, human nature, and money that underpin, or came to underpin, sensibility and thereby justified the system, or at least shifted criticism from it.

The poor widow was a useful device for signaling value: the way a character responded to such a figure indicated that character's virtue or vice. In Charlotte Smith's *Emmeline* (1788), William Godolphin, searching for his fallen sister, Lady Adelina, "gained information as to the place of his sister's residence from the mother of Lady Adelina's woman; who being the reduced widow of a clergyman, resided in the Bishop's alms-houses at Bromley, where her daughter frequently sent her such assistance as her own oeconomy, or the bounty of her lady, enabled her to supply." When he tracks down the widowed mother of his sister's former maid, he "easily found the poor woman, who was paralytic and almost childish. Her letters were read for her by one of her neighbors." This character's condition receives more than its share of narrative attention, given the widowed mother's almost negligible significance to the narrative. She appears in such detail because the pathos of her situation elicits still more sentiment from an already overcharged novel, and because it shows that compassion and not just duty motivates Mr. Godolphin's search.[7]

Using the response to the poor widow as a signal of a character's virtue also allowed authors to comment on larger economic issues. To establish the plausibility of Orlando Somerive's rescue by a humane Indian, the Wolf-hunter, in *The Old Manor House* (1793), for example, Charlotte Smith demonstrates the Wolf-hunter's benevolence with an impeccably pathetic object: a homeless, helpless widow "wandering in the woods," whom he protects. The Wolf-hunter's humanity, demonstrated first through this display, allows Smith to criticize the empire's treatment of native Americans and other indigenous peoples. In *Secresy* (1795), Eliza Fenwick also uses benevolent display toward a widow to establish character and attack British imperialism. Mr. Murden displays his worthiness through his attentive care to a poor widow from India, and Fenwick displays her rejection of British treatment of the Indians by showing an Indian as a proper object of benevolence, a person for whom one ought to feel "fellow feeling" rather than contempt.[8] Smith and Fenwick are among the more radical authors of the 1790s in this critique of empire, but even their use of the poor widow objectifies the widow and her suffering in order to make a point. The characters reacting to the widow are the focus of these authors' attention, not the widows themselves. In both cases, the widow as charitable object allows commentary on the empire, but she also reinforces traditional associations of power and action with men, and passivity and gratitude with women. In feminizing India by personifying it as a devastated widow, Fenwick reconceptualizes the imperial project as paternal and benevolent rather than exploitative, but she does not reconceptualize the relationship between male and female, rich and poor, constructed by sensibility.

The evocation of such pathos is also more about the widow's audience than about the plight of the poor, pitiable widow herself. To be on the side of the forces of good in Smith's and Fenwick's novels is to value the Wolf-hunter's humanity and Mr. Murden's kindness. When Laurence Sterne's Yorick meets Maria's mother in *Sentimental Journey* (1768), he describes her as an "old mother" who, although supposedly running a farm, occupies herself by standing in her doorway, crying with grief for her dead husband and deranged child. Her function in the novel is not to farm, but to serve as a catalyst to sentiment for the male viewer (Yorick) and the middle- and upper-class reader. As Jeffrey Duncan points out, Sterne often combines an outside viewer and poverty to explore "personal emotional experience" and generate and demonstrate sentiment. Matthew Bramble in Tobias Smollett's *Humphry Clinker* (1771) reveals the generosity and benevolence beneath his crustiness when he gives a cow to an unnamed widowed tenant and allows her to pay for it "when she is able," meaning when her farm is making money. Oliver Goldsmith's Vicar in *The Vicar of Wakefield* (1762) gives his salary "to the orphans and widows of the clergy of our diocese; for, having a fortune of my own, I was careless of temporalities, and felt a secret pleasure in doing my duty without reward."[9] It may be a secret from the other characters in the novel, but it is hardly a secret from the novel's readers. Authors like Sterne, Smollett, and Goldsmith may not employ exactly the same forms of sensibility, but their understanding of the relationship between reader and text, or reader and character, is consistent with each other and with sensibility's view of fiction's role in shaping reader response.[10] The suggestion in all these works, as in other sentimental novels, is that the reader who understands the good impulse in these characters is a good person, and the reader who does not may yet be made good by reading the novel.

Women characters illustrate the same dynamic. In *The Widow* (1794) by Mary Robinson, the discovery of a single mother, presumably a widow, sheltering from "the enraged elements" under a tree with her two small children becomes an opportunity to reinforce the moral value of other characters in the novel. This "poor woman" had "two little children; the eldest about five years old; one was in her arms, the other had hid itself under its mother's tattered gown, and was crying, mournfully." While widowed Mrs. Vernon attempts to bully the woman and her children from their meager shelter so she herself might escape the storm, kindly Julia St. Lawrence asks Mrs. Vernon to "consider, the affrighted children had scarcely anything to cover them; the rain will chill their little bosoms, or perhaps the lightning destroy them."[11] Julia's moral worth is established by her attempts to protect the unprotected, which arise from a laudable compassion; Mrs. Vernon's lack of moral worth is established by her rejection of the poor widow and her refusal to feel sympathy; and the reader's moral worth is established by distinguishing between the two models of human behavior and choosing properly.[12]

To evoke a strong reader response, descriptions of such scenes are vivid and heavily visual, almost painterly. Julia St. Lawrence's letter to her friend draws a picture for the audience to evoke the reader's sympathies for the widow and Mrs. St. Lawrence, and against Mrs. Vernon. She does not have to describe the scene to Mrs. Vernon since the unfeeling woman is right there, but the epistolary structure of the novel offers a useful device for establishing her own distance from the scene as a sympathetic observer, and for creating a distant perspective for the novel's audience to generate sympathy. The technique is the same in Margaret Lee's epistolary novel *Clara Lennox* (1797), while the pathos is still thicker. When Mr. Brook writes to Colonel Lavington, describing the death of their mutual friend, Mr. Fielding, and the reaction of his widow, Lady Angelina, "My attention was suddenly roused to the fair and unfortunate widow," he reports, "who, with eyes overflowing with tears, was feebly straining her infant to her bosom, praying the Almighty to bestow on her every blessing." The voyeuristic elements of this scene are underscored by Mr. Brook's emphasis on his own position as a viewer: "'Had you seen the lovely mourner at this melancholy account, clasping her infant to her breast—Farewel!—A long farewel! sighed forth her oppressed soul! (cried she,) whatever fate Heaven shall appoint thy unhappy widow, humbly let her obey the God that has hitherto preserved her!'—A shower of tears then relieved her." The letter form prioritizes the letter writer in these passages—"My attention was suddenly roused"—and reminds Mr. Brook's audience of his position as narrator—"Had you seen the lovely mourner," "(cried she)"—enabling Brook and Lee to transfer the emphasis from the anguish to its observers.[13]

Eighteenth-century novels often present the suffering widow as a still life happened upon by someone who describes it. "I had scarcely reached the threshold, when I perceived a female in deep mourning, sitting at a table drawing," Lady Seymour reports to Mrs. Vernon of her discovery of Julia St. Lawrence (Robinson, *Widow*, 1:56). As early as Tobias Smollett's *Adventures of Peregrine Pickle* (1751), when Peregrine seeks the "forlorn lady in the straw" about whom he had heard at a party, he "found this unhappy widow sitting up in a truckle-bed, and suckling one of her infants, with the most piteous expression of anguish in her features, which were naturally regular and sweet, while the other was fondled on the knee" of another benevolent visitor.[14] Having provided the means of exposing Peregrine's, and the reader's, benevolence and the hard-heartedness of society, and of introducing him to the Lady of Quality, this young widow vanishes from the story. In *Clara Lennox*, Lord Belmont is ushered into Clara's room "where sat this unfortunate widow at a table, with the writing apparatus before her, her cheek reclined on her hand, whilst the table supported her arm, the tears swimming in her eyes, and a gentle smile diffused over her countenance." He concludes, "Never did I see sympathy and sorrow so lively painted on a countenance, as was on her's," underscoring the observational, image-based aspects of the scene (Lee, 1:193–94).

Objective contemplation, because it distances the sufferer from the observer and shifts emphasis from causation to observation, is a centerpiece of sentimental fiction's use of poor widows to respond to socioeconomic conditions. As Markman Ellis shows, in converting poverty into a question of suffering, and suffering into an opportunity for the observer rather than the sufferer to act, sensibility creates a system that emphasizes the giver's virtue rather than the prob-

lem of poverty.[15] When Goldsmith's Vicar explains his charity to orphans and widows, he concludes by reflecting on his own actions: "I
was careless of temporalities, and felt a secret pleasure in doing my
duty without reward" (Goldsmith, *Vicar of Wakefield*, 5). Further, sensibility considers poverty as an issue of individual worth by setting up
the categories of deserving and undeserving poor. Benevolence, in
its practical and literary manifestations, thus reveals itself to be a
form of class conservatism by converting the poor into objects for
the rich's use: the rich employ the poor to generate sympathy within
themselves, reaffirming their own moral worth despite the fact that
their wealth, even when it is land-based, has been accumulated in an
unequal, unregulated, and generally exploitative economy.

Resistance to this objectification signals villainy. In the case of
Robinson's Mrs. Vernon, for example, her refusal to see the poor
widow and her children as pathetic objects renders and reveals her
odious. A similar refusal by a poor widow, however, also makes her
despicable. As a result, efforts by poor widows to act independently
appear sinister in the eighteenth-century novel. When Bernardo, the
hero of Sarah Scott's *The History of Cornelia* (1750), falls ill in the for-
est and is nursed by Madame De Garré, a poor widow living with her
daughter and her spinster sister, he finds himself in a self-centered
and disordered household. Both Mademoiselle De Garré and her
aunt are ignorant and ferociously flirtatious; they fight incessantly
over Bernardo. Bernardo confesses that in such an atmosphere, he
prefers Madame De Garré because she is neglectful. She ignores her
responsibilities as a mother, nurse, hostess, and head of the household, preferring "indolence" above everything else. In seeking the
easiest course rather than the most honest one, she believes her
daughter's lies about Bernardo, attacks him unjustly, and helps her
daughter bring a false suit of breach of contract against him, inflict-
ing more damage on him and his beloved Cornelia. Madame De
Garré uses her independence, however limited by poverty, to indulge her intellectual and moral sloth. As a result, she is neither un-
derstandable nor forgivable, according to the novel.[16]

The poor widow's renunciation of autonomy does not necessarily
preclude her ability to act, but it does preclude her ability to act outside the social hierarchy reinforced by sensibility. Charlotte Smith's
"old lady, the widow of a clergyman" from *The Old Manor House* effects Orlando Somerive's introduction to the Raylands and enables
his happiness and wealth at the end of the novel. She even goes so far

as to bring Orlando to see his relative without an invitation or orders from Mrs. Rayland. In this sense, the clergyman's widow might seem to be taking an inappropriate initiative, acting above her place. Her behavior is legitimated, however, by occurring within a sentimental framework. She acts from "sense and benevolence," two crucial words in sensibility that signal virtue. She is also the recipient of kind offices from the Raylands, being "among the ancient friends of the family, that still enjoyed the privilege of being regularly sent for in the old family coach, once a year" to dine at Rayland Hall (38–39). Smith's clergyman's widow is therefore both a benefactor and a benefactee, firmly situated within the hierarchy of social relations endorsed by sensibility. In bringing Orlando to Rayland Hall, she reciprocates the generosity of the Raylands by ensuring the ultimate preservation of the family estate and name, what the Rayland family holds most dear. And, as if aware of her social unimportance, she then obligingly vanishes forever. Here again the representation of a poor widow reveals the limits of an author's critical stance. While Smith finds fault with people who behave badly within their class, like the Rayland sisters or Philip Somerive, her clergyman's widow underscores how she does not find fault with social hierarchy.[17]

The willingness to be objectified therefore is crucial for establishing the legitimacy of the pathetic object. As actual charitable grants to poor widows indicate, benevolence requires a needy object, and the best needy objects are passive, not diluting the benevolence of the benefactor by making any effort on their own behalf. A community sponsored by Sarah Scott's Millenium Hall (1762) follows the ladies' example by admitting primarily lower-middle-class or poor women, for whom it is a place of refuge. The narrator reports that "in general the ladies chose to admit those who had least, as their necessities were greatest." The women of Millenium Hall also support a clergyman's widow: they "immediately raised her drooping spirits, settled an income upon her, took [a] house, furnished it and lent her some of their girls to assist in making up the furniture, and decorating it, according to the good woman's taste." In *School for Widows* (1791) by Clara Reeve, a widowed tenant of Mrs. Strictland "was lame: she staid at home, did needle-work, and spun wool" until "the widow was laid by with the rheumatism." She and her little family fall almost instantly into poverty, which is hardly surprising, until rescued by Mrs. Strictland, who puts her, her daughter, and her unmarried sister into a new cottage and gives them Mr. Balderson as a boarder. The widow's inability to take care of herself justifies the need for and therefore the system of benevolence. A blacksmith's widow in *Humphry Clinker* delivers her baby and loses her husband nearly upon the same instant, a confluence of events that "deprived her of her senses." Smollett's travelers are so struck with the pathos of her situation that they "did not leave the village without doing something for her benefit—Even Tabitha's charity was awakened on this occasion." Madame Miteau in Scott's *History of Cornelia* is instantly intellectually incapacitated by becoming a widow, and is about to be jailed for debt when she is rescued by Cornelia. Mrs. Fleming in *The Old Manor House* requires the assistance of friends to secure a roof over her and her children's heads.[18]

Benevolence may rescue the helpless, but the focus of the action is the rescue itself. Like working widows, who may work provided it is to restore their class rather than to rise out of it, poor women may be saved from starvation, but only to be reinstated into their original class, and preferably without an accompanying ability to take care of themselves. The clergyman's widow of *Millenium Hall*, for example, grows flowers, not vegetables, in her garden, and without the income provided by the women of Millenium Hall, she would starve once again. The support she receives is intended to reinforce her status as someone too genteel to work, and too dependent to become self-sufficient. When a widow uses her garden to grow vegetables to feed her household, like Mrs. Batson in *School for Widows*, she becomes the object of ridicule. In *Tom Jones* (1747), Henry Fielding's Mrs. Miller plunges immediately into poverty upon being widowed until she is put into business and provided an annuity by Mr. Allworthy. She does not do it on her own and considers herself perpetually indebted to him. Orlando Somerive invites Mrs. Fleming to live with his family; he does not offer her the opportunity to earn an income on her own. Even when established in a position of security, these widows reinforce traditional social relationships. They reflect back the glow of the rescuer and the rescue. Although as widows they are entitled to work to support themselves, they do not shine on their own as productive citizens of the nation.[19]

A more extended example of the role of benevolence to restore original class, and the role of the recipient to be anything but capable, appears in Sarah Fielding's *History of the Countess of Dellwyn* (1759). In this novel, a clergyman's wife works diligently and effectively until the moment of her husband's death, whereupon she is transformed into an incompetent, impoverished, dependent, grateful creature. The family had come to Bristol Hot Wells so the clergyman could recover his health. "[A]s soon as [his wife and daughters] came, they requested [the landlady] to procure some Plain-work for them; and that they had dispatched a great Quantity since they had been there, having worked as hard as possible, and lived with the utmost Frugality in every thing but where the poor sick Man was concerned, for whom they had been most careful to provide every Comfort and Convenience that a much more ample Fortune could have procured him."[20] To provide so well through plain-work is indeed an accomplishment. From the moment that the clergyman's wife becomes his widow, however, there is no further mention of earning income. Instead, the married Mrs. Bilson comes to her aid. As with other working and poor widows, in the transition from wife to widow, a capable woman becomes helpless upon bereavement.

This helplessness is crucial in justifying benevolence, because it offers an excuse for the initial generosity and an excuse for the class system that generosity almost invariably reaffirms. After her daughter has been married off, her other daughters put into service, and the preparations for her own and her daughters' house begun, the clergyman's widow rejoices at her good fortune:

> The poor Widow left the Place with a most grateful heart for all the Favours which had been showered down upon her, and felt all the Consolation her Grief for the Loss of an excellent Husband could admit of, from a true Sense of the great Blessing of having Three of her Children well-provided for. Her pride felt no Wound from thinking Two were in a State of nominal Servitude; for in reality they were used with all the Kindness of Friends; insomuch that many Persons, who have experienced what it is to be dependent under the Denomination of Friends, would rejoice in every Corner of their Hearts to meet with half the same Indulgence. And their Mother, who had flattered herself with no high Expectations for them, poured out her Thanks to the Almighty for their being so placed, that they were rather with protectors of their Youth, and Exemplars for their Conduct, than with Mistresses, where their Dependence was the strongest Security for the kind Treatment they should receive. (96–97)

As Fielding points out, one of the striking aspects of this episode is that although the poor widow is the widow of a clergyman, she has readily, cheerfully in fact, sent two of her children into service. Class considerations remain as inarticulate as the widow herself, who never breaks into direct speech and is rendered speechless by the actions of others. Evidently it is not an uncommon social transition: Clara Reeve may have done so upon the death of her father, a clergyman, and according to the records from the Society for the Relief of Necessitous Widows and Children of Poor Dissenting Ministers, the daughters of the widows of clergymen often went into service. That Fielding makes note of it, however, highlights that it was indeed a class change for these girls, and that what makes that shift (although a shift regarded by benevolent people as highly appropriate) acceptable to the widow is the framework of gratitude in which it takes place. It is not necessarily an unrealistic depiction, but its emphasis in representations of poor widows suggests that it was also a convenient one, especially since it avoids having to acknowledge any other emotions involved in the change. All that remains for poor widows like the widow of the clergyman is dependence and gratitude.

This behavior and attitude, at least, virtuous poor widows perform with considerable aplomb. In response to Mrs. Bilson's first round of kindnesses, the clergyman's widow

> felt her Goodness deeply in her Heart, and therefore had no Flow of Words ready to burst forth in Elocution to express her Thanks; but turned her Eyes, with a quick Transition, alternately on Mrs. *Bilson* and her Daughters, full of the highest Amazement. . . . [T]ender Feeling for her own, and the Offspring of the Man she had loved with an ardent Affection, brought a Flood of Tears to her Relief. She wept, cast up her Eyes to Heaven, could just utter the Words, Good God! And then sunk back in her Chair, as being overwhelmed with the grateful Emotions of her own Mind. (S. Fielding, *Countess of Dellwyn*, 91)

As sensibility became increasingly histrionic, widows were decreasingly able to handle their gratitude. In Sarah Scott's *Sir George Ellison*, published in 1766, Mrs. Maningham becomes irrational upon learning her son will be released from debtor's prison. When George Ellison (not yet a knight) reveals that he will pay off young Maningham's debts, he

> found Mrs. Maningham at his feet, embracing his knees, and shedding such showers of tears, that her joy could find no utterance in words. The excess of her rapture alarmed him, and raised such ap-

prehensions in her son, as moderated his joy. . . . No small time was taken up in calming Mrs. Maningham; she alternately embraced Mr. Ellison with the most lively raptures of gratitude, and her son with joyful congratulations: her sensations seemed too strong for her reason, and it was with great difficulty they restored her to any tolerable composure of mind. (152)

Even when she is recalled to herself, her irrationality persists in her belief that Mr. Ellison is an actual angel. "Mrs. Maningham was inclined to think it really miraculous, and that their benefactor was more than human, supporting this supposition by the very uncommon benignity and sweetness of Mr. Ellison's countenance, which she called truly angelic," the narrator reports but her son, "being less superstitious, looked on him only as the best of men," a contrast that highlights her emotion and her weakness, both virtues in the poor widow (153). A few years later, when *Humphry Clinker*'s Matthew Bramble gives twenty pounds to an unnamed widow in Bath to help care for her consumptive daughter, she "exclaimed in an extacy, 'Twenty pounds! Oh, sir!' and sinking down upon a settee, fainted away—" Upon reviving, "She shed a flood of tears, and cried aloud, 'I know not who you are: but, sure—worthy sir—generous sir!—the distress of me and my poor dying child—Oh! if the widow's prayers—if the orphan's tears of gratitude can ought avail—gracious Providence—Blessings!—shower down eternal blessings'" (Smollett, 49–50).

Tears also play a significant role in signaling virtue and gratitude. When Lord Woodville in Elizabeth Griffith's *The Delicate Distress* (1769) presents a collection of dependent widows to his wife, Lady Woodville reports that his former nurse "knew not in what manner to receive me—humility and joy seemed to struggle in her countenance—I stepped forward, and embraced her—my lord seemed delighted, at what he was pleased to call my condescension." As for the nurse's mother, also a widow, "she blessed, and embraced my lord, while tears of joy, and gratitude, ran down her fair, unfurrowed cheek." Reinforcing their femininity, his nurse—an "extreme good looking woman, about fifty"—also has a daughter, a "very pretty woman, about two-and-twenty; and ready to lye in, of a second child."[21] Motherly and generally nameless, consistently dependent, rejoicing in their dependence and gratitude, these women willingly maintain the class distinctions presented in such scenes of charity. They are clearly deserving of generosity by their gratitude and personal attractiveness, and their primary activity after being bereaved is to reaffirm a system of stratified benevolence based on a traditional, stable social hierarchy. This loss of self-control, whether in the ability to stand or to speak or to restrain tears, indicates the widow's weakness and therefore, her deservingness. The inability to manage her own emotions suggests an inability to manage her misfortunes, which renders the giver's act even more significant.

Novelists used virtuous motherhood to reinforce these behaviors in poor widows, although in actuality, motherhood exacerbated the difficulties of widowhood, particularly when some women had no way of making a living at all. Poor widowed mothers were caught in a terrible bind. Emerging ideas about maternity demanded behaviors only possible in a financially secure and intact family, and incompatible with the realities of impoverished widowhood. The inability of poor widows to conform to society's expectations for mothers was seen not as a failure of the social system or of the expectations, but of the women to be good mothers. Since employment took them away from their children, the reasoning went, they were abandoning them. By the same token, dependence was construed as indigence, which carried its own stigma. Bowers has shown that many women who could not ensure the survival of their children gave them up to the Foundling Hospital at Coram's Fields, but whether they gave up their children or kept them, their failure was seen as an "individual moral problem: mothers fail because they are not properly virtuous," and not as a systemic one.[22] The novel resolved this social ambivalence by shifting attention away from the widows. Their inability to maintain their children allowed the focus to move to those who could, thereby reinforcing the virtue of benevolent wealth. The widow's failure was a foil for highlighting virtuous, wealthy activity, and not important in and of itself.

Admittedly, as the clergyman's widow's emotion in *The Countess of Dellwyn* indicates, even though the eighteenth-century novel used charity to reinforce class divisions, its beneficial effects—saving families from starvation, for example—ought not to be underestimated or unappreciated. Its converse is illustrated in Frances Burney's *Evelina* (1778), in the famous race of the elderly women. The old women who run the race do not have their own names; the men and the crowd give them the names of the men sponsoring them. When one falls, Evelina is prevented from helping her by Lord Merton, "to whom [the old woman] did not belong."[23] At no time do any of the people with the means to help these women do anything for them, and Evelina's attempt to aid one physically highlights her intention's very basic nature as well as the isolation of her act. Burney criticizes the lack of individual charity in the upper classes, since the wager is settled by an ironic corruption of Lord Orville's recommendation that the two men bet on which one "should bring the worthiest object with whom to share" the money wagered (274). This lack of charity is perhaps more striking for its difference from other novelistic men and women who do help the poor, from Defoe's Robinson Crusoe in *Robinson Crusoe* to Smith's Emmeline Mowbray in *Emmeline.*

Consistent with the rising reluctance from those who paid taxes (and bought books) to support parish poor relief, eighteenth-century novels tend to emphasize individual rather than institutional charity. In fact, while history reveals the establishment of a large number of private charities during midcentury and sensibility's rise, the novel takes the trend further by generally demonstrating the relationship between the needy and the charitable as personal and individual. *Millenium Hall*'s beneficiaries usually trace their support back to the particular women who founded the Hall itself. Even Sir George Ellison's workhouse in Scott's *Sir George Ellison* is personal, for although he takes over the care of the poor for the parish, their maintenance depends on him, not even a privately-run organization like Millenium Hall (65–67). In *Sir George Ellison* Scott criticizes parish poor relief outright by comparing the protagonist's private, individual charity favorably to the parish system. Although *Millenium Hall* and *Sir George Ellison* demonstrate Scott's personal brand of sensibility, with its strong emphasis on generous action and community orientation, the appearance of this strategy in earlier and later novels reveals a more general effort by novelists to depict poverty as an issue of individual behavior, not systemic problems. Furthermore, because individual responsibility can rescue the deserving poor (at least according to the novel), many of the widows who experience poverty in the eighteenth-century novel do so transiently, from *Robinson Crusoe*'s "good widow" to Clara Lennox. The individuality of their situation and the solution administered by individual fellow-feeling heightens the sentiment of the situation, and allows the representation of poverty to be both tragic and particular.

It is worth noting that while virtue and wickedness are associated with the country and the city in other economic groups such as the affluent widows discussed in chapter 2, no such distinction exists when it comes to poor widows. In fact, with the exception of Madame De Garré from Scott's *History of Cornelia*, there are really no selfish poor widows in this chapter at all. What wicked poor widows do exist turn out to be criminal widows, and they appear in chapter 5. It would appear that selfishness in poor widows can only be translated to the extreme of wickedness: criminality. Poor widows are virtuous if they are dependent; if they are not dependent, they must be criminal. That means that the unifying issue here is function. Poverty can only be acceptable if it is grateful and dependent, regardless of its residence or associated locales. When the total lack of means, a situation possible even in a wholly agricultural society, appears in an emerging commercial economy, the question is not necessarily the existence of poverty, but participation in the commercial economy as a result of or remedy for it. Hence, when those who are poor insist on threatening the status quo by acting entirely against their assigned class and engaging in the commercial economy, they become criminal and the subject of chapter 5.

In this respect, the representations of working widows and of poor widows are considerably different. Widows like those discussed in this chapter offer another model for the exclusion of women from the commercial economy. By rejecting the idea that work can help such women, and by firmly situating them instead in the hierarchy affirmed by sensibility, the eighteenth-century novel offered a still more emphatic claim for widows' exclusion from the economy. Unlike the novel's affluent widows or working widows, its poor widows do not simply refuse to exercise the power that widowhood confers on them. Instead, they never had or have that power. They crumple instantly in the transition from wife to widow; at the moment that they become legally and socially their own person, they become novelistically nobody at all. And they therefore affirm the idea that others' benevolence, not their own economic action, is necessary to their well-being. As Elizabeth Bergen Brophy summarizes, "The age deprived these unfortunates not only of material means of support but also of the all-important psychological support of social approval and of an important, useful role to play."[24] Furthermore, Tories and Whigs alike could find satisfaction in such a representation, since it always limited female economic activity regardless of whether emerging mercantile capitalism was also a target.

By removing all possibility of the poor widow being a working widow, the eighteenth-century novel also gets around another thorny issue in philanthropic thinking of the time. Increasingly over the course of the century, writers discussing charity emphasized that gifts to those who could work actually corrupted the work force, rather than helped it. People who could work, the theory went, should work. Giving them charity was encouraging idleness and parasitism in the poor. By the 1790s, as Scheuermann points out, writers like Hannah More and Henry Townshend were arguing that divine will created the poor, whose purpose in the cosmos was to labor, and that only poor people who were unable to work should be supported. According to conservative thinkers, "Widespread, unmediated charity ruins societies; not only is the general economy destroyed, but so too are the individual objects of the charity. . . . Labor must be the center of the poor man's existence; the only useful help to give the poor is to give them work." But these ideas were, in different forms, present throughout the development of mercantile capitalism. Even a writer as favorably disposed to the emerging commercial economy as Defoe in the 1720s was uncomfortable with charity that enabled otherwise sound workers to avoid labor.[25] By defining the poor widow as someone who could not work, the novel avoided this problem. Giving charity to the poor widow was a good thing to do because according to the novel, she was far too helpless, dependent, and generally passive to do anything like act on her own behalf, especially in business. According to the novel, the English widow could never be mistaken for the hearty English worker who captured the imaginations and ideas of economic thinkers of the age. The poor widow was the perfect charitable object, represented as the very thing (or person) benevolence was designed for.

Critics have already demonstrated how the sentimental novel used slavery for this purpose. In his examination of the rhetoric and relationships around slavery between 1688 and 1791, Gary Gautier argues that as the landed hierarchy gave ground to capitalism, sensibility took over as an ideology to explain human interaction: the "concept of 'sensibility' grew into a form that could offer ideological support to a hierarchy that was otherwise losing its ideological viability, so the concept of 'race' came to give 'slavery' a new kind of ideological support." This process is more precisely outlined by George Boulukos, who shows that sensibility's emphasis on benevolence to generate gratitude obscures and reinforces the unequal power distribution between those who can afford to be benevolent and those who must, or ought to be, grateful. In the sentimental novel, benevolence is used to test the worth of the benevolent object: if the latter is grateful, his or her subservient position is reaffirmed; if the latter is ungrateful, his or her subordinate position is reaffirmed. Either way, sensibility asserts the superior humanity of the person who can afford to be benevolent over the person who should accept the benevolence.[26]

This dynamic is the same dynamic that exists between the poor widow and the generous benefactor. Instead of race, these novels use class, economic situation, to assert and reinforce the developing mercantile hierarchy. The instinct to be generous is aroused by the plight of the pathetic subordinate, but being generous serves to reiterate the superiority of the benefactor over the recipient. In establishing this relationship, the novel therefore also reaffirms, rather than challenges, the system in which the relationship takes place.

The novel thus participates in several emerging cultural strategies for managing the question of poverty and its sufferers' desperate need to end it. State-instituted tactics for handling poverty consisted primarily of the Poor Law, which, as Van Sant notes, made the poor "invisible." For practical purposes, the mechanism of the Poor Law got poor people off the streets or rendered them "non-persons," people whom the law did not recognize as people who could be given help. By depicting the frequent poverty that attended widows as occasional, nameless, and brief, the novel reflected and also contributed to this attempt. Private efforts such as the Yerbury Almshouses or the foundling hospital at Coram's Fields did the opposite: they "aimed at results *that could be seen*: rescued, reformed, and incorporable 'objects.' In order to gain the voluntary funding on which they depended, these institutions had to generate approval of their aims and sympathy for their objects."[27] By emphasizing the connection between an individual giver and an individual recipient, the novel reflected and also contributed to this effort as well. In short, then, the state rendered the poor invisible as a class and private charities rendered them visible as small, unthreatening, sentimental groups or as individuals in order to generate a sense of sympathy and the reassurance of moral worth that a sympathetic response brings.

The virtuous poor widows of the eighteenth-century novel thus obligingly refuse to acknowledge their right and need to work, but

even sentimental fiction recognized that passive gratitude and obedience were virtues, not inevitabilities. What of the widow who utterly disregards sensibility's limitations and warnings and works anyway, participating in the activities and philosophies of capitalism?
She is, of course, the opposite of the approved, dependent, passive
widow. She is the transgressive, feared, independent, active widow.
And she is the subject of chapter 5.

5

She Put Mercury
into the Morning Milk:
Crime and the Widow

Parting with him! Why, that is the whole scheme and intention
of all marriage articles. The comfortable estate of widowhood
is the only hope that keeps up a wife's spirits. Where is the
woman who would scruple to be a wife, if she had it in her
power to be a widow whenever she pleased?

—John Gay, *The Beggar's Opera*

In August of 1784 in North Riding, John Bayston drank his
breakfast milk, took violently ill upon arriving at work, and was carried home. Attended by his wife, Ellin, and two neighboring widows,
Elizabeth Fletcher and Hannah Sickling, he lingered in agony until
the small hours of the morning, then died. Ellin later confessed to
putting mercury into the milk, evidently so she could marry another
man whom she loved better than John.[1]

In short, sometimes a widow could become a widow on purpose.

This is not a pleasant possibility to contemplate in any century,
but for people in a period attempting to redefine gender relations
among people and with property, and often with each other through
the medium of property, such a possibility was deeply unnerving as
well as morally reprehensible. Nor did the murder of a husband to
achieve widowhood constitute the only terrifying connection between widowhood and criminality. Eighteenth-century society had
evidence that widows might do anything. There was that pesky sexuality which, awakened but unfettered by marriage, might bring destruction to anyone. In March, 1742, for example, Mary Johnson, a

116

widow, evidently having had conjugal relations without the conjugal arrangement, killed her newborn baby rather than face the stigma of bearing an illegitimate child. And there was that unsettling freedom to consider, as well. Without a husband or children to care for, a widow might become monstrously selfish. In August of 1745, Ann Simpson, a widow of New Castle Upon Tyne, put arsenic in the cask of beer that her neighbor, Ann Pearson, also a widow, kept in her kitchen for family consumption and occasional sale. She then stole a large quantity of money and goods from Ann Pearson's house.[2] In fact, the historical record reveals widows acting as legal criminals—violators of the law—in a multiplicity of ways, which made them social criminals—violators of convention. Such a woman was troubling because she was an infanticide, a poisoner, or a thief, but in doing such things, she also contradicted the period's emerging definitions of gender. These women were criminal in one sense because of their actions, and criminal in another sense because they were taking action. It was enough to make you lie awake at night. Or check your morning milk very carefully.

As it happens, there are plenty of criminal widows in eighteenth-century novels, but they do not bear much resemblance to historical criminal widows. London statistics show that for female offenders between the ages of thirty and forty-five, only 10 percent were widows, although they made up a larger proportion of female criminals over forty-five.[3] In contrast, there might be as many as two or three criminal widows per ten characters in a novel. This disparity reinforces what Lincoln Faller suggests underpins the early eighteenth-century fascination with criminal biography: that times of great change yielded the perception that forms of instability like crime were on the rise, and the interpretation of crime as a "sign of the breakdown of traditional social authority."[4] It is therefore not surprising that the novels of the period would feature proportionately more criminal widows than actually existed.

Beyond sheer numbers, the representation of criminal widows is significant for the kinds of crimes and the motives behind them. Historically, fluctuations in the rate of minor property crime correlates with periods of national economic difficulty and is attributed to the rising criminality among populations economically victimized even during the best of times: widows, unmarried women, and mothers who have been abandoned by their spouses. These figures suggest that crime in the actual widowed population is not a regular occupation, but a method for surviving extreme hardship.[5] Although it is true that on occasion in the novel, poverty drives widows to crime (Moll Flanders explains that she would never have become a criminal if she hadn't been reduced to abject poverty of purse and spirit), it is never the only thing, and rarely any thing, that drives them to it. Ferdinand's mother in Tobias Smollett's *Adventures of Ferdinand Count Fathom* (1753) has the opportunity to live in domestic comfort after being widowed for a sixth time, but she opts instead to continue following the army, killing and looting wounded soldiers of both sides, and selling "choice geneva," "clean linnen," and herself to the troops. An affluent London widow in the same novel steals from her lodgers and frames her servants for theft because she enjoys it.[6] Both women choose illegal activity rather than are forced to it by circumstances, and generally speaking, crime in the fictional widowed population almost never has anything to do with economic situation.

Reality and depiction also tend to part ways over the kinds of crimes that widows performed. While the criminal register features widows involved in all sorts of crimes, including murder or attempted murder and arson, novelistic widows perpetrate a more limited range of crimes, and very rarely are involved in violence. They are often, however, adulterers or sellers of innocents. In fact, most of the kinds of crime that these widows undertake have something to do with sexuality. The lasciviousness of wicked widows, discussed in chapter 2, becomes criminal, for example, as it evolves into a mechanism for adultery, fraud, or worse. Eliza Haywood's Lady Mellasin in *The History of Miss Betsy Thoughtless* (1751) readily misappropriates her first and second husband's tremendous resources to support her lover, Oliver Marplus.[7] Her trouble starts because of an uncontrolled appetite for sex, rather than because of financial need. Elizabeth Griffith's Italian widow from *The Delicate Distress* (1769) uses both wealth and sex appeal in a willful attempt to destroy others and to enjoy herself through criminal activities. Griffith's marchioness chases Lord Woodville simply for the pleasure of rekindling his passion for her, ingenuously mislabeling her ambition as "vanity" and "caprice," ordinary female foibles, and falsely assuring Lord Woodville's best friend, Lord Seymour that "I have not the least design, upon his heart."[8] Although Lord Woodville initially resists her invitation to run away with her, he is only prevented from joining her later by a fall from his horse (2:135–36, 2:198).

Such crimes threaten the whole family. In *The Delicate Distress*, Lord Woodville and Sir Harry Ransford are prepared to abandon their families at crucial moments, and while Lord Woodville does not manage it, Sir Harry does. The marchioness's seduction of Lord Woodville almost destroys the rest of the Woodville family: Lady Woodville nearly dies of an illness contracted by caring for her husband's injuries, and their infant son is almost orphaned. In addition to the English families who shiver but fortunately, do not break, the marchioness's own mother, Madame de St. Far, is reduced to penury by her daughter and is forced to beg subsistence from her daughter's enemy, Lord Seymour. As Lord Woodville writes, the revelation of the marchioness's ingratitude and unfilial behavior to her mother simply confirms her depraved nature (2:226).

The eighteenth-century novel extends this string of targets from individual men through their families to property, specifically its proper possession and transmission. As with wicked, affluent widows, widows' adulterous behavior reveals a perceived connection between the sexual acquisition of a man and the material acquisition of property. In seducing and then living with Sir Harry Ransford like but not as a wife, Griffith's marchioness may have been living on his income; she certainly has been claiming a jointure from her late husband's family to which she was not entitled (*Delicate Distress*, 2:189–90). Just as she has claimed men to whom she has no right, and whom she treats as property, so the marchioness lays claim to literal property that also is not hers. When she is placed under house arrest for fraud and debt, she entangles the virtuous Lord Seymour in her crimes and causes his arrest as well (2:190). Infuriated by her behavior, Lord Seymour rages, "if, as I hope, she is not Ransford's wife, she may possibly be reduced to her original poverty, and meet the contempt due to her vices, from all mankind" (2:196–97). He conflates her sexual rapacity with material rapacity, and sees the proper punishment in similar terms.

This depravity, that is, the pursuit of personal desire at the expense of virtuous people, familial as well as social stability, and the preservation of property, shows up in novels throughout the century. Haywood's Lady Mellasin from *Betsy Thoughtless*, an arguably sentimental novel, and Mrs. Gerrarde from Frances Sheridan's definitively sentimental *Memoirs of Miss Sidney Bidulph* (1769) parasitize good men's estates. In paying off her lover, Lady Mellasin not only does considerable economic damage, but also endangers her second husband, Mr. Goodman's estate. The only way he can stop her is to bring a lawsuit, which is eventually concluded by his heir. In the meantime, her daughter learns all the wrong values and consequently, nearly destroys the heroine, Betsy, while these family woes contribute to Mr. Goodman's fatal illness.

In her turn, Sheridan's "widow Gerrarde," twenty-six years old and everything charming, does similar damage. She seduces Mr. Arnold, maligns sentimental heroine Sidney, and causes Sidney's disgrace and separation not only from the husband she loves, but also from her children. Mrs. Gerrarde has already devastated her own late husband, spending his money while he lived on "such pleasures as the country afforded . . . horse-races, assemblies, and such other amusements . . . which, together with expensive treats at home, and card-playing (her supreme delight)," left her in an "indigent state" upon her widowhood, a situation which makes expedient the seduction and milking of Mr. Arnold and the consequent destruction of his family.[9] Once widowed and without the income provided by her own husband, Mrs. Gerrarde must find income provided by someone else's husband. The question of adultery thus extends anxieties over the connection among sexuality, enterprise, and desire in widows to its logical, however appalling, conclusion: that women who have the experience to desire and the freedom to pursue that desire constitute a threat not just to individuals around them, but to the core of English society, the function of property.

The extent of this anxiety over the criminal abuse of property involves other forms of crime, especially and unsurprisingly, theft. In addition to draining estates of money best spent, if at all, elsewhere, *Sidney Bidulph* and *Betsy Thoughtless* also link adultery with another form of attack on the English family and English society: the fraudulent claim on the estate. When she hears that Mr. Goodman is on his deathbed, Lady Mellasin hires an unscrupulous lawyer to forge a will leaving a hefty legacy to her daughter, Flora (Haywood, *Betsy Thoughtless*, 392–93). Fortunately, the suit fails. Things go less well for the virtuous characters in *Sidney Bidulph*. In addition to being devastated by Mrs. Gerrarde, Sidney, as well as her husband, Mr. Arnold, and their children suffer illness, poverty, and in Mr. Arnold's case, death because of "the widow Arnold." Mrs. Arnold is the widow of Sidney's brother-in-law, who initially inherited the extensive Arnold fortune. Although the late Mr. Arnold and his widow had been separated for more than a year, Mrs. Arnold produced a daughter almost nine months after his death, and brought suit in the child's name to re-cover the estate from Sidney's husband on this child's behalf (Sheri-dan, 95–99). A pretty woman with a clever lawyer, the widow Arnold wins, beggaring the younger Mr. Arnold and driving him to his grave. While Mrs. Arnold's adultery predates her widowhood, her fraudulent suit on behalf of her illegitimate child is only possible once she becomes a widow. That makes the widow Arnold an adul-terer, a liar, and a fraud, like Lady Mellasin, as well as a thief and, one might contend, a murderer. Her victory destroys the good little family who should have inherited the estate and disrupts the proper transmission of family property.

When a sexual widow becomes criminal, then, two conversions happen: sexual power becomes the means for criminal ends, and sexuality becomes criminal in and of itself. For her scheming, grasp-ing, damaging, and more to the point, adulterous, fraudulent be-havior, the marchioness in *The Delicate Distress* is described as "unsexed" and "unnatural" (Griffith, 2:188, 2:226). As her crimes become more evident, her attractiveness and right to be called "woman" diminish. Furthermore, meeting the definition for "wom-an" has to do with property manipulation, whether that property in-cludes herself or what would otherwise belong to a man. As Lord Woodville exclaims after recovering from his infatuation, "For though a man may love a woman, that has ten thousand faults, and follies, those faults and follies should be feminine.—Avarice, and in-humanity, are sufficient to unsex the loveliest woman, and strip her of her every charm" (2:226). Eighteenth-century novels are clear about what is at stake: upon the proper transmission of property rests the stability of eighteenth-century society. Violation of this transmission is at the very least a violation of the conventions for defining gender.

Crimes perpetrated by widows against property and against pri-mogeniture are hardly an invention of eighteenth-century literature. As seventeenth-century characters such as Widow Blackacre from *The Plain Dealer* and the Widow from *The Counterfeit Bridegroom* sug-gest, anxieties about the possibility of a woman legatee interrupting the proper disposal of property and therefore of society appear in English literature well before the emergence of the novel.[10] But such characters prevent proper transmission by refusing to hand over what came legally, however unjustly, into their hands. Instead of pre-venting proper transmission, eighteenth-century fiction's criminal widows like Mrs. Arnold and the Italian marchioness reverse it, taking the initiative to flip or undo correct inheritance patterns. Furthermore, Behn and Wycherley's females also demonstrate a problematic sexuality, but it is an aspect of their criminality. For the novel's criminal widows, sexuality is a catalyst of their criminality.

Equally significant is the placement of these crimes in the constellation of crimes perpetrated by widows in the eighteenth-century novel. Crimes against property, including against primogeniture, took on new significance during the eighteenth century as notions of property developed within the changing economic system, and the legal system, including definitions of crime and kinds of crime, adjusted throughout the century to accommodate these changing ideas. As Peter Linebaugh explains, in the relationship between the changing economy and the changing penal code, "we can say, first, that the forms of exploitation pertaining to capitalist relations caused or modified the forms of criminal activity, and, second, that the converse was true, namely, that the forms of crime caused major changes in capitalism."[11] Hence, widows' crimes against property exemplified a cultural sensitivity toward property and crime distinctive to the eighteenth century and colored by attitudes toward sexuality and possession. Widows' crimes against primogeniture arise from a sense that widows' sexual status, economic status, and legal status can make a widow entrepreneurial, and therefore occur out of this confluence of sexual and economic desire and entitlement.

The question of property also becomes entangled with the question of gender in other ways, notably with the victimization of the sentimental heroine. Sometimes that victimization can be reasonably simple: Sarah Fielding's Marchioness of Trente arranges for the kidnapping of Ophelia, the heroine of *The History of Ophelia* (1760), to get her away from Lord Dorchester. The marchioness is an excellent example of why criminality and economic need do not correlate in the emerging novel. As a rich and independent widow, the Marchioness of Trente has not just the cash, horses, and carriage for this plan, but also the necessary collection of houses and dependents, including her widowed cousin Mrs. Herner, who actually does all the work. The marchioness has no compunction about using her wealth and her status to pursue her plans or to take her revenge on those who fail her. When she escapes, Ophelia reports that "The Marchioness of *Trente* was so enraged at Mrs. *Herner*'s having left me a Possibility of Escaping, by which her Schemes were frustrated, and

she exposed, that she refused to see her at her Return to *London,*
where Mrs. *Herner* went, as soon as she found I was irrecoverably
lost." The marchioness's rejection of Mrs. Herner ensures rejection
by others as well, reducing Mrs. Herner almost immediately to
homelessness and poverty.[12] Her desire, including her desire to vent
her rage when thwarted, is her constant motivation, and she uses the
considerable resources that widowhood offers her to gratify that desire. Her crime thus appears on several levels. First, she desires—bad
enough in a society trying to persuade women that if they must want
anything, it should only be to take care of others. Second, she uses
what she has inherited to gratify that desire. Certainly a misuse of an
inheritance. And third, what she desires is not only something for
her own good, but also something for someone else's—the virtuous
heroine's—detriment.

The marchioness's coconspirator, Mrs. Herner, although economically suffering both before and after the kidnapping, also
demonstrates how the novel portrays crime in widows as a matter of
choice rather than of necessity. Mrs. Herner, we are reminded, could
have taken a job rather than become a toady. Instead, regardless of
her views on the kidnapping, she helps the Marchioness of Trente
kidnap Ophelia in order to preserve her cousin's good favor and
handouts: "Thus the poor Woman, for a Subsistence, sold herself to
the most abject Slavery: But she was too proud to take any other
Means of gaining a Support" (Fielding, *Ophelia,* 2:5). Fielding allows
this "slavery" to exact its price on Mrs. Herner just as another kind of
slavery would damage another person. "From a continual servile
Compliance with the Will of another," Ophelia explains in retro-
spect,

> she lost all Liberty of Thought, of which only one's own Meanness
> can deprive one. She entirely forgot the Method of pronouncing the
> Word No; her Language was composed of nothing but Expressions
> of Assent and Affirmatives; and she would contradict her own Senses,
> as often as her violent and capricious Cousin, happened to err. (2:5)

Eventually Mrs. Herner's language is so distorted that when Ophelia
asks to go somewhere, Mrs. Herner's negative is unrecognizable and
Mrs. Herner has to take physical action to stop Ophelia, who
thought she had permission (2:5–6). Although they occupy different
economic situations, both Mrs. Herner and the Marchioness of
Trente treat the young female protagonist as an object and an obsta-

cle, and both use her to achieve their own ambition, whether for money and social standing or for a man.

This connection of money, crime, and widowhood has a very specific commercial flavor from early in the period. *The Temple Rakes* (1735) features Mrs. Villiard, the widowed aunt of Arabella, the intelligent and principled heroine. Mrs. Villiard has had a licentious life, even during her marriage, and in her widowhood has inherited "a very pretty Fortune."[13] Having reached middle age, however, "As the Time of indulging her more sensual Desires was now over, so she resigned herself to an insatiable Avarice, which gradually increased with her Years; and it was with the View of gratifying this Appetite, that she had taken *Arabella* into the House to live with her; having heard such exceeding Commendations of her Beauty, that she did not in the least doubt of making a good Return, in the Disposal of her Person" (23). Overtly linking sexual avarice and financial avarice, the novel uses that connection to indicate how commercial greed leads to emotional and familial breakdown.

Mrs. Villiard's economic abilities and consequent villainy also appear in the person with whom she is making the deal: Mr. D——z, who is not only rich, old, and a man, but also Jewish. Antisemitic stereotypes portray Jews as dishonest, avaricious, and impossible to outsmart in a business deal. So brilliant a financial and sexual strategist is Mrs. Villiard, however, that she manages, despite his misgivings, to get Mr. D——z to increase his financial offer every time he is rejected, pointing out that if Arabella were to become his mistress, "her Niece could not promise to herself any of those Advantages, which young Widows expect upon the Decease of an elderly Husband. Tho' she did not doubt but the Girl's Behaviour, if she could be brought to comply, would sufficiently induce him to provide handsomely for her in his Will" (30).[14] Unlike Arabella's widowed mother in the country, who is desperate for money to support her six children but who would never sell her daughter for cash, Mrs. Villiard is unremittingly venal. The language around her is specifically commercial in nature: "she did not in the least doubt of making a good Return" (23); "well judging that the more she expends this way, the greater would be her Returns in the End" (24); "the Aunt had not yet made any direct Bargain for her niece" (25); she sets "Terms" with Mr. D——z (32); and so on. In addition to the urban, London setting, the vocabulary associated with Mrs. Villiard is also the vocabulary of urban, London-based business, rather than of an agricultural or rural economy. Mrs. Villiard's transformation of desire from desire for sex to desire for money is therefore connected to a specifically commercial economy, an artifact of the moment in which she appears.

Behavior like Mrs. Villiard's crops up repeatedly in mother figures as early as 1722 in Daniel Defoe's *Moll Flanders*, and as late as 1791 in Clara Reeve's *School for Widows*. When Moll discovers that her nameless mother-in-law is really her mother and that her husband is really her brother, she endures a crisis rooted not simply in the economic security her marriage has gained her, but also in the familial security it has brought her.[15] She worries about the effect of this discovery on her husband, her mother, and her own children. The family itself is transgressive, and Moll must decide which act is more damaging: continuing to live in sin, which is unbearable for her, or breaking up the family by leaving her marriage and the colonies.

No such anguish attends Moll's widowed mother.[16] When she learns the news, she pressures Moll "to bury the thing entirely, and to continue to live with him as my Husband," offering Moll considerable financial incentive to do so (146). Although she claims to be considering the good of the family in her opinion, she is asking Moll to do something illegal, immoral, and repugnant to her daughter and the audience. One might accuse Moll's birth mother of favoritism in trying to preserve the ignorant happiness of her son at the expense of the knowing anguish of her daughter, and favoritism, as Toni Bowers notes, is one of the great maternal sins outlined by eighteenth-century writers.[17] One might also accuse Moll's mother of perpetrating and perpetuating a crime, since incest is not just immoral, but illegal. Hence, although Moll calls her "a very Pious sober and religious Woman" (137), Moll's mother also demonstrates a disconcerting comfort with criminal behavior, including exhorting her daughter to continue in the way of crime and sin. Moll's mother's criminal activity is not simply a crime against society, but also a crime against her own children, even though she justifies it by claiming the opposite.

Moll's mother is not the only example of a mother on a quest for economic and familial stability through the exploitation of a daughter or daughter figure, although she is possibly the most atrociously criminal. In an era where social instability through economic change was a cause for anxiety, the ambition to exchange goods (a daughter) for status (class, money) through marrying her off was both acceptable and charged with transgression. In the novel, this use of individuals is often contemptible when it does not violate rank, as in the case of Madam Duval or Madame Cheron, but criminal when it becomes the kind of class movement ultimately regulated by the Hardwicke Act of 1753. In Frances Burney's *Evelina* (1778), Dame Green passes off her own daughter as Sir John Belmont's. "When Mrs. Selwyn asked her how she dared perpetrate such a fraud," Evelina reports, the former midwife and nurse "protested she had no ill designs; but that, as *Miss* would be never the worse for it, she thought it pity *nobody* should be the better," revealing a cool-headed spirit of enterprise that overwhelms the morality of appropriate class consciousness. Sally Godfrey's widowed mother in Samuel Richardson's *Pamela* (1740) was "a person of great art," as Pamela explains, who, "in hopes to draw him in, as she knew that he was heir to a great estate, encouraged his private visits with her daughter." This would indeed be class change: the Godfreys are a "good family," but Mrs. Godfrey is Mr. B——'s landlady. Sally would be rising considerably above her station, although not as much as the virtuous Pamela, who proves her deservingness by withstanding Mr. B——'s pressure. Evil schemes cannot prosper in the Richardsonian moral universe, however; Mrs. Godfrey is too interested in her plan to consider the reality of the situation, which is that Mr. B—— "was known to be unsettled and wild, and that her daughter was young and inexperienced, and far from being indifferent to him."[18] While Mr. B—— abandons Sally, Sally makes her mother's wicked commercial intentions all too visible with pregnancy and self-imposed exile to Jamaica.

The victimization of the sentimental heroine, the sale of innocents, or even just the attempted manipulation of young people like Sally and Mr. B—— makes people into property, property to be acquired and used to generate more wealth. While the acquisition of goods and wealth are indeed admirable commercial behaviors and aims under emerging capitalism, the novel shows that in the hands of widows, both the methods and goals become criminal, at least as applied to certain kinds of people. This attitude in the novel signals a deliberate cultural regulation of interactions with property. After all, like a good capitalist, *Evelina*'s Dame Green is simply tailoring a business plan to fit an economic opportunity.

Legislation such as the Hardwicke Act, designed in part to protect heirs and heiresses, was another manifestation of the period's fears about the changing role of property. Although the concept of women as property and the practice of women as transmitters of property did not change, because of evolving ideas about property, crime against women was considered particularly heinous. That is not to suggest that all rapes were treated alike; on the contrary. But abducting an heiress, either to marry or to rape, was a capital offence even when the heiress later testified to her consent.[19] Crime against women was not therefore a crime against a person, but a crime against property, both literal, as in the estate that she was to inherit or had inherited, and figurative, as in the woman's virginity, which was an item belonging to her family and then her husband.

The novel also complicates these issues by making some criminal widows exploit a daughter or daughter figure. Like the novel's other deplorable widows, criminal widows fail as mothers, and their crimes are linked one way or another to that failure. When Ferdinand's mother in *Ferdinand Count Fathom* insists on continuing her life as a camp follower, making a living by killing and looting wounded men on the battlefield, she not only offers Ferdinand a poor role model, but also offers him a criminal lineage that at least partially explains his career of villainy. Eighteenth-century women were not encouraged to view themselves as autonomous selves able and entitled to engage in self-interested behavior. Womanhood was portrayed as passive, not active; selfless, not self-interested; domestic and private, not entrepreneurial and public. As Toni Bowers points out in *The Politics of Motherhood*, eighteenth-century maternity also followed this construction. Ruth Perry and Felicity Nussbaum demonstrate that women were only allowed to produce at the maternal level. This ideology justifies capitalism, as Laura Brown argues in *The Ends of Empire*, and is a part of the reorganization of the male-dominated society, as Michael McKeon points out in "Historicizing Patriarchy."[20] Widows who took advantage of the rights and opportunities presented by widowhood, however, were hardly being passive, selfless, domestic, and private, but rather active, self-interested, entrepreneurial, and public. Widows who rejected the period's notions of proper female and maternal behavior easily moved into the realm of the criminal, where their refusal to worship their dependents at their own expense rendered them not just figuratively monstrous, but literally criminal.

In fact, the sale of a female dependent is, in addition to adultery, the other most pervasive crime committed by widows in the eighteenth-century novel. One of the features of this crime is that it is perpetrated by widows of all classes—Mrs. Villiard is affluent, for example, Mrs. Godfrey is a landlady, and Mrs. Burton in Clara Reeve's *School for Widows* is a hired nurse. She attempts to procure Captain Maurice's beloved, Donna Isabella, for the Captain with violence. Supposedly nursing Donna Isabella back from the insanity to which Captain Maurice has driven her, Mrs. Burton is actually more concerned with subduing Donna Isabella and bringing her to the Captain's bed (or vice-versa). "They tell me, that, though you have been married to her many months, you have not had courage enough to bed her," she says to Captain Maurice one night, standing at Isabella's bedroom door. "Come in, sir; and I will bring her to your lure, I warrant: you shall go to bed to her now, if you please, upon condition that you give me a pair of gloves, and a favour, to-morrow morning."[21] To "bring Isabella to his lure," Mrs. Burton hog-ties and gags her: "She lay with her face into the pillow, and I fear she would be suffocated. I offered to take her hand.—Oh, madam! how shall I speak it?—her dear hands were tied behind her, and her feet tied together!" (2:212). Fortunately for Donna Isabella, even the Captain cannot stomach this behavior, but that he cannot—he who has caused her husband's death, stolen her property, arranged a sham marriage between them, and driven her insane—reveals the degree of its depravity.

Other criminal widows render this behavior more clearly what it is. An unnamed city widow in Sarah Scott's *History of Cornelia* (1750) takes the orphaned and homeless Cornelia under her wing, offering "lodging at her house, and a recommendation to such persons, as, whatever way of life she fixed upon, should prove sufficient to procure her an easy maintenance." With such an invitation, she persuades Cornelia to stay with her until Cornelia discovers the widow is a procuress, from whom Cornelia must escape with the help of one of the widow's clients. The very real Mother Needham turns up in Mary Davys's *The Accomplish'd Rake* (1727), where she is called "Mother N——d——m" and Jezebella. She imprisons a young lady, offering her to any likely young man who will pay for the privilege of deflowering her. London procuresses like these commit crimes against propriety but also against property, a confluence highlighted, as Kathryn Kirkpatrick points out, by conduct books, which treated a woman's propriety as a commodity that determined her worth in society, especially on the marriage market. Furthermore crime, like commercial behavior, was constructed as "unnatural" in a woman, so abducting or selling these young women is not simply an immoral or illegal treatment of property, but also of gender, once crime is framed as an unnatural act in a woman.[22]

Significantly, however, while eighteenth-century literature provides examples of unmarried bawds who attempt to sell (or do sell) virtuous women to debauched rakes, they are rarely if ever clearly labeled widows. Scott's London bawd is identified as a widow, but she is the exception. There is neither literary evidence that the character delineated by Davys nor historical evidence that the real Mother Needham was a widow. The three women who pimp for Fanny Hill in John Cleland's novel *Fanny Hill* (1749) resemble the Mother Needham described in *The Accomplish'd Rake*, and there are other unscrupulous bawds in other novels, such as Mrs. Modely in *Betsy Thoughtless*, Madam la Mer in Tobias Smollett's *Adventures of Ferdinand Count Fathom* (1753) and Mrs. Miser in Margaret Lee's *Clara Lennox* (1797). None of these procuresses is ever unambiguously identified as a widow, either. Perhaps an explicit articulation was unnecessary; everyone knew that such a woman had to be not just a procuress, but a widow. Or perhaps the lack of this specific identification is a sign of how the category was manipulated: women could encourage people to think of them as widows, a label that enabled them to act autonomously and economically, without having to produce evidence such as a dead husband. The category was useful but ultimately unprovable, since it could be reduced to a self-assumed title and self-assumed clothes. In either case, the association of widow and procuress highlights the association of widowhood and transgression.

The ability to become a widow in the minds of others by appearing as a widow raises another set of issues arising, as the epigraph from *The Beggar's Opera* suggests, out of what could be seen as the desirability of widowhood. The period was not only aware of the appeal of widowhood, but also sensitive to the urge to become a widow. The presence of ambiguous bawds like Mrs. Modely or Mrs. Miser indicates that fortunately, such an urge did not have to be heeded by putting mercury into a husband's morning milk. One also could become a widow simply by announcing oneself a widow in a place where no one had reason to think otherwise. Women could create an identity by putting on the right clothes and saying the right thing, and in the case of widowhood, then could assume liberties that they did not really have.

The ambiguous bawds are only one example of the elasticity of labels, especially when it comes to widows. In *Fantomina* (1725), Eliza
Haywood's eponymous protagonist uses the dress of a young widow
and the name "Mrs Bloomer" to seduce Beauplaisir for a third time.
Beauplaisir finds offering comfort a great aphrodisiac for himself,
and the pretty young widow is a delicious object. In chasing "Mrs
Bloomer," however, Beauplaisir allows himself, all unconsciously, to
be the object of Fantomina's chase, and in seemingly seducing "Mrs
Bloomer," he becomes instead the seduced. While disguise allows
Fantomina one form of freedom, the disguise of a widow allows her
another advantage as well. Using the well-known fact that widows
(unless in highly remarkable circumstances) are sexually experienced, Fantomina can use a new form of adventure, sex with a
knowledgeable woman, to tempt her rapidly sated lover. That Fantomina herself is, by this point, thoroughly sexually experienced herself makes her disguise that much more authentic, easy to assume,
and, paradoxically, honest, even at the same time that she is as nearly
the opposite of a widow—an unbetrothed, unmarried young woman
—as eighteenth-century society can conceive.[23]

The use of a false title of widow is therefore itself a form of crime,
a fraud—a remaking of the self, escaping past sins, disguising something—and like the crimes it is meant to cover, is not to be allowed
to stand. When the countess in Sarah Fielding's *The Countess of Dellwyn* (1759) is divorced for adultery, she takes another name, "passed
at *Paris* for a Widow" and is called "*La belle Anglaise*, and *la belle Veuve*"
by the Parisians. She persuades a rich, handsome, young man to
marry her but his father discovers the fraud and her history and prevents the marriage, reducing the countess to a bad end.[24] Samuel
Richardson is more generous in *Pamela*, although here again, his
false widow never escapes the taint of earlier sexual transgression.
Sally Godfrey goes to Jamaica, where "she is since well and happily
married; passing to her husband for a young widow, with one daughter, which her first husband's friends take care of, and provide for"
(501).[25] Titles such as "la belle Veuve" or Sally Godfrey's calling herself a widow expose the danger of names: their usefulness in signaling identity, and the readiness with which they are assumed and dis-
carded. As Paul Langford points out, the use of honorifics loosened
considerably during the eighteenth century. Money could buy a coat
of arms, but by the second half of the century, most people were
claiming coats of arms without registering with the College of Her-

alds. "Gentleman" was also enormously devalued during the time. Everyone claimed to be a gentleman, including tradesmen, although it was supposed to be a very particular title and rank. Even a label as seemingly definite as "mother" was corruptible, since it was also used to indicate that the woman was a bawd, as in the case of "Mother" Needham, perhaps the most powerful madam in London in the 1720s, and a woman who was certainly not a mother to the young women she corrupted, as Hogarth's *Harlot's Progress* shows.[26]

The potential to manipulate labels can seem dangerous in a society already concerned about social and economic indeterminacy, and more so when the labels have to do with gender. Terry Castle points out in "The Culture of Travesty" that the eighteenth century possessed a "persistent popular urge toward disguise and metamorphosis" that allowed the period's subjects to take advantage of a "cathartic escape from the self and a suggestive revision of ordinary experience," thereby challenging the "ordering patterns of culture itself."[27] As long as someone dressed like a gentleman, for example, he would be treated as one on the basis of his wardrobe alone. In an age fascinated with disguise, the masquerade in particular could serve women well, providing "eighteenth-century women with an unusual sense of erotic freedom."[28] "Disguise obviated a host of cultural prescriptions and taboos," Castle notes. "A woman in masquerade might approach strangers, initiate conversation, touch and embrace those whom she did not know, speak coarsely—in short, violate all the cherished imperatives of ordinary feminine sexual decorum" (169). One striking example of this behavior is when an unnamed widow in *The Accomplish'd Rake* takes on masculine prerogative and proposes marriage to the protagonist, Sir John, while dressed as a handsome young man (Davys, 178–79).

Catherine Craft-Fairchild points out that not all masquerade worked to subvert notions of gender or to generate more freedom for women, but Castle's point is still significant. Masquerade highlighted what Judith Butler calls the performativity of gender, gender's existence as a set of signs and behaviors that conform to expectations of masculinity or femininity and therefore indicate whether one is male or female.[29] While masquerade did not always offer women the "essential masculine privilege of erotic object-choice," as Castle claims, the age recognized that physical disguise could allow a behavioral transformation as well (169, 157). As one eighteenth-century cartoonist pointed out,

Here City Wives, disguis'd in Widows Weeds,
Look out for Sparks to Mend their sev'ral breeds,
These no advantage of their favours make,
Sin not for Gold but Kiss for Kissings Sake. . . .
                    ("The World in Masquerade")

Assuming not just the physical guise but also the titular guise of a widow, that is, extending the masquerade to life rather than to a discrete event, allowed women this freedom, but it was hardly unambivalently understood. Fantomina's manipulation of Beauplaisir and society's roles for women stands until the very end of the story, when she is punished with pregnancy, no offer of marriage, disgrace, and a continental "monastery" (Haywood, *Fantomina*, 248). While disguise is liberating, it is also frightening in its possibility of escape and catharsis.[30]

The issue of the widow-by-disguise, then, poses a significant problem for a society in flux. The question of how to label society's members is only a problem if that society is seeking new ways of categorizing its members rather them embracing the breakdown of categories, but eighteenth-century novels' association of widowhood and crime suggests that that society was indeed seeking some form of social certitude. *Moll Flanders* offers perhaps the clearest view of novelists' grappling with questions of identity, although as the other novels discussed in this chapter should indicate, it is hardly the only work to offer such a perspective.

Moll Flanders's complicated and ambiguous identity lies at the heart of her story. She is definitely a widow at various times in the novel, and she is probably a widow at others, but she also may be married at the same time as many of these widowhoods. For example, after her first husband dies, she really is a widow with two children under the age of five and "about 1200 *l.* in my pocket" (Defoe, *Moll Flanders*, 102). Once she hands her children over to her in-laws, furthermore, she is "left loose in the World, and being still Young and Handsome, as everybody said of me, *and I assure you I thought my self so*, and with a tollerable Fortune in my Pocket" (103; Defoe's emphasis). She moves to London, acquires the appellation the "pretty Widow," and is "resolv'd now to be Married or Nothing, and to be well Married or not at all" (103). Her marriage to the draper (104) is something of a disaster—when he is arrested for debt, they part ways, never to hear from each other again—but as late as her imprisonment in Newgate, she is still mentioning that he might still be alive (177, 180, 236). "I was a Widow bewitched," she says at one point; "I had a Husband, and no Husband" (108). Sometimes other husbands as well haunt her remarriages throughout the novel, so Moll is simultaneously presented as a widow and a married woman.

Her identity as a widow, however fraudulent, allows Moll to engage in different kinds of business, and to reveal different behavior, such as marriage, as aspects of business. Her first remarriage may be from desire, but future marriages have much if not everything to do with "Circumstances," that is, the threat of poverty and starvation, which "made the offer of a good Husband the most necessary Thing in the World to me" (122). To exploit the male desire for a rich and appropriately virtuous wife, Moll repeatedly presents herself as a widow, which almost always enables her to get the husband she needs or wants (159, 183, 185, 186, 197). Although the narrative as well as Moll are unclear about whether she really is one, the use of this title, this identity, makes Moll a comprehensible person in society, and therefore a player in the marriage market and a survivor.

This assumed identity is profitable in other business ventures, as well. Describing one criminal episode, Moll explains, "I had taken up the Disguise of a Widow's Dress; it was without any real design in view, but only waiting for any thing that might offer, as I often did" (311), a statement that could stand as a larger description of Moll's life after her gentleman draper leaves her. Whether she really is a widow or not—and the existence of that pesky draper of hers, as she reminds readers from time to time, challenges that claim's veracity—the term "widow" carries meaning for the people she meets that enables them to understand her and her to employ them. That Moll literally is able to put on and off the dress of a widow when fleecing a mercer (311–25) actualizes what happens linguistically: the term is a label that may be employed to cover or create an understanding of a woman, but that does not necessarily express the full identity of the woman using the label. It provides a category for people to understand her, but it also offers an opportunity for Moll to exploit, since people's expectations attend the category. The slippage between what other people in the novel construe Moll to be when they hear "widow" and what the reader knows Moll to be reveals the flexibility of such a term, and opens up the idea that transgression arises from escaping traditional, accepted definitions of female behavior and identity, which is what by definition widowhood does. Regardless of the reality of her claims to widowhood, the use of the title "widow" reveals how the category conceptualizes her for a society that otherwise has little room to understand and accommodate a woman in her situation, a woman either granted or claiming autonomy. "Widow" makes room for Moll to act as an independent woman in a society that does not have much space for independent women, and it creates a way of understanding Moll that is incomplete but effective on at least some levels.

That incompleteness recurs repeatedly as the novel examines the problems of categorization for women. As a small child, Moll says she wants to be a "gentlewoman," which means different things to different people. For Moll, "being a Gentlewoman, was to be able to Work for myself, and get enough to keep me without that terrible Bug-bear *going to Service*, whereas they meant to live Great, Rich, and High, and I know not what" (50; Defoe's emphasis). Moll points to a woman who "mended Lace, and wash'd the Ladies Lac'd-heads" as a gentlewoman, but who, she is told, also "is a Person of ill Fame, and has had two or three Bastards" (50, 51). This dichotomy within the figure used to define "gentlewoman" exemplifies the slippage Defoe establishes within the term. Ironically, the woman does define "gentlewoman" for Moll in many ways, since Moll also has assorted illegitimate children and acquires her share of "ill Fame," although she gives up her needle for a life of crime. According to her Nurse, the Mayoress, and other women who "made themselves Merry" with Moll's aspirations, Moll never achieves "genteel" status as they understand it, and instead accomplishes only the disreputable, transgressive things that this unnamed woman embodies. Nevertheless, however, Moll is a gentlewoman according to her own definition throughout the novel, right up to the end when she manages her last, "Lancashire husband" and her two estates around Chesapeake Bay.

Moll seeks self-sufficiency rather than leisure, and she undertakes anything necessary to achieve it. Although she seems to discover that the best independence is that conferred by affluence, the lengthy and detailed section outlining Moll's life of crime and her spectacular success in amassing a fortune suggests that it is not the comparatively leisured life in the colonies that is most exciting for her, but rather the autonomous, entrepreneurial life of crime in London. That she loves her Lancashire husband best, as she professes, that she repeatedly refers to him as a gentleman and says his pleasures are in hunting rather than farming (411), and that she is also the manager of their finances and the dominant one in the relationship, is probably not a coincidental confluence of events. By the end of the novel, one might argue, entrepreneurial Moll has managed to combine the best aspects of marriage (love, companionship, children, and presumably, sex) and of widowhood (independence, control of the estate and of herself) all at the same time. But that she has done so through a life of crime, and is telling the story after illegally returning to England (and therefore in the midst of still more law-breaking), taints what might otherwise appear as a triumphant female participation in the possibilities of a fluid, commercial economy. Considering that in other texts, Defoe wrote against what Faller calls "the prevalent suspicion that modern economic life was the pursuit of criminal ends by other means," opposing the eighteenth-century "'scandal' that trade was inherently dishonest and so comparable to theft," Moll's simultaneous criminal and commercial existence suggests that for Defoe, female participation in "modern economic life" was the problem, not modern economic life itself.[31] Other writers, like the more conservative Sarah Fielding, might also take issue with the economic system, but Defoe's Moll Flanders reveals that discomfort with the presence of women holds these writers and their depictions together.

There is another significance to Moll's simultaneous existence as widow and wife: since Moll is both a widow and not a widow, she is both transgressive and not transgressive. As a widow, she is transgressive in the sense that all widows are transgressive against gender roles for women and a patriarchal society that paradoxically creates the very thing that transgresses. So as a not-widow (that is, as a still-married woman), Moll should be not-transgressive, as well. After all, married women conform to the roles laid out by eighteenth-century English society. But in fact, Moll is also transgressive as a married woman, because she is bigamous. This paradox parallels the situation in which women in eighteenth-century English society found themselves. Whatever their condition, it smacks of the transgressive, because female sexuality is always on the brink of bursting forth from the bounds that male-dominated society has put on it. As Mary Poovey explains, the image of the Proper Lady, as she calls it, is designed as a model for containing woman's tendency to transgress, but that means that by definition, the Proper Lady contains within her the concept of transgression. The Proper Lady is therefore always on the brink of transgression, always having within herself the potential for it.[32] And this, of course, is precisely what the widow does as well; since by definition the widow is even more overtly inherently transgressive than other women, the widow must work doubly hard to bring herself within the bounds of the Proper Lady.

Widowhood as understood in the eighteenth century is a condition always already transgressing and always already between definitions. The novel's criminal widows thus reveal that for the eighteenth century, crime and widowhood can be conceptualized as the same thing, the same form of transgression. They differ in degree, but not in kind. Not all novelistic widows are criminals, of course, but the nature of the historical and novelistic crimes underscores another way in which widows could generate anxiety in their society. The novel's criminal widows are criminal because of the enterprising investment of resources and exercise of rights that characterize commercial and male society, but that they also have access to as widows. The conflation of sexual and material desire underscores the access that widows have to sexuality, either their own or that of the dependents in their care, and to opportunities to gratify that desire whether in sex, property, or money. For a woman to want anything was problematic enough and from being initially disquieting, became the ultimate in the derangement of desire and acquisition that characterized emerging capitalism for the age.

The reason for the number and kind of novelistic widows might then be explained: these women exemplify attributes of unregulated, emergent capitalism that particularly would have made people fearful, including the satiation of one's individual appetite regardless of the cost to others, the ability to change self and class rapidly, the ability to buy the hallmarks of prestige that originally only accrued to birth, and so on. Criminal widows thus bring together several contemporaneous strands of anxiety: the anxiety about female autonomy that a widow generated anyway; the anxiety about the possibilities of the new commercial, not agrarian system; the anxiety about what this new commercial system might do to definitions and systems like class and gender; and the anxiety about the seeming amorality of the new commercial system's potential. Lastly, collapsing the categories of "widow" and "criminal" not only outlines a warning to women who might contemplate widowhood or the new society with equanimity or pleasure, but also goes further, criminalizing the widow who acts on the powers that her status and her commercial economy grant her.

6

A State of Alteration, Perhaps of Improvement: Jane Austen's Widows

> The Musgroves, like their houses, were in a state of alteration,
> perhaps of improvement. The father and mother were in the
> old English style, and the young people in the new.
>
> —Jane Austen, *Persuasion*

"Do you think me destitute of every honest, every natural feeling?" Jane Austen's Lady Susan asks her sister-in-law, Mrs. Vernon, after attempting to prevent Mrs. Vernon's marriage; driving her own late husband into bankruptcy; torturing her daughter for all sixteen years of Frederica's life and trying to force her to marry a man she rightly detests; lying to just about everyone; and seducing married men, affianced men, and Mrs. Vernon's beloved brother. "The idea is horrible," Mrs. Vernon replies diplomatically, but in fact, Lady Susan is destitute of every honest and natural feeling.[1] She is exactly what affluent widows at their worst are supposed to be: selfish, unmaternal, manipulative, exploitative, enterprising, and more interested in money than in emotion.

Although she revised it around 1805, Austen did not publish *Lady Susan* and the work is very different from her completed and published novels, regardless of whether it contains the seeds of later technique and subject matter. Terry Castle points out that *Lady Susan* "has more of an eighteenth-century feeling to it than some of Austen's later works" and compares Austen's themes, devices, and techniques to Samuel Richardson, Henry Fielding, and Charlotte

137

Lennox. I would add that Lady Susan herself derives from the eighteenth rather than the nineteenth century, and despite revision remains imprinted with her original invention in the 1790s. Certainly as "a survivor, a woman who refuses to be a passive victim" and therefore a "villain," she clearly shows the mark of the eighteenth century.[2] More specifically, her tremendous powers of attraction and her desire to captivate and manipulate men as well as to control her daughter nearly defines earlier wicked, affluent widows. Her competition with other women, especially her vicious rivalry with her sweet-tempered daughter, reinforces eighteenth-century fears of dangerous sexuality in the widow and that sexuality's ability to overwhelm correct maternal urges. In fact, Lady Susan comprises almost all the qualities associated with affluent, wicked widows in eighteenth-century novels, and that she manages to escape being a cardboard cutout is testament to Austen's talents rather than to the inherent quality of those conventions.

Austen's published novels, however, at least as demonstrated by her widows, involve very different thinking about gender, economics, and society than that demonstrated by Lady Susan. As a familiar character type, Lady Susan displays attitudes characteristic of an earlier stage in the development of a mercantile capitalist society than Austen's later widows display. We can speculate about why Austen did not revise and publish Lady Susan as she revised Elinor and Marianne and First Impressions.[3] Whatever the reason, one thing is clear: Lady Susan displays sensibilities and conventions more consistent with a time struggling to comprehend and justify changes to an entire economic system, while the later, published novels display sensibilities and conventions more consistent with a time struggling to understand how to maximize the good in changes that had become a foregone conclusion.

Jane Austen's completed novels are crammed with widows—twelve significant widows in six books, in fact. Sense and Sensibility (1811) features Mrs. Dashwood, whose widowhood catalyzes the action of the novel; Mrs. Ferrars, whose widowhood creates one of the crises of money and marriage in the novel; Mrs. Smith, whose widowhood creates another crisis of money and marriage; and Mrs. Jennings, whose actions so facilitate both plot and commentary. In contrast to these women, Mansfield Park (1814) offers Mrs. Norris, possessed of an emotional miserliness matched only by her economic stinginess, and Mrs. Rushworth, possessed of a narrow-mindedness about social class that becomes a tragic intractability in all kinds of relationships. *Pride and Prejudice* (1813) has the famous Lady Catherine de Bourgh. It also, one might argue, features the phantom widowhood of Mrs. Bennet. *Persuasion* (1817) sketches Lady Dalrymple, whose appearance is too brief to be anything but iconic, and three more substantial characters: Lady Russell, whose well-meaning but unquestionably snobbish advice has created the obstacle which hero and heroine must clear; Mrs. Clay, whose designs on Sir Walter Elliot, Anne's father, threaten the family; and Anne's friend Mrs. Smith, who exemplifies what damage marriage can inflict on women and to what depths, as a result, they might be forced in widowhood. A similar figure is the confused Mrs. Thorpe from *Northanger Abbey* (1817). Further down the economic chain is *Emma*'s Mrs. Bates (1815), who, with her daughter and grand-niece, embody the fall from gentility and independence into genteel poverty and dependence that often accompanied widowhood in the eighteenth and nineteenth centuries.[4]

Although these women, like their literary ancestresses, express views about the connections among gender, society, and the changing economy, they also enjoy significant differences from the widows of eighteenth-century novels. Their increased complexity reveals not just a greater comfort with the category of "widow," but a greater comfort with the commercial economy. Austen's widows consistently complicate old dichotomies with a hybrid of characteristics associated formerly with feudal agrarianism or unstable commercialism. They indicate a view of economics that balances between the old and new systems without demonizing or deifying either one.

Austen's stance on class and gender has been the subject of considerable debate. On the one side there are scholars like Margaret Kirkham, Mary Poovey, and Claudia Johnson, who wish to claim Austen for the revolutionaries, liberals, or feminists, and who read Austen as criticizing the structures of her time. On the other side there are scholars like Marilyn Butler, David Aers, and Edward Said, who read Austen as conservative, a proponent of traditional values and certainly not a feminist. My Jane Austen occupies the middle ground between these positions: she is no radical, but neither is she a reactionary. I agree with Paul A. Cantor that Austen seeks to infuse the aristocracy with the same "new energy and discipline of the middle class" embodied by the Naval officers of *Persuasion*, as well as with Alistair Duckworth that Austen worries that "economic considerations will outweigh and overcome moral considerations in human conduct." As Susan Fraiman argues, while Austen certainly espouses some conservative views about England and empire, class and economics, she is also well aware of how those institutions—England, empire, class, economics—can be restrictive, especially to women. Austen was a critic and her novels critique certain values, institutions, and systems while accepting others. Austen's economic attitude negotiates between an indictment and an endorsement of the old feudal agrarian order and the new commercial system, her understanding of the system shaded by an acceptance of some possibilities within the system as well as a rejection of other possibilities; as John Dussinger observes, "Austen's fictional world resists either / or solutions." It is not just class change that fascinates Austen, but kinds of class change. This nuanced understanding manifests itself in a plethora of representations that together as well as individually express the complexity of Austen's conceptualization.[5]

Austen's life can account for some of her attitudes toward class, gender, and economics. Money and social status were always issues in her family, as her brothers each had to make his way in different professions without the leg-up of substantial financial or social support from their father. Upon the death of Austen's father, furthermore, the women of the family—Austen's mother, his widow; Austen's sister, Cassandra; and Austen herself—found themselves considerably impoverished, and without the help of the Austen brothers, would have found making ends meet extremely difficult. David Nokes points out that Austen was acutely aware throughout her life and especially after her father's death of the precariousness of female fortune. Furthermore, with brothers in the navy, business, the landed gentry, and the clergy, Austen was intimately connected to the range of military, economic, social, and religious concerns of the day. Her social circle during her formative years was also, according to Claire Tomalin, quite diverse, including families from the professional, business, landed, clerical, and aristocratic classes. That community was alert to the issues of the time, such as abolition and the questions of human rights that slavery involved.[6]

Austen's widows also reflect a situation larger than the specific facts of Austen's life, however; they reflect how the changing socioeconomic situation in England enabled new attitudes toward that situation. By the time Austen was writing in the early decades of the nineteenth century, the socioeconomic situation in England had changed and the balance of power and of cultural perception had shifted. Commercial values, particularly those propounded by sensibility, had become much more mainstream, as the popular response to the trial of Queen Caroline in 1820 indicated. When George IV attempted to divorce her, the popular press represented her as a lady in distress and as neglected domesticity incarnate. The king's rejection of her was portrayed as a repudiation of domestic virtues associated with his popular father, George III, and with what essentially had become a middle class, in favor of a hedonistic selfishness associated with the aristocracy, the government, and corruption. The middle class was also a tremendous literary force, consuming and supporting the dissemination of literature, and therefore of cultural values, through institutions such as booksellers, subscriptions, and lending libraries. Men and women of commercial and landed families readily married across class lines and this social and familial mixing led, as did the economic, political, and cultural power, to a merger of values.[7]

Whatever advantages this change might have brought some groups, however, historians such as Leonore Davidoff and Catherine Hall, Maxine Berg, and Bridget Hill describe a very difficult economic reality for women by the opening decades of the nineteenth century.[8] Throughout the eighteenth century, women were being excluded practically and ideologically from the commercial economy, and by the opening years of the nineteenth century that exclusion had had a noticeable effect on the role of women in their society. Efforts to limit widows' rights also continued, culminating in the Dower Act of 1833, which eliminated a widow's legal right to one-third of her husband's estate and rendered her dependent on the terms of his will, rather than on the law. As Barbara Benedict explains, "In Austen's society, where the identities of women and men, the roles of servants, merchants, and every social class, and the nature of socializing were all changing. . . . [t]he arenas of privacy seeped into areas of public display, even while increasingly rigid gender roles apparently asserted their separation." The situation for women in general and widows in particular had worsened as a result of efforts throughout the eighteenth century to exclude women from access to public, commercial activity; Austen's novels "evince a deep responsiveness to economic and cultural shifts occurring during the years of revolutions, trade wars, imperial adventurings, and slavery," and consequently "register cultural anxieties created by the new economic systems and the social disruptions."[9]

A comparison of two widows from *Sense and Sensibility*, Mrs. Ferrars and Mrs. Smith, reveals how Austen modified eighteenth-century conventions used for widows, especially affluent ones, as well the economic attitudes that those conventions represented. At first glance, Mrs. Ferrars appears to be the eighteenth-century's affluent villain-widow exemplified by Madame Duval and Madame Cheron. Nearly invisible and deprived of direct speech throughout almost the entire novel, Mrs. Ferrars nevertheless maintains a strong presence. She desires money and power for her children and complete obedience from them. For her elder son, Edward, Mrs. Ferrars "wanted him to make a fine figure in the world in some manner or other. His mother wished to interest him in political concerns, to get him into parliament, or to see him connected with some of the great men of the day" (*S and S*, 13). When her negotiations to marry Edward to a Miss Morton, who "has thirty thousand pounds" (226), are thwarted by his secret engagement to Lucy Steele, Mrs. Ferrars's response typifies the unmaternal behavior of earlier negative, affluent widows. First, she attempts to bribe and then threaten Edward with money (224–25). Next, she reorders the family by reordering its finances, making Robert, the second son, heir to the Norfolk estate and the family money (226–27). In fact, what Mrs. Ferrars wants is to have her own power repeatedly confirmed by her children. She loves (according to her definition) Robert more than Edward because Robert thinks of himself and his mother as Mrs. Ferrars directs, and he and Lucy earn her good will by giving Mrs. Ferrars what she desires: their obedience and willing self-humiliation. Unlike Edward and Elinor, Robert and Lucy behave commercially, making themselves in the image of the market's demands in the interest of acquiring money. As for Mrs. Ferrars, she seeks confirmation of her economic and emotional power over her sons, two powers that she incorrectly regards as one. Her manipulation of wealth, particularly to control her adult male children, as well as her preferred habitation in London argue for Mrs. Ferrars's place in an eighteenth-century novel as a negative widow.

Sense and Sensibility's complement to Mrs. Ferrars is Willoughby's aunt, Mrs. Smith. She is invisible throughout the novel and depends on Willoughby and Mrs. Jennings, at least at first, to present her to others. Initially introduced as a hindrance to Willoughby's inheritance, Mrs. Smith takes on another aura as the story unfolds and Willoughby becomes thoroughly unreliable. Mrs. Smith expects practicality and honor from young men, particularly Willoughby, and when she learns that he has seduced and abandoned a young lady, she casts him off (274). What she taketh away, however, she can also restore with "voluntary forgiveness . . . stating his marriage with a woman of character, as the source of her clemency" (322). Mrs. Smith upholds a moral code opposite to Mrs. Ferrars. While they both withhold an inheritance from young men because of their heirs' displeasing behavior, Mrs. Ferrars punishes her son's honorable behavior while Mrs. Smith rewards, or would reward, her nephew's. Mrs. Ferrars finds young women threatening—she never simply approves the independent choice of her sons—but Mrs. Smith finds the endorsement of a "woman of character" reassuring. For one woman, the relationship between widow and heir is about power and manipulation for her own gratification; for the other, it is about adherence to a larger, nobler set of values than her own desires. That Mrs. Smith resides in the country while Mrs. Ferrars resides in the city further reinforces this distinction between country and city, good and bad.

These two women appear to conform to expectations established in the previous century's novels: virtuous affluent widows are associated with the country and use their wealth to nurture their communities, mother their family and friends, and practice benevolence, while associations with the city often indicate selfishness and transgressive interest in managing money, including the control of dependents and the gratification of sexual desire. But Mrs. Ferrars and Mrs. Smith also escape these expectations. The dependents they manipulate are men, not women, and they do not receive the usual punishment or reward. Mrs. Ferrars concludes the novel essentially satisfied with her lot and surviving very nicely, whereas her literary predecessors tended to suffer unhappy or fatal ends. Mrs. Smith concludes the novel converted from tyrannical relative to morally-upright relative in everyone's perception without once appearing in her own right to present herself to others and without changing her modus operandi: like Mrs. Ferrars, using money to bring her relative into compliance with her expectations. Both women, in fact, display characteristics more often separated into different characters in eighteenth-century novels, and usually valued clearly as positive or negative attitudes or behavior. Separately and together, they complicate earlier images and the issues that shaped those images in the novel.

In fact, as a group Austen's affluent widows, particularly Lady Catherine de Bourgh, Mrs. Rushworth, and Mrs. Norris, repeatedly adjust the models for affluent widowhood. They do not support the tension between the country and the city or their associations with land-based socioeconomic stability or commercial instability explored in earlier novels, the positive associations with behaviors classified as benevolent, or the models of mothering applied to those earlier figures. At first glance, like Mrs. Ferrars, *Pride and Prejudice*'s Lady Catherine seems to be a wicked, affluent widow. She is overbearing, interfering, officious, unintelligent, unaccomplished, bigoted, and selfish. She takes on the duties of a magistrate although as a woman she is not authorized to do so, and she attempts to control everything around her, right down to the Collins's cuts of meat (*P and P*, 112, 109). She is a poor mother: her daughter Anne is "pale and sickly," unsociable, and unaccomplished (108, 117). When displeased, Lady Catherine uses her position and her money to menace other people, such as her famous conversation with Elizabeth Bennet at Longbourn (230–34). She concludes the novel deeply ensconced at Rosings and in unhappiness, two places where she appears to belong.

From the perspective of a study of widowhood in the novel, however, the primary problem with Lady Catherine is not what she does, but the fanaticism with which she does it. Anne de Bourgh may not have turned out well, but that seems to be because of too much maternal interest, rather than too little. In fact, instead of neglecting them, Lady Catherine worries profoundly over her family—she and her sister planned the marriage of their children, she cares about the family name, and she keeps a sharp eye on Anne. She remains active in a network of friends, especially women friends, supplying governesses for people she knows, often from the dependents of her dependents (110). And no one in her estate is too mean for her concern, for "whenever any of the cottagers were disposed to be quarrelsome, discontented or too poor, she sallied forth into the village to settle their differences, silence their complaints, and scold them into harmony and plenty" (112).[10] If anything, this behavior resembles that of the ladies of Sarah Scott's *Millenium Hall* (1762), who bring a group of quarrelsome, gossipy poor women into a state of grace with God and with each other so, as one testifies, "now we love one another like sisters, or indeed better, for I often see such quarrel."[11]

Her interest in the well-being of her tenants extends to the principles of estate management. She is a country widow not a city widow, and she believes in the consolidation of estates for the preservation of family rather than for profit. This last concern reveals perhaps most clearly that Lady Catherine is not a commercially minded, self-interested, wicked widow like Lady Galliard from Mary Davys' *The Accomplish'd Rake* (1727) or Lady Booby from Henry Fielding's *Joseph Andrews* (1742); in fact, she clearly shares these characteristics with the virtuous Mrs. Strictland from Clara Reeve's *School for Widows* (1791). She is a virtuous affluent widow taken to a logical extreme. While her activities are described in a different tone than that used for activities in *School for Widows* or *Millenium Hall*, they are still the same. Much of what makes Lady Catherine such a negative figure is just how determinedly she follows rules for behaving like a good affluent widow, working to maintain the old agrarian stability, not only opposing change but restoring or maintaining a system that does not have much change built into it. Lady Catherine's dogmatism and lack of imagination and flexibility indicate stagnation of all kinds, an inability as well as a refusal to change; she is the aggregate of virtuous affluent widowhood's qualities taken to excess. She suggests the failure rather than the success of the aristocracy and the agrarian system, the worst that such a system of nurturing and stability has to offer.

Mrs. Rushworth from *Mansfield Park* offers another, briefer example of Austen's hyperbolizing the qualities expected of positive affluent widows. Mrs. Rushworth could be the great lady of the great house, but her adherence to the values of agrarian society makes positive action impossible and reveals the problematic aspects of those values. She is a "well-meaning, civil, prosing, pompous woman, who thought nothing of consequence, but as it related to her own and her son's concerns" (*MP*, 105). She too has few accomplishments to boast of, as her primary skill is the recounting of family history (113). Mrs. Rushworth can only conceive of marriage in terms of breeding and money. When Mrs. Norris hints that Julia Bertram and Henry Crawford might marry, Mrs. Rushworth replies, "Yes, indeed, a very pretty match. What is his property?" and later adds, "Four thousand a year is a pretty estate," conflating in her use of the word "pretty" the attractiveness of a person with the attractiveness of an estate, and of two handsome people forming a couple with the attractiveness of two moneyed people forming a couple (144). At the end of the novel, her refusal to keep private Maria's defection emphasizes how a strict adherence to tradition not only represses possibilities, but also represses even the chance for redemption or renewal. It does not excuse Maria's fault by any means, but Mrs. Rushworth's insistence on a narrowly construed set of values and protocols also leaves no room for innovation or flexibility. According to this widow's behavior, too much of the old order is destructive.

Characters like Lady Catherine or Mrs. Rushworth complicate earlier novelistic models of affluent, landed widowhood and thereby suggest a more nuanced view of the socioeconomic situation of the time and its connection to gender. At the same time, Austen also uses widows to criticize commercialism. Mrs. Norris from *Mansfield Park* illustrates how too much commercial enterprise can be destructive. She lives in the country, in a house supplied by her brother-in-law, and calls herself "a poor helpless, forlorn widow, unfit for any thing, my spirits quite broke down," protesting that "Here I am a poor desolate widow, deprived of the best of husbands, my health gone in attending and nursing him, my spirits still worse, all my peace in this world destroyed, with barely enough to support me in the rank of gentlewoman, and enable me to live so as not to disgrace the memory of the dear departed" (*MP*, 63). Her manipulation of this image to screen enterprising motives and actions as well as her view of marriage as a combination of estates, not people, reveals that at heart Mrs. Norris is a shamelessly selfish trader. She commodifies everything, including people and especially her late husband, for whose loss she "consoled herself . . . by considering that she could do very well without him, and for her reduction of income by the evident necessity for stricter economy" (58). In fact, at the death of her husband, Mrs. Norris has no children, no dependents, and six hundred pounds a year (63). Her self-applied adjectives are stock descriptive phrases for widows, useful to Mrs. Norris in her efforts to protect her autonomy and hoard her wealth, but not accurate. The "poor, forlorn widow" who has lost love, health, wealth, and status becomes a figure to be invoked but hardly a reality for Mrs. Norris, who wouldn't have the faintest sense of obligation should she meet such a woman in reality.

For Mrs. Norris, everything is a commodity, every relationship and event an opportunity to augment her stock of valuable items. Money, of course, she parts with reluctantly. She refuses to travel at her own expense and to take on the added emotional and financial expense of Fanny as a companion, even though she has the means (367, 62). She dispenses what she calls love sparingly and erratically, like Mrs. Ferrars, playing favorites with her nieces according to their potential to achieve a high exchange value, that is, to make a good marriage. As Eileen Cleere points out, Mrs. Norris substitutes a fascination with preservation and with money for maternal behavior, nursing her monetary wealth while squandering the family around her.[12] Even visits to other peoples' houses become opportunities for profit for Mrs. Norris, who returns from Sotherton loaded with "gifts" she has extorted from the servants (*MP*, 132).

Mrs. Norris's efforts to conserve her own wealth transcend virtue for vice. She reveals how the stereotype of the good widow who maintains the resources at her disposal can become an evil, and how a refusal to spend money requires, in its way, the same determination, discipline, and ingenuity as commercial activity supposedly undertaken in the city. In this sense, Mrs. Norris epitomizes the worst of both landed and commercial values, insisting on the preservation of status at all costs while extracting supplies from everyone around her but paying nothing for them in any coin, emotional or financial. Mrs. Norris also demonstrates how a love of property and cash suppresses nurturing, rendering the materialistic widow an unfit mother. Like Lady Catherine and Mrs. Rushworth, Mrs. Norris is an extreme example of a value system.

Mrs. Norris is also a striking figure for another reason. Although she espouses almost entirely commercial values and behavior, she is still tied to the country and the aristocracy. She is therefore a mixed figure like *Sense and Sensibility*'s Mrs. Smith and Mrs. Ferrars, combining the landed and the commercial. While Austen uses some of her widows to attack the extremes of landed or commercial activity and values, overwhelmingly her widows represent a hybrid economic sensibility, a world where old agrarianism and new commercialism are no longer at odds, but are rather working out a merged identity. This merger was familiar to English society by the time Austen was writing: members of the gentry and the commercial classes had been intermarrying for some time, as the subjects of Amanda Vickery's study of Yorkshire families indicate.[13] Furthermore, this broad economic sensibility appears not just in the way Austen's widows combine landed and mercantile concerns, but also in the sheer range of economic classes that they occupy.

Like earlier novelists, Austen is aware that widowhood can impose great hardship on a woman and her family. Unlike earlier novelists, however, Austen does not sentimentalize this problem. Instead, she offers a balance of dependence and hard work as a mode for handling this fall from financial stability. Perhaps the poorest of Austen's widows is Mrs. Bates from *Emma*, and she is also the character through whom Austen most overtly rejects the sentimental modes of poor widowhood described in chapter 4. Mrs. Bates is a beautifully sketched portrait of an elderly, infirm, poor widow. Although film adaptations of *Emma* have used the Mrs. Bates-Miss Bates relationship for comic effect—the Miramax production reduces Mrs. Bates's deafness to Sophie Thompson's comically useless eruptions of "Pork!" to inform her mother about the subject of the conversation, and the A&E production offers a scene where everyone's desire to be helpful deprives Mrs. Bates of her refreshment—there is nothing comic about the Mrs. Bates of the novel.[14] She is compassionately portrayed—Mr. Knightley actually uses the word "compassion" about the family—and it is Emma's transformation to understanding not just Miss Bates and Jane Fairfax but also Mrs. Bates, which is to say, Emma's acquisition of the same compassion with which the novel treats Mrs. Bates, that lies at the heart of *Emma*.

Mrs. Bates is a "good old lady" (Austen, *Emma*, 101, 298), a "harmless old lady" (11), and a "quiet neat old lady" (99). She is marginal narratively and by virtue of her financial, social, and physical condition. As the narrator explains, "Mrs. Bates, the widow of a former vicar of Highbury, was a very old lady, almost past every thing but tea and quadrille. She lived with her single daughter in a very small way, and was considered with all the regard and respect which a harmless old lady, under such untoward circumstances, can excite" (11). From the vicarage, the Bates's have been reduced to a "very moderate sized apartment, which was every thing to them" on the "drawing-room floor" in a house on Highbury's main street that "belonged to people in business" (99). Their means are extremely straitened, a fact that Austen raises repeatedly. Mr. Weston says they have "barely enough to live on," Mr. Knightley calls them "poor," Emma says they live in "Poverty," and the narrator notes that Miss Bates's "middle of life was devoted to the care of a failing mother, and the endeavour to make a small income go as far as possible" (125–26, 246, 56, 12). Compounding Mrs. Bates's difficulties are common physical ailments of the elderly. She does not move around much on her own. Her eyesight is failing and in addition to spectacles, she requires her daughter to read her the contents of Jane's letters (100–101). Unsurprisingly, her hearing is also going, as Miss Bates often notes: "By only raising my voice, and saying anything two or three times over, she is sure to hear; but then she is used to my voice" (101). Age and infirmity conspire to keep Mrs. Bates just beyond complete comprehension much of the time (103, 248).

Mrs. Bates and her family manage this financial, social, and physical marginality through a dignified dependence on others. They rely on the kindness of the community not only for company, but also for subsistence, and the community in turn regards the Bates household rather protectively. Mr. Elton gives Mrs. Bates the vicarage pew because she is going deaf, thereby attending to her spiritual needs (112). Emma sends a hind-quarter of pork, Mr. Knightley sends all his remaining apples, Mr. Perry the apothecary is willing to attend Jane in her illness free of charge, and as Mr. Weston explains to Frank, "I must give you a hint, Frank; any want of attention to [Jane] *here* should be carefully avoided. You saw her with the Campbells when she was the equal of everybody she mixed with, but here she is with a poor old grandmother, who has barely enough to live on. If you do not call early it will be a slight" (110, 154–55, 104, 125–26; Austen's emphasis). The community is watching, in other words. Do the right thing by these people. In *Emma*, poverty and the fall into it require compassion, and there is nothing ridiculous or sentimental about them.

The historical record indicates that without the acceptance of responsibility for women like the Bates's by people who could afford to look after them, class and the English family alike threatened to destabilize. The reality for women without the safety net of community support, however conditional, was devastating. Family members were not always willing or able to support a widow and her family. As Cynthia Curran explains, widows from the middle class who did not inherit sufficient resources to maintain themselves and their families were usually from or married to families with the same economic pressures. Without family, widows had only the community to fall back on before reaching starvation. In 1820, Ann Burder applied from London to the overseers of her home parish in Mundon for poor relief. "Gentlemen/ I beg leave to inform you of the Death of my Dear Husband which took place this Morning about twenty minutes before Six as such humbly hope you will allow what you may think necessary for his funeral," she writes, and implores them to send her some money for the support of her children.[15] The urgency of the letter, including its composition hours after the death of her husband, indicates how quickly the widow of a working man in the early nineteenth century could be stripped of everything. Private religious charities such as the Society for the Relief of Necessitous Widows and Children of Protestant Dissenting Ministers were also available to support the widows of clergymen such as Mrs. Bates, although as the appendix and chapter 4 discuss in more detail, private organizations subsidized only those who met a rigorous set of requirements, and it could take months to be approved and then to receive payments. Without the support of neighbors, widows who did not inherit affluence or the means to generate income such as a business easily could lose everything.

Emma's responsibility for Mrs. Bates and her family recognizes the reality of such women's precarious position and thereby constitutes a rejection of the individualized, emotional focus of a sentimental perspective. This compassion is also conditional, however. The Bates's poverty is very real, but it is not cause for a disruption of the social order. The Westons are entitled to feel themselves injured by Jane's secret engagement to Mr. Weston's son, as the oft-repeated expressions of Jane's remorse suggest, and their acceptance of the young lady is attached to the warmth and selflessness of the aunt and grandmother. It is Mrs. Bates's disinterest that secures everyone's admiration for her at a moment when she could hardly be faulted for rejoicing in her own and her daughter's, as well as Jane's, good fortune that Jane is marrying the heir to the Churchill fortune. When the Westons call on the Bates family upon the announcement of the engagement,

> The quiet, heartfelt satisfaction of the old lady, and the rapturous delight of her daughter—who proved even too joyous to talk as usual, had been gratifying, yet almost an affecting, scene. They were both so truly respectable in their happiness, so disinterested in every sensation, thought so much of Jane; so much of everybody, and so little of themselves, that every kindly feeling was at work for them. (274)

The Bates women procure kindness from the Westons precisely because Mrs. and Miss Bates are "respectably" happy, that is to say, "disinterestedly" so, thinking of everyone "and so little of themselves." What would have been their reception, even after so many years of living in the community, had they even for a moment mentioned their delight that their medical care would not depend on Mr. Perry's good will, one wonders? Hence, while Mrs. Bates is not a sentimental figure, the emphasis on her and her daughter's deservingness seems to suggest that her positive depiction depends to at least some extent on more old-fashioned values of community benevolence and class stability. Austen compels even Emma and her readers to see Mrs. Bates and the reality of her situation—not to see it is "badly done," as Mr. Knightley asserts—and therefore to move compassion beyond the selfishness of personal gratification it had under sentiment, while preserving the social stability that sentiment promoted.

The rewards for this revision of sentiment include a practical rather than sentimental community benevolence that makes it possible for Mrs. Bates and her family to avoid commodifying their only resource, Jane Fairfax. Although Austen famously likens the conditions under which Jane is forced to work, i.e., the exploitation of young women of a certain class and education in order to provide cheap governesses, to the slave trade (196), Austen is equally clear that there is nothing shameful with Jane's working provided that it is voluntary. Furthermore, Jane's engagement to Frank Churchill is clearly a love match, since she feels guilty about the secret, wounded by his behavior, and certain about breaking off the engagement. Jane's behavior is not about sale and neither, crucially, is Mrs. Bates's. Mrs. Bates is not trying to sell her granddaughter, either as a governess or as a wife. She understands and accepts, although she may not enjoy, the situation to which she has fallen.

The figurative sale of daughters, in fact, is one of the methods for addressing financial hardship that Austen criticizes the most. Again, as with Austen's affluent widows, it is not commercial behavior per se that provokes Austen's criticism, but certain aspects of commercialism. Widows are allowed to be self-sufficient, but they are not allowed to employ dependents as the agents of their salvation. As Mrs. Thorpe from *Northanger Abbey*, Mrs. Bennet's phantom future widowhood from *Pride and Prejudice,* and Mrs. Dashwood from *Sense and Sensibility* demonstrate, some things may be commodified, particularly their own resources such as emotional resilience or ability to work, but other things, especially their children, may not.

Northanger Abbey's Mrs. Thorpe underscores the point made by Mrs. Bates: that only certain methods for economic change are acceptable. Mrs. Thorpe depends on her children to rescue her from financial difficulty, something even more clearly disapproved in Mrs. Bennet, rather than on herself or other adults. Mrs. Thorpe is the widow of a lawyer at Putney and "not a very rich one; she was a good-humoured, well-meaning woman, and a very indulgent mother" (*NA*, 30). She accepts her children's word on everything. Deluded by her son John's "vanity and avarice" (213), Mrs. Thorpe shares Isabella's disappointment when Mr. Morland offers his son a living at four hundred pounds a year upon his son's engagement (120–21). Her children are grasping, ambitious, self-interested, and entirely commercial, but Mrs. Thorpe is a doting woman who begins and ends the novel ignorant about her children and others. She is not wealthy in terms of money, experience, or knowledge, and while understandably excited by what she believes is her daughter's marrying very much above her fortune, she is not really an agent in bringing it about. Other widows, of course, are the agents of such ambition— Madame Cheron and Madame Duval do everything in their power to ensure that their young charges marry as well as possible, for example—but Mrs. Thorpe is simply too dependent on her children to manage such a feat, which is precisely her problem. Here a lack of agency, the use of children as a substitute for one's own action, is the issue.

Mrs. Bennet is also too dependent on her children as a means for negotiating her impending widowhood. While it has not yet taken place and might never take place—"Let us flatter ourselves that *I* may be the survivor," Mr. Bennet suggests (*P and P*, 89; Austen's emphasis)—Mrs. Bennet does indeed face a very real problem. The estate is entailed away from her and her daughters to Mr. Collins, he is not a very considerate person, and Mr. and Mrs. Bennet have not saved anything during their marriage. Mrs. Bennet's hysteria makes it an irritating subject, but the reality she faces is actually grim: she will lose her home and almost all of her income, and whatever unmarried daughters remain will have too little money to attract a suitor of comparable class, prompting Maaja Stewart to contend that *Pride and Prejudice* of all of Austen's novels "expresses the most anxiety about the economic vulnerability of women."[16] Nevertheless, Mrs. Bennet cannot seem to employ the best part of commercial or landed values. Everything must be immediate gratification, an instant fix. Her emotional luxuriousness is matched by her inability to save (*P and P*, 200). She is also a spendthrift of knowledge—her gossiping alone is a squandering of information and propriety—and of experience, as she is utterly unable to learn from anything that happens, such as forgetting Lydia's transgressions the moment that Lydia's marriage is announced (198). And while she is ambitious that her daughters should marry well, she will do nothing to facilitate such success that comes at any cost to her own pleasure—she will not save to increase their dowries, for example, or change her behavior to present a more proper and genteel front. It is not the phantom widowhood understandably haunting her waking hours that makes Mrs. Bennet the object of Austen's ridicule, but the way that Mrs. Bennet addresses this future state: indulging herself at every turn and wasting every resource available, except her daughters, for easing its effects. Hence, while she lives in the country, enjoys gentility, and faces a very real dire future, Mrs. Bennet is also commercial: ambitious, greedy, and selfish, trading in people and things to achieve her own pleasures.

Mrs. Dashwood from *Sense and Sensibility* also mismanages her assets. She has come down considerably in life upon the loss of her husband, a situation made more acute by her interest in irresponsibility (as framed by Austen) and her disinterest in responsibility. Again, Austen equates emotionalism with being a spendthrift: the same person who lavishly indulges in emotion equally lavishly spends money. Mrs. Dashwood is "every thing but prudent," a "woman who never saved in her life" trying to live in a higher style than her finances will support (*S and S*, 6, 12, 22, 25). Her lack of emotional and financial discipline puts her family in danger, exposing Marianne to the gossip and censure of the neighborhood and to heartbreak from Willoughby, and exacting long periods of silent suffering from Elinor. As the narrator notes reprovingly, "common sense, common care, common prudence, were all sunk in Mrs. Dashwood's romantic delicacy" (74). Nor is she able to accumulate any resources such as experience, a valuable but dangerous commodity in the eyes of earlier novelists and an equally valuable but less dangerous one for Austen. Mrs. Dashwood's wishful thinking causes her to disregard Elinor's warnings that something is amiss between Marianne and Willoughby and to indulge in the same wishful thinking about Brandon that she has about Willoughby. Doggedly insisting on discovering that the best course of action is the one she most prefers, Mrs. Dashwood also actualizes the threat of damage to the sentimental heroines, thus nearly destroying both adult daughters' chance for happiness. This refusal to take care of valuable resources such as knowledge, money, or people, and to indulge instead in self-gratification at the expense of those resources, reveals the importance of balance between the old and new systems in the Austenian universe.

These widows are well-meaning; however, they are poor managers of themselves, others, and their resources, and for that they receive their fair share of criticism. Viewed with Mrs. Smith and Mrs. Clay of *Persuasion*, all of these widows reveal a sophisticated effort on Austen's part to work out an ethics of female economic activity that allows women to manage their resources benevolently while avoiding the exploitation inherent in mercantile capitalism and the passive dependence espoused by gender ideology.

Like *Emma*'s Mrs. Bates, *Persuasion*'s Mrs. Smith offers a view of the genuine hardships that can strike a widow. Mrs. Smith has not only fallen into poverty by the loss of her husband, who "had left his affairs dreadfully involved." She also has been struck with illness, "a severe rheumatic fever, which finally settling in her legs, had made her for the present a cripple," and isolation, since her illness and financial means require her to live "in a very humble way, unable even to afford herself the comfort of a servant." As a result, she is "of course" essentially a social outcast, "almost excluded from society" (101). She is a "poor, infirm, helpless widow, receiving the visit of her former protegée as a favour" (101); Anne "could scarcely imagine a more cheerless situation in itself than Mrs. Smith's. She had been very fond of her husband,—she had buried him. She had been used to affluence,—it was gone. She had no child to connect her with life and happiness again, no relations to assist in the arrangement of perplexed affairs, no health to make all the rest supportable" (101). Furthermore, the loss of financial security and health has reduced her to uncomfortable living quarters and physical dependence on others (101–2). Austen has deprived her of even the most tenuous supports for a widow, such as an annuity from investments or family aid. Duckworth summarizes, "Mrs. Smith, a minor character in Jane Austen's last novel, is important as the final embodiment of a fate that haunts all her novels. Here at last is the entirely unsupported woman, reduced to bare existence without husband, society, or friends."[17]

Mrs. Smith's situation is compounded by the disdain of an unfeeling society, expressed in Sir Walter's tirade against his daughter's acquaintance:

A Mrs. Smith. A widow Mrs. Smith,—and who was her husband? One of the five thousand Mr. Smiths whose names are to be met with every where. And what is her attraction. That she is old and sickly. Upon my word, Miss Anne Elliot, you have the most extraordinary taste! Every thing that revolts other people, low company, paltry rooms, foul air, disgusting associations are inviting to you. But surely, you may put off this old lady till to-morrow. She is not so near her end, I presume, but that she may hope to see another day. What is her age? Forty? (Austen, *Persuasion*, 104)

When Anne surprises him by pointing out that Mrs. Smith is not the stereotypical aging widow but instead a young woman of thirty, Sir Walter insists on marginalizing her by calling her "A poor widow, barely able to live, between thirty and forty" (104). Here Sir Walter articulates most plainly that it is not simply her class, but also her widowed status that makes her an object of contempt.

The urban Mrs. Smith has only herself to depend on, and her response to her situation and isolation is an active one. She has a resilient spirit which gives her the emotional strength to grapple with adversity. She

had moments only of languor and depression, to hours of occupation and enjoyment. How could it be?—[Anne] watched—observed—reflected— and finally determined that this was not a case of fortitude or of resignation only.—A submissive spirit might be patient, a strong understanding would supply resolution, but here was something more; here was that elasticity of mind, that disposition to be comforted, that power of turning readily from evil to good, and of finding employment which carried her out of herself, which was from Nature alone. It was the choicest gift of Heaven; and Anne viewed her friend as one of those instances in which, by a merciful appointment, it seems designed to counterbalance almost every other want. (102)

Her nurse, Mrs. Rooke, teaches her to use her hands and Mrs. Smith busies herself "making these little thread-cases, pin-cushions and card-racks" which Nurse Rooke sells to recuperating patients (102). Mrs. Smith thus possesses a commercial strength of character that allows her to keep herself busy making goods for sale. She also possesses sufficient gentility to avoid handling the actual transactions for herself: Austen gives her an infirmity precisely designed to keep her in pathetic but genteel seclusion and thereby to avoid engaging in the crassness of actually exchanging goods and cash.

Because of her hunger for gossip and her sale of knitted thread-cases to the convalescent, Mrs. Smith seems to display an unsettling venality and cynicism. A close reading of Mrs. Smith reveals that the knitted objects "supply [her] with the means of doing a little good to one or two very poor families in the neighborhood" (102). Either Mrs. Smith is giving knitted card racks to "very poor families in the neighborhood," a generous but probably not very useful impulse, or she is using the proceeds from the sale of her card racks to do "a little good" to those families. In that case, Mrs. Smith is not simply helping herself, although it is imaginable that she is also using those profits for herself; she is also helping those more unfortunate than herself. She therefore seems to possess some of the proper benevolence that other novelists required of women of her original class. Furthermore, she exemplifies the danger to women in a volatile and patriarchal society; she really is in a dreadful situation. She commissions Nurse Rooke to sell knitted thread-cases to more affluent people during their recoveries, exploiting people in a moment of weakness, but she is not unequivocally nefarious or selfish. This money is for bed and board or for charity to others, not for luxury. As a result, Mrs. Smith can be seen as a mixed commercial figure. She takes advantage of the widow's right to go into business and seizes an economic opportunity, and Austen justifies her with a good reason for her activities and sufficient gentility to avoid the filthy lucre of her earnings herself. Overall, Mrs. Smith's enterprise receives at least some understanding as a necessary if problematic undertaking for a single woman of no fortune, family, or health.

Austen more overtly problematizes the way Mrs. Smith handles Anne, however, because she does commodify her friend. That Mrs. Smith does not once attempt to dissuade Anne from what Mrs. Smith has good evidence will be an unhappy marriage is certainly disquieting. Her claims that Mr. Elliot might have changed, that a sensible woman might make him a good man, and that family harmony ought to be preserved have enough credibility to render her silence dubious or ambiguous. Nevertheless, they cannot reverse the impression that Mrs. Smith was prepared to sell Anne down the river, a phrase particularly appropriate given the nature of Mrs. Smith's lost property: plantations in the West Indies. Like Sir Thomas Bertram's reliance on income generated by slave plantations in *Mansfield Park*, Mrs. Smith's dependence on income derived from the exploitation of slaves should be read as a subtle mark against her. Mrs. Smith, like Sir Thomas, is ready to use the bodies at his disposal for her own gain, whether they are slaves in the Caribbean or Anne Elliot, whose transfer to Mr. Elliot hopefully would facilitate the recovery of these estates and their income for Mrs. Smith. That there is no certainty that a married Anne could persuade her husband to such a thing simply underscores the commercialism of Mrs. Smith's plan: it is risky, it is self-interested, it is profit-oriented, and it commodifies others.

It is a slippery slope and Austen shows it to be so, but she also suggests that the line can be drawn somewhere. Selling a person is not acceptable, but selling knick-knacks to people is. Mrs. Smith is not granted complete success, just as she is not unmitigatedly positive. Her fortunes are only partially reversed by an "improvement of income, with some improvement of health, and the acquisition of such friends to be often with," and Wentworth puts "her in the way of recovering her husband's property in the West Indies; by writing for her, acting for her, and seeing her through all the petty difficulties of the case, with the activities and exertion of a fearless man and a determined friend" (167), but significantly, she neither recovers all her health nor all her fortune. This temperate success indicates an incomplete endorsement of Mrs. Smith and all that she represents, a respect for her very real economic, financial, physical, and emotional situation but a discomfort with some of the capitalistic commodifying behaviors it drives her to. She is poor—but she rises again; she is ill—but she recovers to some extent; she is a city-bound widow—but she owns property.

Another and potentially more successful entrepreneur is Mrs. Clay from *Persuasion*. Mrs. Clay is certainly the villain among the women of the novel. Her physical appearance—"freckles, and a projecting tooth, and a clumsy wrist" (23)—signals her spotted character. Lady Russell, in contrast, "sits so upright!" (143). Mrs. Clay emotionally seduces Sir Walter and Elizabeth Elliot, effectively edging out Anne for what little attention her sister and father spare from themselves. After Anne arrives in Bath,

> On going down to breakfast the next morning, she found there had just been a decent pretence on the lady's side of meaning to leave them. She could imagine Mrs. Clay to have said, that "now Miss Anne

was come, she could not suppose herself at all wanted;" for Elizabeth was replying, in a sort of whisper, "That must not be any reason, indeed. I assure you I feel it none. She is nothing to me, compared with you;" and she was in full time to hear her father say, "My dear Madam, this must not be. As yet, you have seen nothing of Bath. You have been here only to be useful. You must not run away from us now. You must stay to be acquainted with Mrs. Wallis, the beautiful Mrs. Wallis. To your fine mind, I well know the sight of beauty is a real gratification."

He spoke and looked so much in earnest, that Anne was not surprised to see Mrs. Clay stealing a glance at Elizabeth and herself. (95–96)

All of her efforts are designed to culminate in marrying Sir Walter himself. Anne and Mr. Elliot are very concerned, and as Mrs. Smith summarizes to Anne, all of Bath society recognized that Mrs. Clay "is a clever, insinuating, handsome woman, poor and plausible, and altogether such in situation and manner, as to give a general idea among Sir Walter's acquaintance, of her meaning to be Lady Elliot, and as general a surprise that Miss Elliot should be apparently blind to the danger" (137). She is not simply a woman from the professional classes attempting to marry into the peerage (and who has conveniently forgotten her "additional burthen of two children" [11]). Were she doing it solely for love and with a proper sense of her good fortune, like Jane Fairfax, she would be acceptable. But Mrs. Clay is an operator. She has no compunction about what she attempts, and no concern for anything except herself.

Part of what makes Mrs. Clay so dangerous is the fact that she does not sport all the stereotypical hallmarks of the wicked widow or the criminal widow of novels past. Despite her teeth, complexion, and "clumsy wrist," Mrs. Clay "was young, and certainly altogether well looking, and possessed, in an acute mind and assiduous pleasing manners, infinitely more dangerous attractions than any merely personal might have been" (23). These qualities, both the physical and the mental, hide what is more obvious in her father, Mr. Shepherd, Sir Walter's "friend" and attorney who advises and has what the narrator suggests is a "hold" on Sir Walter (8). Both Mrs. Clay and Mr. Shepherd possess a self-interested, profit-oriented, and not entirely honest spirit and drive. Her father's ability to get other people to suggest unpleasant things so he can seem more appealing to Sir Walter is a skill that Mrs. Clay herself possesses: "She was a clever young woman, who understood the art of pleasing; the art of pleasing, at least, at Kellynch-hall" (9). In this respect she has advantages that Mrs. Smith lacks, having a family to fall back on upon being widowed after an "unprosperous marriage" (11). Rather than maintain Mrs. Clay in decorous retirement, however, Mrs. Clay's family's support is enterprising, designed to acquire wealth, and with her full complicity. She and her father work together to capitalize on his influence and position with the family. She attends the meeting where Sir Walter agrees to rent Kellynch, for "her father had driven her over, nothing being of so much use to Mrs. Clay's health as a drive to Kellynch," the narrator reports dryly (13). Her youth, attractions, and intelligence may make her unlike older wicked widows in earlier novels, but they do make her like the younger ones such as the marchioness from Elizabeth Griffith's *The Delicate Distress* (1769).

Austen treats this enterprise with some equivocation, particularly when she places it in relief against the poor behavior of the aristocracy in *Persuasion*. Although Mrs. Clay spends the majority of the novel in Bath and goes to London at the novel's end, for example, she first appears where she was born and bred, the country, so she is both rural and urban. She also enjoys an ambiguous ending. It is simply unclear whether she has been seduced or persuaded by Mr. Elliot, or whether she has done the seducing or persuading; either way, she has a chance of achieving her ambitions: "She had abilities, however, as well as affections; and it is now a doubtful point whether his cunning, or hers, may finally carry the day; whether, after preventing her from being the wife of Sir Walter, he may not be wheedled and caressed at last into making her the wife of Sir William" (167). In fact, Mrs. Clay is certainly much smarter than the old, landed money with whom she has dealings. Only Anne, the protagonist, appreciates and understands all aspects of Mrs. Clay but then again, Anne is attracted to the enterprising spirit herself. While Mrs. Clay is certainly no poster child for the middle class, she is also no unconditional indictment of the commercial spirit, either. She suggests that the separation of traditional agrarian values and new commercial ideology is really an illusion, and that anyone insisting on the separation of the systems is an easy mark for those who understand the reality and complexity of the new social order.

What the collection of Austen's widows suggest is a balanced combination of landed and commercial activity, and the idea that this balanced combination can be achieved in women through appropriate activity, even appropriate maternal activity. As Benedict argues, "Rather than opposing commercialization, Jane Austen dramatizes commercial culture as the arena for moral choice. Her work shows especially the way literary commodification shaped middle-class female identity at the beginning of the nineteenth century," and that that identity is not corrupt but positive provided it is tempered: "Middle-class femininity is regulated consumption, discreet display, the social performance of private taste."[18] Not only do correct femininity and commercial society comfortably coexist, but also for Austen, correct maternal behavior and commercialism do as well. Mrs. Jennings of *Sense and Sensibility* and Lady Russell of *Persuasion* epitomize how the landed, the commercial, and the family can all be suitably blended. These are women who are both positively economically conscious and positively interested in daughters, suggesting that a blend of old and new, landed and mercantile, aristocratic and bourgeois is not just appropriate, but necessary.

Mrs. Jennings and Lady Russell both illustrate the virtues of combining the landed and the commercial societies. Mrs. Jennings's insistence on gratifying her own urges, especially of gathering and disseminating information and conjecture not rightly hers, aligns her with selfish affluent widows, and especially criminal, affluent widows of earlier novels who spend their resources doing what they enjoy most, rather than what is best for others. Certainly her insistence on viewing the world as a series of sentimental romances complicates and irritates already difficult and painful situations for many characters, especially Elinor and Marianne. In spite of the romance story, however, Mrs. Jennings appreciates the commercial aspects of marriage—"[Y]ou have taken Charlotte off my hands, and cannot give her back again," she reminds Mr. Palmer, "So there I have the whip hand of you" (*S and S*, 96). She also gossips with an energy besides which *Persuasion*'s Mrs. Smith's gossip sessions pale. She "exultingly" tells a crowd of guests that Colonel Brandon must have gone to London about "his natural daughter" (59). Surely this is not information that Colonel Brandon wishes broadcast to the neighborhood, but Mrs. Jennings does not consult his wishes in telling it, only her own. She does the same with Marianne's "broken engagement" as she styles it, with Willoughby (164–65). It is no coincidence that as "the widow of a man, who had got all his money in a low way," Mrs. Jennings's ability and energy for gossip is at its height in London, where she keeps her own residence (193). In these respects, she seems directly descended from negatively portrayed, commercially minded, city-oriented affluent widows who appear in earlier novels.

Mrs. Jennings is redeemed, however, by her maternalism. As Dussinger notes, "her busy talk is never really malicious, as Elinor comes to learn and later instructs her sister, but shows a genuine interest in others and always has something to communicate."[19] She is a caring mother to her daughters, especially when Charlotte Palmer goes through the difficult and dangerous ordeal of childbirth (*S and S*, 207). Unlike the selfish affluent widows of earlier texts, she is willing if not determined to think well of sentimental heroines, even when they are not really sentimental heroines, like Lucy Steele. Her enterprising efforts to get young women married to fine and economically superior young men, while occasionally more crassly than romantically articulated, are genuinely generous and kindly. Her first inclination, in fact, is to like other people, especially the young women whom wicked affluent widows generally find threatening. Mrs. Jennings takes to the Dashwoods right away—"from the first [she] had regarded [Elinor] with a kindness which ensured her a large share of her discourse"—and assumes virtues in her cousins, the Steeles—"I believe there is not a better kind of girl in the world, nor one who more deserves a good husband," she says of Lucy (48, 225). While her judgment of character is weak, she does take pleasure in their successes.

Ultimately, the commercial and romantic narratives that she invents or seeks about young women give way to a redemptive maternalism that she applies to other women, mothers and daughters alike. When Marianne falls dangerously ill at Cleveland, "The rapid decay, the early death of a girl so young, so lovely as Marianne, must have struck a less interested person with concern," but for Mrs. Jennings, Marianne is more than the conventional broken-hearted sentimental heroine (265). She appreciates Marianne, who "had been for three months her companion, and was still under her care, and she was known to have been greatly injured, and long unhappy" (265). She also understands how Marianne's illness would affect Elinor, not only respecting Elinor's feelings but also, unlike other characters in the novel, appreciating her even more than Marianne: "The distress of her sister too, particularly a favourite, was before her" (265). Significantly, Mrs. Jennings understands Marianne's illness as a mother, thinking that "as for their mother, when Mrs. Jennings considered that Marianne might probably be to *her* what Charlotte was to herself, her sympathy in *her* sufferings was very sincere" (265; Austen's emphases). In short, Mrs. Jennings possesses positive and negative characteristics. She is neither all good nor all bad, much the same way that she is neither a country figure nor a city figure, and this "mixed" status suggests that the affluent widow no longer embodies the same anxieties that she once did. Mrs. Jennings thus combines the best and the worst of both systems, overall demonstrating how the combination of commercial and landed values can be a positive event.

If Mrs. Jennings represents the acceptable merger of maternal, landed, and commercial interests in women from the business end of society—her late husband was in trade, after all—Lady Russell offers a view of it from the landed end of society. Lady Russell's mothering, interest in innovation, and ability to reconcile and renew offer an image of how the aristocratic ideology of a land-based society can successfully, if painfully, adjust to the ideology of the capitalist system. Like Mrs. Jennings, Lady Russell does have good qualities. She is a "sensible, deserving woman" (*Persuasion*, 4), a

> woman rather of sound than of quick abilities, whose difficulties in coming to any decision in this instance were great, from the opposition of two leading principles. She was of strict integrity herself, with a delicate sense of honour; but she was as desirous of saving Sir Walter's feelings, as solicitous for the credit of the family, as aristocratic in her ideas of what was due to them, as any body of sense and honesty could well be. She was a benevolent, charitable, good woman, and capable of strong attachments; most correct in her conduct, strict in her notions of decorum, and with manners that were held a standard of good-breeding. She had a cultivated mind, and was, generally speaking, rational and consistent. (8–9)

She loves her late friend's children, especially Anne, who is overlooked and exploited by her selfish sisters and father. When Anne is denied her share of affection from her immediate family, "Lady Russell's composed mind and polite manners were put to some trial on this point, in her intercourse in Camden-place. The sight of Mrs. Clay in favour and Anne so overlooked, was a perpetual provocation to her there" (96). But her indignation is also tempered, or interrupted, by her more worldly interests. The passage continues, "and vexed her as much when she was away, as a person in Bath who drinks the water, gets all the new publications, and has a very large acquaintance, has time to be vexed" (96).

In fact, for most of the novel Lady Russell is not terrifically good on the subject of family when it comes to the individuals, the flesh and blood involved in the concept of family. Returning from a visit to the Musgroves, she complains to Anne that "Uppercross in the Christmas holidays" is too noisy and busy for her because of the multitude of children. Lady Russell has no trouble with the noise and busy-ness of the adult scene, however. "No," notes the narrator of the "rumble," "bawling," and "ceaseless clink" of Bath, "these were noises which belonged to the winter pleasures; her spirits rose under their influence; and, like Mrs. Musgrove, she was feeling, though not saying, that, like Mrs. Musgrove, nothing could be so good for her as a little quiet cheerfulness" (88–89). Despite her years of attention to the Elliot girls, Lady Russell is not interested in hands-on mothering. While she gives lectures, carriage rides, or books to the daughters of her late, loved friend, she is simply not comfortable with children and the concept of family that having children around indicates. Her similarity to Mary Musgrove in this regard is an ominous indicator of detachment arising from selfishness.

Lady Russell does excel at managing family when it comes to names, titles, and the hierarchy of rank both within a family and surrounding it. She is a snob. She has no difficulty with Sir Walter and Elizabeth's attendance on Lady Dalrymple, also a widow, who represents exactly the frozen, autocratic elements of the aristocracy that Austen most criticizes. Nearer to home, Lady Russell deplores the neglect that Anne suffers not just because it slights Anne, but also because it slights an Elliot in favor of a non-Elliot, putting a poor upstart widow in place of the dutiful daughter. "[N]ever had [Elizabeth] pursued [her will] in more decided opposition to Lady Russell, than in this selection of Mrs. Clay; turning from the society of so deserving a sister to bestow her affection and confidence on one who ought to have been nothing to her but the object of distant civility" (12), and Lady Russell "was almost startled" that Sir Walter and Elizabeth were taking Mrs. Clay to Bath "as a most important and valuable assistant to the latter in all the business before her. Lady Russell was extremely sorry that such a measure should have been resorted to at all—wondered, grieved, and feared—and the affront it contained to Anne, in Mrs. Clay's being of so much use, while Anne could be of none, was a very sore aggravation" (23).

Words like "deserving," "important," "valuable," and "use" suggest her view of the sisterly relationship and indicate that Lady Russell is more interested in what it means to be family than in feelings.

This understanding of family relationships extends to the creation of family, that is, to marriage. Lady Russell "had prejudices on the side of ancestry; she had a value for rank and consequence, which blinded her a little to the faults of those who possessed them. Herself, the widow of only a knight, she gave the dignity of a baronet all its due" (9). This "prejudice," a loaded word in Austen's oeuvre, explains why Lady Russell is so prepared to have Anne marry Mr. Elliot: "She could not imagine a man more exactly what he ought to be than Mr. Elliot; nor did she ever enjoy a sweeter feeling than the hope of seeing him receive the hand of her beloved Anne in Kellynch church, in the course of the following autumn" (107). In addition to her refusal to see the actuality for all the convention, here Lady Russell also reiterates the evils of marrying off young women for convenience's sake that appear at the end of *Sense and Sensibility*. It is the same sentiment in *Pride and Prejudice* that would marry Darcy to Anne de Bourgh and Georgiana Darcy to Bingley, both clearly unions to be avoided. Lady Russell is not consulting Anne's character when she wishes the marriage, but rather Anne's station and her age. In attempting to persuade Anne to consider the match, she says,

> I own that to be able to regard you as the future mistress of Kellynch, the future Lady Elliot—to look forward and see you occupying your dear mother's place, succeeding to all her rights, and all her popularity, as well as to all her virtues, would be the highest possible gratification to me.—You are your mother's self in countenance and disposition; and if I might be allowed to fancy you such as she was, in situation, and name, and home, presiding and blessing in the same spot, and only superior to her in being more highly valued! My dearest Anne, it would give me more delight than is often felt at my time of life! (105–6)

Anne's organization of the move to Bath and her care for the children at Uppercross, Louisa at Lyme, and the poor at Kellynch indicate that she would indeed be a good Lady Elliot. As she well knows, however, she would also be a most unhappy wife to Mr. Elliot. Lady Russell only considers the first aspect of this marriage: not the relationship, but the alliance and disposal of property. In hoping to place Anne in the same station as her mother, Lady Russell also ignores the fact that Anne's mother had a lot to put up with in Sir Walter, and that it was only Lady Elliot's management that kept the estate from being encumbered with debts to begin with. When Anne tells Lady Russell, "We would not suit," the reminder of the function of personality and temperament in making a good marriage goes entirely over Lady Russell's head (105).

Lady Russell's inability to comprehend the objections to a marriage between Anne and Mr. Elliot is precisely the same blindness that she demonstrated in objecting to Anne's marriage to Captain Wentworth, whom she calls a "young man, who had nothing but himself to recommend him, and no hopes of attaining affluence, but in the chances of a most uncertain profession, and no connexions to secure even his farther rise in that profession" (19). His character, which "bewitches" Anne, merely irritates Lady Russell, who "saw it very differently.—His sanguine temper, and fearlessness of mind, operated very differently on her. She saw in it but an aggravation of the evil. It only added a dangerous character to himself. He was brilliant, he was headstrong.—Lady Russell had little taste for wit; and of any thing approaching to imprudence a horror. She deprecated the connexion in every light" (19). It is Wentworth's spirit of enterprise that bothers Lady Russell, his refusal to accept his place in the world and his imagining that he can become a man of consequence that alienates her:

> Captain Wentworth had no fortune. He had been lucky in his profession, but spending freely, what had come freely, had realized nothing. But, he was confident that he should soon be rich;—full of life and ardour, he knew that he should soon have a ship, and soon be on a station that would lead to every thing he wanted. He had always been lucky; he knew he should be so still. (19)

But it is also this combination of qualities that makes Wentworth desirable for Anne. He is not like Mr. Elliot: he does not marry for money and he does not insist on inheriting it. As a member of the Navy, he is a member of a "meritocratic" system that *Persuasion* "celebrates."[20] In other words, Wentworth is a self-made man whom the novel endorses by marrying him to its heroine. Lady Russell's initial rejection of Wentworth and acceptance of Mr. Elliot arises from her adherence to traditional hierarchical notions and a rejection of capitalism's flexibility and potential. And she does so, as the novel's conclusion indicates, against the values espoused by the novel.

In fact, what Lady Russell needs is considerable reeducation to bring her into conformity with the values of *Persuasion*. She stands, after all, on the brink of negativity: for all her good maternal qualities and her abode in the country, she prefers the values of a dying, stagnant system, and as a widow of the city, she consistently damages the heroine through her insistence on her own views. To achieve the redemption denied widows like Lady Catherine and Mrs. Rushworth, Lady Russell must change her mind about enterprise and the validity of certain forms of commodification.[21] Lady Russell repeatedly insists on Anne's being shown to the world: "Anne had been too little from home, too little seen. Her spirits were not high. A larger society would improve them. She wanted her to be more known" (11). Later, deploring the engagement to Wentworth, the narrator exclaims for her, "Anne Elliot, so young; known to so few, to be snatched off by a stranger without alliance or fortune" (19). Why this emphasis on Anne's "being known"? Because "being known" is being displayed in front of a large array of eligible young men. When Anne is still unmarried at twenty-two, Lady Russell wants her considerably less exposed, that is, "respectably removed from the partialities and injustice of her father's house" by marriage to Charles Musgrove (20). Anne is just at the age when any further fruitless exposure reveals the staleness of the wares. It is time to settle on a buyer, for "however Lady Russell might have asked yet for something more, while Anne was nineteen, she would have rejoiced to see her at twenty-two" accepting that offer (20). Anne's rejection of Charles Musgrove's suit may not do him or Mary, the Elliot who marries him, much good, but it does save her for Wentworth, the appropriate man, in spite of Lady Russell's wishes.

Lady Russell is, however, "a very good woman" and Austen allows her to develop, unlike Lady Catherine, Mrs. Rushworth, or Mrs. Ferrars. As the novel concludes, Austen lists the tasks that Lady Russell must undertake:

> She must learn to feel that she had been mistaken with regard to both; that she had been unfairly influenced by appearances in each; that because Captain Wentworth's manners had not suited her own ideas, she had been too quick in suspecting them to indicate a character of dangerous impetuosity; and that because Mr. Elliot's manners had precisely pleased her in their propriety and correctness, their general politeness and suavity, she had been too quick in receiving them as the certain result of the most correct opinions and well

regulated mind. There was nothing less for Lady Russell to do, than
to admit that she had been pretty completely wrong, and to take up
a new set of opinions and of hopes. (165–66)

Nothing simpler. Nevertheless, if Lady Russell's "second object was
to be sensible and well-judging, her first was to see Anne happy. She
loved Anne better than she loved her own abilities; and when the
awkwardness of the beginning was over, found little hardship in at-
taching herself as a mother to the man who was securing the happiness of her other child" (166). Hence, while Lady Russell's understanding of the world, her mode of valuing and interpreting people,
have all been rejected by the novel, Lady Russell herself is redeemed
by her very genuine love for Anne. Anne and Wentworth's marriage
enacts the convergence of landed agrarianism with trade and empire, and Lady Russell's ability to accept that marriage as a good
thing, eventually to love it "as she ought," enacts not just the fact of
the convergence but the ideological shift involved in it. The fact that
she is a widow is significant to this function in the novel, for the
widow herself possesses the same potential contained in the union
of Anne and Wentworth. Allowing the widow this ideological shift
suggests a concurrent gesture at the same ideological shift for
women.

   Jane Austen's widows, like widows of earlier texts and periods,
thus offer insight into the attitudes toward gender and economics
possible at the start of the nineteenth century. Affluent widows like
Mrs. Ferrars or Mrs. Smith from *Sense and Sensibility* show how a combination of behaviors and values not only had become imaginable,
but also had transcended the associations of good and bad that
tended to gather around landed and commercial action and attitude. The rest of Austen's widows suggest reasons why Austen would
espouse this hybridization of behavior and belief. Widows like Lady
Catherine and Mrs. Norris show how either system—the landed or
the commercial—are inadequate without infusions of values and behaviors from the other. Widows like Mrs. Bates or Mrs. Clay reinforce
the necessity for this balance, and widows like Mrs. Jennings and
Lady Russell model how that balance among class and gender might
be accomplished. Individually, Austen's widows offer different per-
spectives on the multitude of concerns facing women living in the
middle stages of emerging mercantile capitalism and the industrial
revolution. As a group, they show how at the beginning of the nineteenth century, it was becoming possible to see the old agricultural

society and the new commercial society merging rather than conflicting, and to consider ways in which that could, should, or did take place.

The figure of the widow permeates the eighteenth-century novel, a phenomenon that testifies to the period's anxieties about its own cultural developments. The eighteenth-century widow possessed rights and therefore potential unlike other women, and consequently escaped the gender conventions assigned to women to identify them as such. Instead, she laid claim to signs of both masculinity and femininity, and possessed the frightening power to self-transform socially and economically. In earlier periods, her status often resulted in depictions resulting from her anomalous state. In the eighteenth century, her status became still more frightening as the world around her took on many of her characteristics, or as she could be seen to embody the characteristics of the changing world around her. The novel responded to the widow in the same way that it responded to economic and cultural developments: with efforts, many of them grounded in sensibility, to contain the explosive potential for change and instability. As a sign of the times and as a figure full of the opportunity to exploit those times to the fullest, the widow can be understood not simply as one of the ciphers of the age, but also as one of the keys for understanding the relationship of the emerging novel to the eighteenth century.

Appendix
Charity to Widows in
Eighteenth-Century England

CHANGES TO THE SOCIOECONOMIC SYSTEM IN ENGLAND DURING THE eighteenth century changed many aspects of the fabric of society and the economic balance of the different classes. They also exacerbated many existing problems in the agrarian system, since England continued to depend on agriculture while adding the virtues and flaws of a mercantile system to its distribution and production of agricultural materials. These changes affected country and city, agricultural and commercial aspects alike. Of particular note is the impact they had on poverty, both in terms of generating and maintaining a population of impoverished people, and in terms of the responses to poverty that characterized the age. Although institutional remedies for poverty, such as the parish poor law, were available, they were implemented in such a way as to make it extremely difficult for the poor actually to use the system. In contrast, a rising number of private organizations took up the charge to address, although not to eradicate poverty.

Common perception, then and now, associates indigence with the city, but in fact poverty attacked rural as well as urban dwellers. Although urban migration swelled the cities, especially London, and exerted tremendous pressure on urban infrastructure and society, many dispossessed people stayed in the country and sometimes were driven to crime or riot to obtain the necessities of existence such as food or firewood, especially during poor harvests. Conversely, the spectacular harvests of 1730 to 1750 drove down food prices considerably, helping urban dwellers buy food but devastating the rural areas and swelling the ranks of the rural poor. In general, the pressures of the changing economy increased class unrest in both city and country, and it is therefore no surprise that discontent and urban migration were seen as threats to the established order. When the poor were described during this period, it was often as "throngs, swarms, or hordes."[1]

To respond to urban and rural poverty, individual and institutional charitable programs sprang up both in cities and in the country and throughout England and Wales.[2] *The Reports of the Society for Bettering the Condition and Increasing the Comforts of the Poor* record a number of "personal services," including a rudimentary soup kitchen run by "Mrs. Shore of Norton-Hall, Derbyshire" which dispensed soup several times a week during the winter, and mention the gift made by the Reverend Mr. Dolling in Hertfordshire of one shift apiece to thirty-seven poor women every Christmas. The *Reports* also describe schools, poor houses, and "friendly societies," many of which owed their existence to the efforts of wealthy or socially-minded individuals.[3] Institutions such as the Wolborough Feoffees and Widows' Charity in Devon served a sturdy population despite locations in small towns. In London, organizations such as the Lambeth Asylum and the Marine Society, founded to keep poor girls and boys, respectively, off the streets and to train them for a trade; the Magdalen Society for Penitent Prostitutes; and the foundling hospital at Coram's Fields addressed the young and old members of the indigent population.

Records such as the Essex Pauper Letters and those of private organizations from London and the provinces reveal a robust population of poor people, especially poor women, throughout England. Between 1716 and 1765, eight charitable lying-in institutions appeared in London alone. By 1772, the Royal Maternity Charity, a London organization that provided at-home midwifery for poor women, was delivering more than five thousand women per year, a number of births that accounted for almost one-third of the baptisms in the Bills of Mortality.[4] Despite the small sums disbursed and the stringent criteria for admission to the aid rolls of organizations like the Wolborough Feoffees in Devon, there were enough destitute widows to keep the lists full. When the Yerbury Almshouses in Wiltshire reported the death of one of their six widows, they generally found a replacement by the next quarter. These data suggest that the country as well as the city housed a large number of insolvent widows, women whose situations were so "distressful" that they were willing to wait months for their small grants of money to be transmitted to the far reaches of the countryside.

This surge in charitable organizations included a number that were particularly designed to look after poor widows. London headquartered the Society for the Relief of Necessitous Widows and Children of Poor Dissenting Ministers, which supported widows from Canterbury to Carmarthen, York to Dover, in tiny towns such as Caln as well as in large cities such as Liverpool and London. In the country, Westley's Charity gave money to widows of local clergymen in the Church of England. The Yerbury New Almshouse in Wiltshire and the Wolborough Feoffees and Widows' Charity in Devon appear to be real-life counterparts of almshouses described in Sarah Fielding's *The History of the Countess of Dellwyn* (1759), Sarah Scott's *Millenium Hall* (1762), and Charlotte Smith's *Emmeline* (1788).

Overall, charitable disbursements were not large, although amounts varied and institutions sometimes increased their stipends over time. Westley's Charity gave whatever seemed appropriate to the individual case, although there are no surviving records from the eighteenth century of what those amounts might have been.[5] Other charities were more regulated in their disbursements. The Widows' Charity in Wolborough gave its "objects of charity" five pounds a year, as directed by the indentures, until or nearly until the nineteenth century. The Yerbury Almshouses gave widows less than four pounds annually until 1768, when their allowance was increased to four pounds per annum apiece, with a maximum of six widows receiving funding at any one time. Raises and the payment schedule alike were infrequent and irregular for the rest of the century, but by 1800, widows were receiving eight pounds per annum apiece.[6]

Some charities rendered a widow's children self-sufficient by giving aid in apprenticing them or sending them out to service. In *The Reports of the Society for Bettering the Condition and Increasing the Comforts of the Poor*, for example, the Reverend John Brewster recorded that between 1796 and 1798, the charity at Greetham spent £32.14s.6d on eleven children being apprenticed or going into service, and £18.15s.6d for another group of six (158). The organization also paid £1.1s "for clothing one girl for service" and 10s.6d "for partly clothing one boy for sea" (159). The Society for the Relief of Necessitous Widows consistently funded apprenticeship and service through the eighteenth century, giving £10 to children being apprenticed and £5 to children going into service, which seemed like princely sums for the times. It frequently funded more than one child in a family, as well. The Waugh family, for example, managed to bind out four children with the Society's help: Elizabeth in 1788, Agnes in 1790, James in 1792, and Margaret in 1796.[7]

These institutions limited the definition of "deserving poor" in a variety of ways, thereby limiting the population of eligible women. One method was to narrow the definition of "need" to those utterly destitute of resources. Petitioners were required to show extreme poverty; even occasional help from a brother was enough to disqualify one applicant (Yerbury 2074.45). Until 1796, the Rules for the Society for the Relief of Necessitous Widows and Children of Poor Dissenting Ministers dictated that a widow was eligible for aid only if she earned less than £20 per year, regardless of how many children she had. After 1796, the rules distinguished between widows with and without children, and between widows with few children or many. In order to receive aid after 1796, an English widow without children could not earn more than £20 a year. The eligibility cap rose if she had children, starting with £24 for a widow with three children and adding £2 per child ad infinitum. It was even more difficult for Welsh widows, who had to be earning less than £15 and have at least one child to qualify for the Society's aid. Welsh widows were allowed £1.5 of income per child, so a Welsh widow with three children had to earn less than £18 to receive funding (OD 14, 25–26). It was possible, therefore, to be extremely poor and still be too financially secure to obtain relief.

It is hard to know how these sums translated into practical economic power, but Roy Porter and John Carswell have supplied some figures for comparison. Most laborers earned one shilling a day during the eighteenth century, and therefore did not earn the thirty to forty pounds per year needed to support a family. Nor could they afford to eat in a London pub, where a meal cost about one and a half shillings for most of the century—nearly two days of pay. Well-paid menservants earned ten pounds per year in addition to food, lodging, clothes, and tips from visitors to the house; well-paid women servants earned about half that.[8] Charitable institutions gave grants ranging from three to ten pounds per year, which, unlike the salaries of servants, might have had to support a family of any number of children.

Charity during the eighteenth century was generally conservative in purpose. These organizations dispensed aid to regulate poverty but not to eradicate it, and their care in selecting "deserving objects" indicates not only how poor a widow had to be to obtain help, but also the character and reputation she had to possess. Charitable awards therefore could be understood as charitable rewards for conforming to certain expectations. The Widows' Charity in Devon required that its recipients be restricted to widows

> such as have lived the greatest part of their time within the County of Devon and City of Exon, They shall be of the Age of fifty years or above of good report of Civill Conversation of Quiet behaviour Serving God, Frequenting the Church three times every Week at the Least if they or any of them shall either entertain any Man to Lodges within the said Habitation or be married, or shall live incontinently or justly suspected of Incontinence, or be Evil reported of, or be of an intemperate Spirit of a Gadder or running about from House to House, or a Tatler or Busy Body or a Scold, or a giver of Reproachful Language of provoking Words She that is so Accused and proved to be so, Shall forfeit and loose their Habitation and their Maintenance and one of better behaviour shall shall be setled in her Room place and Stead by the Trustees their Heirs and Assigns for ever hereafter. . . .[9]

Applications to the Yerbury Almshouses reveal that "worthy" applicants possessed certain similarities. They had married artisans (carpenters, shoemakers, weavers) and had grown up and lived their adult lives in Trowbridge or its immediate environs. The questions posed by the examiner from the Almshouses suggest that the trustees of this fund, like the trustees of the Widows' Charity in Devon, were looking for pious mothers about fifty years of age from the immediate area who had children out of the home or about to leave for apprenticeships or service, and who therefore would not need much help in launching their offspring (Yerbury 2074.45).

There is evidence that these organizations preferred women who would be appropriately grateful and dependent, and not too demanding. Widows who did not meet these criteria were treated summarily, since failing to meet them rendered the women "undeserving." At the February 21, 1771 meeting of the London Society for the Relief of Widows of Dissenting Ministers, word came that Rebecca Drewitt had "misbehaved in respect of the Money allowed for the placing out her Son Apprentice" and the Managers of the Society ordered "That her Annual Donation be suspended till she clears the Complaint to the Satisfaction of the Treasurer." In April, the committee "Ordered That her Annual Donation be not paid to her," although there is no evidence in the record that she had the opportunity to respond to the charges or even knew about them beforehand. An entry in the records of the Society for the Relief of Necessitous Widows and Orphans of Poor Dissenting Ministers refusing Jane Shields ten pounds to apprentice a child is followed immediately by the information that Mrs. Elizabeth Lambe has bequeathed five hundred pounds—it was not a lack of funds, but a careful manipulation of them that informed the Society's decision (OD 4). This determination to use charity to exert control is epitomized by William Wilberforce's 1798 statement that institutions should not "supply the poor in general with money, but rather *to lay it out for them;* as the surest way of directing the relief economically and with effect" (*The Reports . . . of the Poor* 297; original emphasis).

Consequently, while organizations might be willing to prevent children from becoming dependent, they did not extend the same interest to their mothers. Once widows had fallen into dependency, they were expected to remain there. The Wolborough Feoffees and Widows' Charity provided housing and a small annuity for four widows, and the Yerbury Almshouses also subsidized housing for up to six widows who could show extreme need, but neither organization made a gesture toward helping the women get off the aid rolls. Grants to widows did not enable them to start a business or a school, for example, or to get the education or training that would have made entrepreneurial efforts possible.[10] Overall, charity reinforced the status quo—the poor stayed poor, the rich stayed charitable. The relationship was constructed to perpetuate indefinitely the dependence of the one and the benevolence of the other, cementing both the dynamic and each particular player in his or her role.

The historical record also reveals, however, that widows sometimes found ways to resist the directive for passive gratitude. Widows rejected the assumption underpinning this kind of benevolence—that poverty is not about class, but about unfortunate individuals—by forming communities. For example, the widows of the Yerbury Almshouse were almost uniformly illiterate, but the quarterly receipt records in the 1760s reveal that one literate member often taught at least one other member to write. In 1749, the widows of the Wolborough Feoffees and Widows' Charity could not obtain their payments. A series of letters indicate that the women as a group attempted on their own, several times, to obtain their funding, approaching the earl twice and finally forcing him to apply his steward to the task (Courtenay 7:5; Courtenay 8:3, 11).

Widows appear to have challenged the system as individuals as well, fighting with the managers of charities for aid. Consistent with studies that show that the poor exploited the system any way they could, and often very successfully, widows affiliated with institutional charities often did so as well. Tim Hitchcock notes that indigent widows with children struggled to use the London workhouse system to their advantage, to obtain as much support for themselves and their children as possible.[11] Widows who were removed from the roster of recipients of annual donations by the Society for the Relief of Necessitous Widows and Children doggedly petitioned to be restored and frequently were. Although Rebecca Drewett's petitions for reinstatement were rejected on May 5, 1773 and February 2, 1774, at the October 7, 1778 meeting, the Managers Committee recorded that they had heard and corroborated good things about her, and so they granted her petition at the November 4 meeting. Jane Shields had a similar experience in her effort to apprentice her children. Although the Managers Committee rejected her request for reimbursement of the binding fees, between October, 1789 and May, 1790 Mrs. Shields repeatedly wrote the committee to reverse its decision (OD 4). She obtained funding for other children later.

These cases illustrate the very real control exercised by charitable organizations over the recipients of aid, but they also reveal the determination and tenacity of these women in obtaining what was necessary for the survival and success of their families. Such women might call to mind Daniel Defoe's "good widow" from *Robinson Crusoe* (1719) but as chapter 4 discusses at greater length, these are not behaviors or characteristics represented by the eighteenth-century novel as a whole. After *Robinson Crusoe*, poor widowhood is modeled in fictional narrative as dependent, unenterprising, and grateful, a state relating directly to maternal instincts and behavior. The poor widow reaffirms economic distinctions of the period by enabling the affluent to demonstrate their benevolence and by enabling wealth to circulate along familiar charitable routes, and not along new, commercial ones. The novel's poor widows illustrate the inhumanity of individuals rather than the problems of wealth distribution. They also simultaneously illuminate and uphold the problems and contradictions faced by actual poor widows, who had to be resourceful and tenacious with those resources, but pious, unobtrusive, and fully domesticated.

Notes

CHAPTER 1. INTRODUCTION

1. The idea of a new, capitalist, commercial system deserves some explanation, if not justification. Scholars such as Fernand Braudel, Amanda Vickery and Lillian Robinson argue that the economic system that eventually became the recognizably commercial society in place by the mid-nineteenth century was the product of gradual development from the fifteenth century, and Vickery and Robinson add that to ascribe significant change to any period, especially explosive change, is simply inaccurate. As Braudel observes, however, the idea of gradual evolution does not also preclude explosive development during the eighteenth century. My study builds on this recognition and applies instead the narrative of eighteenth-century economic development established by scholars such as Catherine Hall and Leonore Davidoff, Geoffrey Holmes and Daniel Szechi, Neil McKendrick, Maxine Berg, C. P. Hill, and John Carswell, who acknowledge that although trade and manufacture had been developing gradually in England since the Middle Ages, the market situation from the late seventeenth century onward was considerably different, and the period during which England changed over from a stable, agriculturally-based nation to a "polite, commercial people," as Paul Langford has it. Fernand Braudel, *The Wheels of Commerce*, trans. Siân Reynolds, vol. 2, *Civilization and Capitalism, 15th–18th Century* (New York: Harper & Row, Publishers, 1982); Amanda Vickery, *The Gentleman's Daughter: Women's Lives in Georgian England* (New Haven: Yale University Press, 1998); Lillian S. Robinson, "Woman Under Capitalism: The Renaissance Lady," in *Sex, Class, and Culture* (Bloomington: Indiana University Press, 1978), 150–77; Leonore Davidoff and Catherine Hall, *Family Fortunes: Men and Women of the English Middle Class, 1780–1850* (Chicago: The University of Chicago Press, 1987); Geoffrey Holmes and Daniel Szechi, *The Age of Oligarchy: Pre-Industrial England, 1722–1783* (New York: Longman Publishing, 1993); Maxine Berg, *The Age of Manufactures, 1700–1829: Industry, Innovation and Work in Britain*, 2nd ed. (New York: Routledge, 1994); C. P. Hill, *British Economic and Social History, 1700–1982*, 5th ed. (London: Edward Arnold Ltd., 1985); John Carswell, *The South Sea Bubble*, rev. ed. (Thrupp, Stroud: Sutton Publishing Limited, 2001); Paul Langford, *A Polite and Commercial People: England, 1727–1783* (Oxford: Clarendon Press, 1989).

2. As England changed from a traditional agricultural society to a commercial one, the values attached to country and city changed. The physical appearance of city and country were transformed by the doubling of the population during the eighteenth century, by the expansion of urban areas, and by new methods of crop rotation. The population of England in 1701 was 5.058 million and 83 percent of it lived in the country, but by 1800 the population had risen to 8.664 million and only 72 percent lived there. London in particular had grown with the century's increased urbanization: from five hundred and seventy-five thousand in 1700, London in 1800 numbered nine hundred thousand people. When large numbers of the dispossessed streamed into London, they brought all the ills that accompany dislocation and impoverishment: crowding, filth, disease, and crime. Bridget Hill, *Women, Work, and Sexual Politics in Eighteenth-Century England* (New York: Basil Blackwell Inc., 1989), 16–17, 19.

Associations with the country or with the city became code for understanding any given position or person within the new economic system, and the values embedded in these associations could be manipulated to express views on the new or the old systems. London in particular was viewed as a corruptor of values, where the freedom and anonymity of a large metropolis could readily lead to vice and violence. The country became idealized as the place where agricultural traditions resided. It was both the nostalgic refuge of anticapitalist agrarians and the place to which successful merchants retreated once they had made their fortunes. In politics, for example, the Tories were generally associated with the country, old money, and the landed interest, while the Whigs were associated with the city (London), the new economic system, and new money. To declare oneself a Tory or a Whig was, especially at the beginning of the century, to declare affiliation with a set of values and a part of English geography.

3. William Warner's discussion in *Licensing Entertainment* of the evolution of the novel's reputation over the course of the eighteenth century is so thorough as to be definitive. The eighteenth century hosted a continuous debate about novels, but the terms of that debate changed over time. Before about 1750, the debate about reading novels was about whether one should read them at all. They were attacked for being lies and were therefore highly suspect. After about 1750, Warner explains that the "issue for debate became much less whether to read than what kind of novel should be read, and what kind should be written" (8). In either case, the problem for novels throughout the century was finding validation with the reading public, whether as a genre or as specific manifestations of that genre. That struggle appears in the novels examined here, as they participate in the conceptualization of eighteenth-century society as it changes under tremendous economic developments. William Warner, *Licensing Entertainment: The Elevation of Novel Reading in Britain, 1684–1750* (Berkeley: University of California Press, 1998).

4. Barbara Todd, "The Remarrying Widow: A Stereotype Reconsidered," in *Women in English Society, 1500–1800*, ed. Mary Prior (New York: Methuen & Co., 1985), 71; Esther Cope, "'The Widdowes' Silvar': Widowhood in Early Modern England," in *"The Muses Females Are": Martha Moulsworth and Other Women Writers of the English Renaissance*, ed. Robert C. Evans and Anne C. Little (West Cornwall, CT: Locust Hill Press, 1995), 192; Merry E. Weisner, *Women and Gender in Early Modern Europe* (Cambridge: Cambridge University Press, 1993), 59.

5. B. Todd, "Remarrying Widow," 55.

6. J. Douglas Canfield, *Tricksters and Estates: On the Ideology of Restoration Comedy* (Lexington: The University Press of Kentucky, 1997), 6, 1–2, 33.

7. Helen Burke, " 'Law-suits,' 'Love-suits,' and the Family Property in Wycherley's *The Plain Dealer*," in *Cultural Readings of Restoration and Eighteenth-Century English Theater*, ed. J. Douglas Canfield and Deborah C. Payne (Athens: University of Georgia Press, 1995), 95.

8. Aphra Behn and Thomas Betterton, "The Counterfeit Bridegroom: or the Defeated Widow," in *English Dramas* (London: L. Curtiss, 1677).

9. Mary Poovey, *The Proper Lady and the Woman Writer: Ideology as Style in the Works of Mary Wollstonecraft, Mary Shelley, and Jane Austen* (Chicago: The University of Chicago Press, 1984), 6.

10. Until and continuing through the eighteenth century, marriage was women's primary occupation and preoccupation, and also one crucial mechanism in the circulation of goods and property. Women carried estates, plate, cash, and other forms of wealth between families when they married out of one and into another. Marriage's role as a significant economic event remained fairly constant during the eighteenth century, although scholars such as Olwen Hufton and Kathryn Kirkpatrick report various signs that the goods transferred in marriage changed. Money became a larger factor in the process, as did cash, furniture, and jewels.

While the system of piggybacking wealth onto a woman did not in and of itself constitute a radical challenge to the status quo, by the eighteenth century, it could be used to facilitate class change and therefore class instability. The rising merchant class intermarried with landed families, exchanging commercially gained wealth and inherited bloodlines. As a result, John Gillis notes, the "control of courtship, particularly that of heirs and heiresses, remained essential" despite other economic changes taking place during the period. This effort to control marriage appears most clearly in Lord Hardwicke's 1753 Clandestine Marriage Act, which was designed to protect young heirs from fortune hunters or foolish choices made in the heat and inexperience of youth. The act's language only poorly covered another intent, however: to reduce the opportunities for anyone, not just fortune hunters, to rise through marriage. As such, it was perceived by some as a form of class suppression. Olwen Hufton, "Women Without Men: Widows and Spinsters in Britain and France in the Eighteenth Century," in *Between Poverty and the Pyre: Moments in the History of Widowhood*, ed. Jan Bremmer and Lourens van den Bosch (New York: Routledge, 1995), 127; Kathryn Kirkpatrick, "Sermons and Strictures: Conduct-Book Propriety and Property Relations in Late Eighteenth-Century England," in *History, Gender and Eighteenth-Century Literature*, ed. Beth Fowkes Tobin (Athens: University of Georgia Press, 1994), 204; John R. Gillis, *For Better, For Worse: British Marriages, 1600 to the Present* (New York: Oxford University Press, 1985), 135; Douglas Hay and Nicholas Rogers, *Eighteenth-Century English Society* (New York: Oxford University Press, 1997), 37; Christopher K. Brooks, "Marriage in Goldsmith: The Single Woman, Feminine Space, and 'Virtue,' " in *Joinings and Disjoinings: The Significance of Marital Status in Literature*, ed. JoAnna Stephens Mink and Janet Doubler Ward (Bowling Green, OH: Bowling Green State University Popular Press, 1991), 20.

11. The Hardwicke Act attempted to control marriage through a variety of mechanisms, under the theory that controlling marriage would allow the state to

control population, in terms of quantity (how many people were born) and quality (how well they were raised, what kind of contributors to empire they would become), and property transmission. The Hardwicke Act declared only marriages performed publicly and entered into the Register to be legal and legitimate, thereby nullifying existing as well as future marriages based on the traditional verbal agreement between two parties. According to Eve Tavor Bannet, the theory behind this decision was that only people willing to commit publicly to a monogamous union should be permitted to propagate, and that the public's knowledge of this commitment would help keep people together. It was designed therefore to ensure that only legitimate children were produced, and that only families committed to raising them would do so. At the same time, the Hardwicke Act recognized that women conveyed property through marriage, and also were considered property. By making it more difficult to effect clandestine marriages, and by making it a capital offense to kidnap an heiress, the act moved to protect primogeniture, patriarchal control of property and women, and marriage's role in the transmission of property. Eve Tavor Bannet, "The Marriage Act of 1753: 'A Most Cruel Law for the Fair Sex,'" *Eighteenth-Century Studies* 30, no. 3 (1997): 233–54.

12. B. Hill, *Women, Work*, 242–43, 253; Peter Earle, *The Making of the English Middle Class: Business, Society and Family Life in London, 1660–1730* (Berkeley: University of California Press, 1989), 172–73, 50–51.

13. B. Hill, *Women, Work*, 245–48, 94; Gillis, *British Marriages*, 113; Ruth Perry, "Women in Families: The Great Disinheritance," in *Women and Literature in Britain, 1700–1800*, ed. Vivien Jones (Cambridge: Cambridge University Press, 2000), 120.

14. Laura Brown, *Fables of Modernity: Literature and Culture in the English Eighteenth Century* (Ithaca, NY: Cornell University Press, 2001), 3, 13; Terry Mulcaire, "Public Credit; or, The Feminization of Virtue in the Marketplace," *PMLA* 114 (October 1999): 1029–42. A female figure representing Commerce or other incarnations of related concepts such as Credit became increasingly common starting in the early eighteenth century, and due to the efforts of Whig promoters of the new economy. Terry Mulcaire's study of this figure offers a persuasive reading of her significance, demonstrating that representing the economy as a volatile, desirable, and desiring female figure shifted economic discourse from aristocratic, concrete terms (money = gold, for example) into the terms currently in use (money = gold, paper, credit, etc.). Mulcaire's study falls short, however, on the issue of gender. While the use of a desiring and desirable female figure to represent the actuality and potential of the new economy is certainly a dramatic and significant reconceptualization of not just economics, but also society and social relationships, it is not the liberating opportunity for women that he implies (1038). Lady Credit is meant to be desirable to men, not to women, after all, and she is an object, not a subject for those men. Furthermore, Mulcaire's convincing analysis of this figure as capricious and "magical" should underscore how the traditional association of irrationality and unpredictability with women was in use once again, albeit for a new subject: a credit-based, commercial economy. While seemingly powerful female figures such as Lady Credit or Commerce offer new modes of understanding in a new economic and social atmosphere, these figures also reinforce the separation of actual women from those economic opportunities and practices.

15. Thomas Bowles, "The *Bubbler's Medley,* or, a *Sketch* of the *Times*: Being Europe's *Memorial* for the *Year* 1720," August 10, 1720, British Museum Collection of Prints and Drawings, 1689–1790; Kirkpatrick, "Conduct-Book Propriety."

16. Toni Bowers, *The Politics of Motherhood: British Writing and Culture, 1680–1760* (Cambridge: Cambridge University Press, 1996), 14, 28, 95.

17. For a more extensive discussion of definitions of femininity and motherhood during the period, see Bowers, *Politics of Motherhood*; Felicity Nussbaum, "'Savage' Mothers: Narratives of Maternity in the Mid-Eighteenth Century," *Eighteenth-Century Life* 16 (February 1992): 165–84; and Ruth Perry, "Colonizing the Breast: Sexuality and Maternity in Eighteenth-Century England," *Eighteenth-Century Life* 16 (February 1992): 185–215.

18. Elise F. Knapp, "'Your Obedient Humble Servant': An Epistolary Account of Marriage and Widowhood in Eighteenth-Century Sussex," *Studies on Voltaire and the Eighteenth Century* 304 (1992): 783, 786; B. Hill, *Women, Work,* 244–45; Elizabeth Bergen Brophy, *Women's Lives and the Eighteenth-Century English Novel* (Tampa: University of South Florida Press, 1991), 227-28.

19. Susan Staves's *Married Women's Separate Property in England, 1660–1833* (Cambridge: Harvard University Press, 1990) offers a particularly thorough examination of the changes to widows' legal status over the course of the eighteenth century. She points out that while changes to widows' inheritance, especially the transition from dower to jointure, were touted as beneficial to surviving spouses, there were no corresponding changes to widowers' inheritance laws (103, 96, 115, 116), a suspicious disparity indeed.

20. Liz Bellamy, *Commerce, Morality and the Eighteenth-Century Novel* (Cambridge: Cambridge University Press, 1998); Gillian Skinner, *Sensibility and Economics in the Novel, 1740–1800: The Price of a Tear* (New York: St. Martin's Press, Inc., 1999); April London, *Women and Property in the Eighteenth-Century English Novel* (Cambridge: Cambridge University Press, 1999).

21. As Adam Smith explains it in *The Theory of Moral Sentiments*, "And hence it is, that to feel much for others and little for ourselves, that to restrain our selfish, and to indulge our benevolent affections, constitutes the perfection of human nature; and can alone produce among mankind that harmony of sentiments and passions in which consists their whole grace and propriety." Adam Smith, *The Theory of Moral Sentiments*, ed. D. D. Raphael and A. L. Macfie (1750; repr., Indianapolis: The Liberty Fund, 1979), 43–44.

22. L. Brown, *Fables of Modernity,* 1, 3.

23. This tracing of sensibility's rise and fall depends on the representation of the widow in eighteenth-century novels, but it is confirmed by seminal studies such as Janet Todd's *Sensibility: An Introduction*. As Todd notes, sentiment's heyday had passed by the early 1780s, but its influence lingered in other modes such as the Gothic and the Romantic. Todd also distinguishes the novels of the 1760s and 1770s from sentiment's earlier narrative productions based on the function of emotion: "The novel of sentiment of the 1740s and 1750s praises a generous heart and often delays the narrative to philosophize about benevolence; the novel of sensibility, increasingly written from the 1760s onwards, differs slightly in emphasis since it honours above all the capacity for refined feeling." I do not employ these terms in this study, as they suggest a break and distinction between novels of one decade and the next, but I do acknowledge in this study the difference be-

tween sensibility's early novels and those of its peak and decline. Janet Todd, *Sensibility: An Introduction* (London: Methuen & Co., 1986), 7–9.

CHAPTER 2. FEAR AND PROPERTY

1. Oliver Goldsmith, "The Revolution in Low Life," in *British Literature 1640–1789: An Anthology*, ed. Robert DeMaria, Jr. (1762; repr., Oxford: Blackwell Publishers Ltd, 1996), 1052–53; Oliver Goldsmith, "The Deserted Village," in *British Literature 1640–1789: An Anthology*, ed. Robert DeMaria, Jr. (1770; repr., Oxford: Blackwell Publishers Ltd, 1996), 55, 275, 64–65.

2. Maaja A. Stewart, *Domestic Realities and Imperial Fictions: Jane Austen's Novels in Eighteenth-Century Contexts* (Athens: University of Georgia Press, 1993), 20.

3. Gillian Skinner, "Women's Status as Legal and Civic Subjects: 'A Worse Condition than Slavery Itself'?" in *Women and Literature in Britain, 1700–1800*, ed. Vivien Jones (Cambridge: Cambridge University Press, 2000), 103–4; Tobias Smollett, *The Adventures of Ferdinand Count Fathom*, ed. Jerry C. Beasley and O. M. Brack, Jr. (1753; repr., Athens: University of Georgia Press, 1988), 235–36, 328, 355–56.

4. Clara Reeve, *The School for Widows. A Novel. In Two Volumes* (Dublin: William Porter, 1791), 2:44–45.

5. Robert D. Spector contends, for example, that Smollett's women, while used at times to criticize the ideology behind ideal femininity, are also minor and often caricaturized depictions. Reeve, in contrast, made women's experience central to her novels, and her female characters, while conventional in many ways, are also recognizably, sometimes brilliantly human. Robert D. Spector, *Smollett's Women: A Study in an Eighteenth-Century Masculine Sensibility* (Westport, CT: Greenwood Press, 1994). For other discussions of Smollett's use of women, more generally, to comment on trade's social impact, see Robert P. Irvine, *Enlightenment and Romance: Gender and Agency in Smollett and Scott* (New York: Peter Lang, Inc., 2000) or Susan P. Jacobsen, "'The Tinsel of the Times': Smollett's Argument against Conspicuous Consumption in *Humphry Clinker*," *Eighteenth-Century Fiction* 9, no. 1 (October 1996): 71–88.

6. Sarah Scott, *The History of Cornelia* (1750; repr., London: Routledge / Thoemmes Press, 1992); Frances Sheridan, *Memoirs of Miss Sidney Bidulph* (1769; repr., New York: Pandora Press, 1987), 385.

7. Sarah Scott, *A Description of Millenium Hall* (1762; repr., New York: Viking Penguin, 1986), 19.

8. Ruth Perry, "Bluestockings in Utopia," in *History, Gender and Eighteenth-Century Literature*, ed. Beth Fowkes Tobin (Athens: University of Georgia Press, 1994), 162, 163.

9. Arlene Fish Wilner, "Education and Ideology in Sarah Fielding's *The Governess*," *Studies in Eighteenth-Century Culture* 24 (1995): 318; "The Finish'd Rake; or, Gallantry in Perfection," in *The Finish'd Rake; or, Gallantry in Perfection (Anonymous); The Secret History of Mama Oello, Princess Royal of Peru (Anonymous); The Masterpiece of Imposture (Elizabeth Harding); The Temple Rakes, or Innocence Preserved (Anonymous)*, ed. Josephine Grieder (1733; repr., New York: Garland Publishing, Inc., 1973), 35.

10. Margaret Anne Doody, "Frances Sheridan: Morality and Annihilated Time," in *Fetter'd or Free? British Women Novelists, 1670–1815*, ed. Mary Anne Schofield and Cecilia Macheski (Athens: Ohio University Press, 1986), 329.

11. Matthew Lewis, *The Monk* (1796; repr., New York: Oxford University Press, 1989). Admittedly, Elvira was not born of a noble family, like Sidney Bidulph, nor inherited vast sums, like Madame Duval. On the contrary, she was born into the working class, depends financially on her sister, Leonella, and aspires to the financial support of Raymond de las Cisternas. Nevertheless, Elvira does not belong among the poor widows of chapter 4. Although she is the daughter of a shoemaker, she shows no signs of her class origins. Elvira does not work or live off charity; she is beautiful and well-bred. She was also the wife of the Condé de las Cisternas. As Lorenzo realizes when he meets her, "In spite of her being the Mother of Antonia, Lorenzo could not help expecting to find in Elvira Leonella's true Sister, and the Daughter of 'as honest a pains-taking Shoe-maker, as any in Cordova.' A single glance was sufficient to undeceive him. He beheld a Woman whose features, though impaired by time and sorrow, still bore the marks of distinguished beauty: A serious dignity reigned upon her countenance, but was tempered by a grace and sweetness which rendered her truly enchanting. Lorenzo fancied that She must have resembled her Daughter in her youth, and readily excused the imprudence of the late Condé de las Cisternas" (203). She deserves to be the wife of the Marquis de las Cisternas; she deserves to be among the nobility. As a result, although Elvira appears to have returned to the poverty from which she sprung, given her innate qualities and the position the novel wishes us to allow Antonia, her class status is actually much higher.

12. Toni Bowers, *The Politics of Motherhood: British Writing and Culture, 1680–1760* (Cambridge: Cambridge University Press, 1996), 158–59.

13. Charlotte Smith, *The Old Manor House*, ed. Jacqueline M. Labbe (1793; repr., Toronto: Broadview Press Ltd., 2002), 444, 449.

14. Ann Radcliffe, *The Castles of Athlin and Dunbayne. A Highland Story* (1789; repr. of 1821 edition, New York: Arno Press Inc., 1972), 102, 106–7.

15. William Godwin, *Things As They Are or The Adventures of Caleb Williams*, ed. Maurice Hindle (1794; repr., New York: Penguin Books, 1988), 19.

16. Mary Davys, "The Accomplish'd Rake, or Modern Fine Gentleman," in *The Reform'd Coquet; or Memoirs of Amoranda, Familiar Letters Betwixt a Gentleman and a Lady, and The Accomplish'd Rake, or Modern Fine Gentleman*, ed. Martha F. Bowden (1727; repr., Lexington: The University Press of Kentucky, 1999), 132, 130.

17. Davys, *Accomplish'd Rake*, 146–47, 154; Henry Fielding, "Joseph Andrews," in *Joseph Andrews and Shamela*, ed. Douglas Brooks-Davies (1742; repr., New York: Oxford University Press, 1990), 252–56.

18. Martha F. Bowden, introduction to "The Accomplish'd Rake, or Modern Fine Gentleman" by Mary Davys in *The Reform'd Coquet; or Memoirs of Amoranda, Familiar Letters Betwixt a Gentleman and a Lady, and The Accomplish'd Rake, or Modern Fine Gentleman*, ed. Martha F. Bowden (Lexington: The University Press of Kentucky, 1999), Ix–xlvi.

19. Frances Burney, *Camilla; or, The Picture of Youth*, ed. Edward A. Bloom and Lillian D. Bloom (1796; repr., New York: Oxford University Press, 1972), 251; Sarah Fielding, *The History of Ophelia* (1760; repr., New York: Garland Publishing, Inc., 1974), 1:155–56; Henry Fielding, *The History of Tom Jones*, ed. R. P. C. Mutter (1747; repr., New York: Penguin Books, 1985), 677.

20. Gary Gautier, "Marriage and Family in Fielding's Fiction," *Studies in the Novel* 27 (Summer 1995): 113.

21. Frances Burney, *Evelina* (1778; repr., New York: W. W. Norton & Co., 1965), 42.

22. Mary Robinson, *The Widow, or a Picture of Modern Times. A Novel, in a Series of Letters, in Two Volumes* (London: Hookham and Carpenter, 1794), 1:147, 1:167, Robinson's emphases.

23. There has been some discussion about *Tristram Shandy*'s classification as a sentimental novel, and the juxtaposition here with a conventionally sentimental novel like Griffith's highlights the ways in which *Tristram Shandy* is different. Here as elsewhere in this study I consider *Tristram Shandy* a sentimental novel less for its use of recognizable conventions from that tradition—although episodes like the story of Le Fever are, as Frank Brady has noted, quintessentially sentimental—than for its overall idea that people are held together by bonds of fellow-feeling. Scholars such as John Mullan and Bernard Harrison may disagree about the strain of sensibility Sterne employed, but they make a convincing case for *Tristram Shandy* as a sentimental novel. For more discussion of Sterne as a novelist of sensibility, see for example Frank Brady, "Tristram Shandy: Sexuality, Morality, and Sensibility," *Eighteenth-Century Studies* 4, no. 1 (Autumn 1970): 41–56; John Mullan, *Sentiment and Sociability: The Language of Feeling in the Eighteenth Century* (Oxford: Oxford University Press, 1988); Bernard Harrison, "Sterne and Sentimentalism" in *Commitment in Reflection: Essays in Literature and Moral Philosophy* (New York: Garland Publishing, Inc., 1994): 63–100; George E. Haggerty, "Amelia's Nose; Or, Sensibility and Its Symptoms," *The Eighteenth Century* 36, no. 2 (Summer 1995): 139–56; Ian Campbell Ross, *Laurence Sterne: A Life* (Oxford: Oxford University Press, 2001); Laura Jane Ress, *Tender Consciousness: Sentimental Sensibility in the Emerging Artist— Sterne, Yeats, Joyce, and Proust*, vol. 59, American University Studies, series 3: Comparative Literature (New York: Peter Lang, Inc., 2002); or James Rodgers, "Sensibility, Sympathy, Benevolence: Physiology and Moral Philosophy in *Tristram Shandy*" in *Languages of Nature: Critical Essays on Science and Literature* ed. L. J. Jordanova (New Brunswick, NJ: Rutgers University Press, 1986), 119–58.

24. Elizabeth Griffith, *The Delicate Distress*, ed. Cynthia Booth Ricciardi and Susan Staves (1769; repr., Lexington: The University Press of Kentucky, 1997), 1:68; Laurence Sterne, *The Life and Opinions of Tristram Shandy, Gentleman*, ed. Melvyn New and Joan New (1760–67; repr., New York: Penguin Books, 1997), 456–57.

25. Brady, "Tristram Shandy," 52; Elizabeth Kraft, "Laurence Sterne and the Ethics of Sexual Difference: Chiasmic Narration and Double Desire," *Christianity and Literature* 51, no. 3 (Spring 2002): 363–85; George Haggerty, "Satire and Sentiment in *The Vicar of Wakefield*," *The Eighteenth Century* 32, no. 1 (Spring 1991): 25–38.

26. Elizabeth Bergen Brophy, *Women's Lives and the Eighteenth-Century English Novel* (Tampa: University of South Florida Press, 1991), 229, 230–31, 27, 228.

27. Charlotte Smith, *Emmeline, the Orphan of the Castle* (London: T. Cadell, 1788); Ann Radcliffe, *The Mysteries of Udolpho* (1794; repr., Oxford: Oxford University Press, 1980), 144; Robinson, *Widow*, 1:181; Eliza Fenwick, *Secresy; or, The Ruin on the Rock*, ed. Isobel Grundy, 2nd ed. (1795; repr., Toronto: Broadview Press Ltd., 1998), 142, 337.

28. Barbara M. Benedict, *Framing Feeling: Sentiment and Style in English Prose Fiction, 1745–1800* (New York: AMS Press, Inc., 1994), 175.

29. Tobias Smollett, *The Expedition of Humphry Clinker*, ed. Angus Ross (1771; repr., New York: Penguin Books, 1985); Burney, *Evelina*, 148.

30. Laura Brown, *Ends of Empire: Women and Ideology in Eighteenth-Century English Literature* (Ithaca, NY: Cornell University Press, 1993).

31. George Boulukos, "The Grateful Slave: A History of Slave Plantation Reform in the British Novel, 1750–1780," in *The Eighteenth Century Novel*, vol. 1, ed. Susan Spencer (New York: AMS Press, Inc., 2001); Gary Gautier, "Slavery and the Fashioning of Race in *Oroonoko, Robinson Crusoe*, and Equiano's *Life*," *The Eighteenth Century* 42 (2001): 161–79. For a more extensive discussion of sentimental fiction's role in promoting a race- or class-based system to reinforce a stable hierarchy, see chapter 4.

32. Peregrine Pickle's plan to "make prize of a rich heiress, or opulent widow" to secure his future offers the fortune-hunter's perspective on this issue. Reeve, *School for Widows*, 2:85–87; Tobias Smollett, *The Adventures of Peregrine Pickle, in which are included Memoirs of a Lady of Quality*, ed. James L. Clifford (1751; repr., London: Oxford University Press, 1964), 397.

33. Stewart, *Jane Austen's Novels*, 12.

34. Eliza Haywood, "The British Recluse; or, The Secret History of Cleomira, Supposed Dead," in *Popular Fiction by Women, 1660–1730: An Anthology*, ed. Paula R. Backscheider and John J. Richetti (1722; repr., Oxford: Clarendon Press, 1996), 162; Smith, *The Old Manor House*, 429–30.

35. Ann Radcliffe, *The Italian* (1797; repr., New York: Oxford University Press, 1990).

36. Penelope Aubin, "The Adventures of the Count de Vinevil And his Family," in *Popular Fiction by Women, 1660–1730: An Anthology*, ed. Paula R. Backscheider and John J. Richetti (1721; repr., Oxford: Clarendon Press, 1996); Smith, *Emmeline*; Eliza Haywood, *The History of Miss Betsy Thoughtless*, ed. Christine Blouch (1751; repr., Toronto: Broadview Press Ltd., 1998); Margaret Lee, *Clara Lennox; or, The Distressed Widow. A Novel. Founded in Facts. Interspersed with an Historical Description of the Isle of Man* (London: J. Adlard, 1797).

37. Like Elvira from Lewis's *The Monk*, Scott's Mrs. Tunstall and Mrs. Blackburn are not made affluent when they become widows. Mrs. Tunstall's husband leaves her penniless except for the charity of her father and George Ellison, and the Blackburn estate is being held in trust for her son by George Ellison. These women either were born or married into affluence, however, and are being maintained in that situation, which explains their presence in this chapter. Sarah Scott, *The History of Sir George Ellison*, ed. Betty Rizzo (1766; repr., Lexington: The University Press of Kentucky, 1996).

38. Clara Reeve, "The Old English Baron: A Gothic Story," in *The Old English Baron and The Castle of Otranto* (1777; repr., London: J. C. Nimmo and Bain, 1883), 52.

39. It is worth noting that when Mrs. Trunnion in Smollett's *Peregrine Pickle* is approached by her family and Jack Hatchway about taking Jack as a second husband, as her late husband wished, she "received his proposal with a becoming reserve, and piously wept at the remembrance of her husband, observing, that she should never meet with his fellow." Even when she consents, as everyone wishes her to do, "it was determined, that the day of marriage should be put off for three

months, that her reputation might not suffer by a precipitate engagement." Smollett, *Peregrine Pickle*, 422.

40. Daniel Defoe, *Robinson Crusoe*, ed. Michael Shinagel (1719; repr., New York: W. W. Norton & Co., 1975). For a more extensive discussion of this character, see chapter 4.

41. Kate Ferguson Ellis, *The Contested Castle: Gothic Novels and the Subversion of Domestic Ideology* (Urbana: University of Illinois Press, 1989), 100, 122.

42. Boulukos, "The Grateful Slave."

43. As J. M. Beattie remarks, "It is this relative freedom that lies behind the dismay at the evil effects of city life expressed by so many commentators in the eighteenth century. Those who saw in the circumstances of life in the city the encouragement of social disorder, rebelliousness, and crime, especially condemned the freedom that life allowed to the young. Poverty and crime and the weakening of the social bonds were the product, in this view, of the licence that urban life granted to the poor to come and go at will, to dress like their betters, to entertain themselves as they chose at theatres and pleasure gardens, and to gamble and drink without restraint in the thousands of taverns that catered to them. No matter what might be thought about the validity of such analyses, they do contain a central truth—that life in the city was on a different order from life in a village or even a market town." J. M. Beattie, "The Criminality of Women in Eighteenth-Century England," *Journal of Social History* 8, no. 4 (1975): 99.

44. Raymond Williams, *The Country and the City* (New York: Oxford University Press, 1973); Gerald MacLean, Donna Landry, and Joseph P. Ward, "Introduction: The Country and the City Revisited, c. 1550–1850" in *The Country and the City Revisited: England and the Politics of Culture, 1550–1850,* ed. Gerald MacLean, Donna Landry, Joseph P. Ward (Cambridge: Cambridge University Press, 1999), 1–23; Beattie, "Criminality of Women."

45. See chapter 5 for a discussion of the illegal ways in which widows use young women as capital or as goods.

46. Samuel Richardson, *Clarissa* (1747; repr., New York: Penguin Classics, 1987).

47. Williams, *The Country and the City;* Beth Fowkes Tobin, "Arthur Young, Agriculture, and the Construction of the New Economic Man," in *History, Gender and Eighteenth-Century Literature,* ed. Beth Fowkes Tobin (Athens: University of Georgia Press, 1994), 179–80.

48. Tobin, "New Economic Man," 184; Bridget Hill, *Women, Work, and Sexual Politics in Eighteenth-Century England* (New York: Basil Blackwell Inc., 1989), 49.

49. Stewart, *Jane Austen's Novels*, 12–13.

Chapter 3. Diligent and Sentimental Labor

1. Papers for the Society for the Relief of Necessitous Widows and Children of Protestant Dissenting Ministers, Dr. Williams's Library.

2. Bridget Hill, *Women, Work, and Sexual Politics in Eighteenth-Century England* (New York: Basil Blackwell Inc., 1989), 85; Peter Earle, *The Making of the English Middle Class: Business, Society and Family Life in London, 1660–1730* (Berkeley: University of California Press, 1989), 172. For a more extensive discussion of the trades that closed to women during the eighteenth century, see chapter 1.

3. As Paula McDowell points out, women, specifically widows, were significant players in all aspects of the print culture. The Ann Dodds (mother and daughter) and the Nutts (Elizabeth and her daughters Catherine, Ann, and Sarah) were London's primary suppliers of newspapers before 1750, and also sold other popular print material, such as pamphlets and tracts. The elder Ann Dodd's imprint appears on Alexander Pope's *Dunciad*, and it appears that Ann Snowden, the widow of a printer, must have been subsidizing John Dunton, since he owed her a considerable sum of money at the time of his bankruptcy. Paula McDowell, "Women and the Business of Print," in *Women and Literature in Britain, 1700–1800*, ed. Vivien Jones (Cambridge: Cambridge University Press, 2000), 142–43, 146.

4. John R. Gillis, *For Better, For Worse: British Marriages, 1600 to the Present* (New York: Oxford University Press, 1985), 113, 119–30.

5. Leonore Davidoff and Catherine Hall, *Family Fortunes: Men and Women of the English Middle Class, 1780–1850* (Chicago: The University of Chicago Press, 1987), 305–6.

6. B. Hill, *Women, Work*, 143, 247.

7. For example, the widow of a gaoler could take up her husband's occupation—between the Glorious Revolution of 1688 and the American Revolution in 1775, slightly more than 25 percent of British jails were run by a woman at some point—but the widow of a shoemaker could not. Olwen Hufton, "Women Without Men: Widows and Spinsters in Britain and France in the Eighteenth Century," in *Between Poverty and the Pyre: Moments in the History of Widowhood*, ed. Jan Bremmer and Lourens van den Bosch (New York: Routledge, 1995), 136, 133–35.

8. Sarah Scott, *A Description of Millenium Hall* (1762; repr., New York: Viking Penguin, 1986), 12–14; Frances Sheridan, *Memoirs of Miss Sidney Bidulph* (1769; repr., New York: Pandora Press, 1987), 322–23; Margaret Lee, *Clara Lennox; or, The Distressed Widow. A Novel. Founded in Facts. Interspersed with an Historical Description of the Isle of Man* (London: J. Adlard, 1797), 2:138, 2:115. Echoes of this avoidance of contact with money appear in a much later novel, Ann Radcliffe's *The Italian* (1797), in which the heroine Ellena and her aunt work, "pass[ing] whole days in embroidering silks, which were disposed of to the nuns of a neighboring convent, who sold them to the Neapolitan ladies" and selling "copies from the antique," drawings of "originals in the royal museum." In this case as well, the work is performed by women who remain ensconced in the home, and the actual exchange of goods for cash takes place outside the home, transacted by other people, and invisibly. Neither Ellena nor her aunt is a widow, however, although the late date and this same careful separation of virtuous heroine from cash transaction suggests that by the end of the century, distance from cash exchange was a sign of virtue. Ann Radcliffe, *The Italian* (1797; repr., New York: Oxford University Press, 1990), 9, 24.

9. Davidoff and Hall, *Family Fortunes*, 287; Clara Reeve, *The School for Widows. A Novel. In Two Volumes* (Dublin: William Porter, 1791), 1:30; Sarah Fielding, *The Governess, Or, The Little Female Academy* (1749; repr., Project Gutenberg: Carnegie-Mellon University), 1–2.

10. Peter King, "Female Offenders, Work and Life-Cycle Change in Late-Eighteenth-Century London," *Continuity and Change* 11 (1996): 77; J. M. Beattie, "The Criminality of Women in Eighteenth-Century England," *Journal of Social History* 8, no. 4 (1975): 106.

11. Sarah Scott, *The History of Sir George Ellison*, ed. Betty Rizzo (1766; repr., Lexington: The University Press of Kentucky, 1996), 46.

12. Samuel Richardson, *Pamela; or, Virtue Rewarded*, ed. Peter Sabor (1740; repr., New York: Penguin Books, 1988), 478, 108.

13. Henry Fielding, *The History of Tom Jones*, ed. R. P. C. Mutter (1747; repr., New York: Penguin Books, 1985), 625.

14. Sarah Scott, *The History of Cornelia* (1750; repr., London: Routledge / Thoemmes Press, 1992), 45–50.

15. McDowell, "Women and the Business of Print," 138; B. Hill, *Women, Work*, 245, 247.

16. Earle, *Making the English Middle Class*, 160–66.

17. Gillian Skinner, *Sensibility and Economics in the Novel, 1740–1800: The Price of a Tear* (New York: St. Martin's Press, Inc., 1999), 12, 91, 99.

18. Laurence Sterne, *The Life and Opinions of Tristram Shandy, Gentleman*, ed. Melvyn New and Joan New (1760–67; repr., New York: Penguin Books, 1997), 507–10.

19. For a more extensive discussion of ideas about maternity in the eighteenth century, see chapter 1.

20. William Godwin, *Things As They Are or The Adventures of Caleb Williams*, ed. Maurice Hindle (1794; repr., New York: Penguin Books, 1988), 245–46; Scott, *Sir George Ellison*, 171; Reeve, *School for Widows*, 2:58, 2:63.

21. Daniel Defoe, *Moll Flanders* (1722; repr., New York: Penguin Classics, 1989), 46, 48–51.

22. The eighteenth-century novel's preference for widowed mothers preparing their children to be economically self-sufficient over widows' preparing themselves to be self-sufficient is also an issue that arises in the disbursement of charitable sums and opportunities. Whether charities should help widows take care of their families themselves, or should look after the families and preserve a widow's dependence on the charity, is a subject discussed at greater length in chapter 4 and in the appendix.

23. Tobias Smollett, *The Adventures of Peregrine Pickle, in which are included Memoirs of a Lady of Quality*, ed. James L. Clifford (1751; repr., London: Oxford University Press, 1964), 544.

24. April London, *Women and Property in the Eighteenth-Century English Novel* (Cambridge: Cambridge University Press, 1999), 122; Sara Gadeken, "'A Method of Being Perfectly Happy': Technologies of Self in the Eighteenth-Century Female Community," in *The Eighteenth Century Novel*, vol. 1, ed. Susan Spencer (New York: AMS Press, Inc., 2001), 217. Gadeken's reading of *The Governess* as an example of a female alternative to the male, Lockean framework is persuasive, although the conclusions she draws about the significance of this alternative are, I would argue, less so. Gadeken argues that people misread *The Governess* because they use a Lockean framework to judge its values. She contends that "*The Governess* has been read as a fable designed to encourage women's happy acceptance of domestic repression or maternity, part of what Nancy Armstrong calls 'literature devoted to producing the domestic woman.' . . . Such literature promotes the formation of a specifically female domestic realm in contrast to a masculine public realm of politics and business, a realm that is proclaimed as the most important institution of moral formation," and she rejects "those who place *The Governess* within this tradition [to] argue that the text works to repress the girls into domesticity" (228). Her

argument and objections to other critics pose an internal contradiction. While she says that *The Governess* proposes an alternative, female community, she also rejects critics who accuse it of creating a "specifically female domestic space." Gadeken and these critics agree on the nature of the space; they disagree on its valuation. As my work with a wide collection of novels indicates, just because this is alternative space does not mean that it is not encouraging women's acceptance of domestic repression or maternity, or a specifically female domestic realm different and considerably more indirectly connected to the public, commercial realm.

25. Sheila Rowbotham, *Hidden from History: 300 Years of Women's Oppression and the Fight Against It*, 3rd ed. (London: Pluto Press, 1990), 3; Merry E. Weisner, *Women and Gender in Early Modern Europe* (Cambridge: Cambridge University Press, 1993), 66. The transition from midwifery to man-midwifery has been the subject of considerable scholarship. See, for example, Jean Donnison, *Midwives and Medical Men: A History of Inter-Professional Rivalries and Women's Rights* (New York: Schocken Books, 1977), 21–41; Adrian Wilson, *The Making of Man-Midwifery: Childbirth in England, 1660–1770* (Cambridge: Harvard University Press, 1995); Irving Loudon, review of *The Making of Man-Midwifery*, by Adrian Wilson, *Bulletin of the History of Medicine* 70 (1996): 507–15; Bronwyn Croxson, "The Foundation and Evolution of the Middlesex Hospital's Lying-In Service, 1745–86," *Social History of Medicine: The Journal of the Society for the Social History of Medicine* 14 (2002): 27–37; and Lisa Forman Cody, "The Politics of Reproducing: From Midwives' Alternative Public Sphere to the Public Spectacle of Man-Midwifery," *Eighteenth-Century Studies* 32 (Summer 1999): 477–95. As Loudon, Croxson, and Cody point out, traditional theories that it was either the rise of technology (forceps) or the rise of antimidwife misogyny are inadequate to explain the cultural shift. Cody in particular shows that an epistemological shift in notions of public and private adhering less to medicine in general than to man-midwifery and midwifery in particular enabled the dramatic transition, and Croxson describes how the rise of charity hospitals contributed to it.

26. Donnison, *Midwives and Medical Men*, 28; Society for Bettering the Condition and Increasing the Comforts of the Poor, *The Reports of the Society for Bettering the Condition and Increasing the Comforts of the Poor*, vol. 1. (London, York, Bath, Newcastle, Durham, Hull, Salisbury, Exeter, Manchester, Gloucester, 1798), 126–27.

27. Sterne's Midwife and more broadly, women in *Tristram Shandy* reveal a sympathy for women that transcends the chivalry underlying sensibility. Wonkyung Yang and Elizabeth Kraft, for example, describe ways in which throughout his fiction, Sterne values women's experience and perspective. As Martha Bowden puts it, Sterne and Tristram Shandy each "generally affirms the importance of women." According to Bowden, the interconnectedness of the structures of *Tristram Shandy*, especially those involving women, reflect Sterne's view of the interconnectedness of society: "His acknowledgement, doubly stated, in characters and the construction of the work, emphasizes the presence and importance of the women in a text in which they have conventionally been considered marginal." Wonkyung Yang, "Childbirth and Female Midwifery in Laurence Sterne's *Tristram Shandy*," *The Journal of English Language and Literature* 44 (Winter 1998): 789–806; Elizabeth Kraft, "Laurence Sterne and the Ethics of Sexual Difference: Chiasmic Narration and Double Desire," *Christianity and Literature* 51 (Spring 2002): 363–85; Martha Bow-

den, "The Interdependence of Women in *Tristram Shandy*: A Chapter of Eyes, Sausages and Sciatica," *English Language Notes* 31 (June 1994): 46.

28. Elizabeth Inchbald, *A Simple Story*, ed. J. M. S. Tompkins (1791; repr., Oxford: Oxford University Press, 1988), 6.

29. Charlotte Smith, *The Old Manor House*, ed. Jacqueline M. Labbe (1793; repr., Toronto: Broadview Press Ltd., 2002), 402–3, 414. Popular illustrations of elderly women almost always depict them as long nosed and long chinned, with narrow faces, sunken eyes, and thinning hair. See, for example, the figures in "Courtship for Money / Faisant Amour pour L'Argent" (1771) by Philip Dawe, or an untitled cartoon from 1776 by W. Humphrey. Reeve's Mrs. Gilson is essentially the textual rendition of this visual type: "an old woman with a sharp pair of eyes, and her nose and chin were like nut crackers." Philip Dawe, "Courtship for Money / Faisant Amour pour L'Argent," in "The Satire of Marriage," Print Collection of the New York Public Library and the British Museum Collection of Prints and Drawings, 1689–1790 (1771); W. Humphrey, Untitled cartoon, in "The Satire of Marriage," Print Collection of the New York Public Library and the British Museum Collection of Prints and Drawings, 1689–1790 (1776); Reeve, *School for Widows*, 1:263–64.

30. Jeanine M. Casler, preface to *School for Widows*, by Clara Reeve, ed. Jeanine M. Casler (1791; repr., Newark: University of Delaware Press, 2003): 16–18. Other ideas in *School for Widows*, particularly those pertaining to marriage and widowhood, are consistent with mainstream thought and reveal that Reeve was far less than a radical social theorist. While she advocated choosing one's spouse carefully, for example, Reeve also advocated making the most of a bad marriage, as Mrs. Darnford and Mrs. Strictland, who is discussed in chapter 2, do. (Part of Mrs. Gilson's work, it should be noted, is helping Mrs. Strictland find a way to achieve détente with her irascible husband). Similarly, and like many others in her society, Reeve also adamantly opposed remarriage for widows under any circumstances.

31. Mellor sees this alternative tradition as a branch of Romanticism rather than of sensibility, and suggests that it not only offered a viable ideology for women but also ultimately triumphed, since its celebration of the novel over other genres, especially poetry, has certainly come to pass. Viewed as a rejection or alternative to the patriarchal Romanticism of writers like Coleridge, William Wordsworth, or Keats, female Romanticism appears as a rare success for women. Seen as an adaptation of sensibility and a culmination of ideas on gender and economics that were developing through the eighteenth century, however, female Romanticism seems a more ambiguous achievement. Anne K. Mellor, "A Criticism of Their Own: Romantic Women Literary Critics," in *Questioning Romanticism*, ed. John Beer (Baltimore: The Johns Hopkins University Press, 1995), 39, 31, 33, 47–48; Mellor's emphasis.

32. A related instance of this shift is Mrs. Lyne from Scott's *Sir George Ellison*. Mrs. Lyne's work life existed only as long as her married life lasted: she and her husband were caretakers to the mentally incompetent Sir William Ellison. Scott has Sir William and Mr. Lyne die at the same time so Mrs. Lyne will not be a working widow, and has Sir George Ellison reward Mrs. Lyne with an annuity so lavish that she can retire to a life of leisure and present her life's savings to her daughter as a wedding gift (190). While Mrs. Lyne is never, technically, a working widow, she is evidence of a preference that work lead to women's leisure, that women work in

tandem with their husbands if at all, and that widows not work for their own subsistence.

33. Earle, *Making the English Middle Class*, 167.

CHAPTER 4. POOR, PATHETIC, AND POSITIVE

1. Daniel Defoe, *Robinson Crusoe*, ed. Michael Shinagel (1719; repr., New York: W. W. Norton & Co., 1975). Another of Defoe's widows who often encountered poverty, the more famous and problematic Moll Flanders, will appear in chapter 5.

2. As C. P. Hill explains, prior to 1696, when the Bank of England was founded, banking was primarily a private and personal arrangement between someone with a good safe, like a goldsmith, and someone with money who needed it stored. In exchange for holding the money, the goldsmith was allowed to make loans, collect interest, and so on with the funds he or she was holding. In this sense, Crusoe's "good ancient widow" really is serving as a bank. Banking as it is currently practiced did not take hold until 1716, when private banks began to appear. C. P. Hill, *British Economic and Social History, 1700–1982*, 5th ed. (London: Edward Arnold Ltd., 1985), 140–41.

3. Toni Bowers, *The Politics of Motherhood: British Writing and Culture, 1680–1760* (Cambridge: Cambridge University Press, 1996), 4–5; Amy Louise Erickson, introduction to *Working Life of Women in the Seventeenth Century*, by Alice Clark, 3rd ed. (New York: Routledge, 1992); Society for Bettering the Condition and Increasing the Comforts of the Poor, *The Reports of the Society for Bettering the Condition and Increasing the Comforts of the Poor*, vol. I. (London, York, Bath, Newcastle, Durham, Hull, Salisbury, Exeter, Manchester, Gloucester, 1798), 167.

4. Donna T. Andrew, *Philanthropy and Police: London Charity in the Eighteenth Century* (Princeton: Princeton University Press, 1989); Mona Scheuermann, *In Praise of Poverty: Hannah More Counters Thomas Paine and the Radical Threat* (Lexington: The University Press of Kentucky, 2002), 21–22.

5. Scheuermann, *Hannah More*, 34; Paul Langford, *A Polite and Commercial People: England, 1727–1783* (Oxford: Clarendon Press, 1989), 6.

6. Ann Jessie Van Sant, *Eighteenth-Century Sensibility and the Novel: The Senses in Social Context* (Cambridge: Cambridge University Press, 1993); Markman Ellis, *The Politics of Sensibility: Race, Gender and Commerce in the Sentimental Novel* (Cambridge: Cambridge University Press, 1996); John Mullan, *Sentiment and Sociability: The Language of Feeling in the Eighteenth Century* (Oxford: Oxford University Press, 1988); Gillian Skinner, *Sensibility and Economics in the Novel, 1740–1800: The Price of a Tear* (New York: St. Martin's Press, Inc., 1999).

7. Charlotte Smith, *Emmeline, the Orphan of the Castle* (London: T. Cadell, 1788), 3:128, 3:129.

8. Charlotte Smith, *The Old Manor House*, ed. Jacqueline M. Labbe (1793; repr., Toronto: Broadview Press Ltd., 2002), 365–66; Eliza Fenwick, *Secresy; or, The Ruin on the Rock*, ed. Isobel Grundy, 2nd ed. (1795; repr., Toronto: Broadview Press Ltd., 1998), 94–89, 109

9. Laurence Sterne, "A Sentimental Journey" in *"A Sentimental Journey through France and Italy By Mr. Yorick" with "The Journal to Eliza" and "A Political Romance,"* ed. Ian Jack (1768; repr., New York: Oxford University Press, 1984), 113; Jeffrey L. Duncan, "The Rural Ideal in Eighteenth-Century Fiction" in *The Country Myth: Mo-*

tifs in the British Novel from Defoe to Smollett, ed. H. George Hahn (New York: Peter Lang, Inc., 1990), 265–66; Tobias Smollett, *The Expedition of Humphry Clinker*, ed. Angus Ross (1771; repr., New York: Penguin Books, 1985), 33; Oliver Goldsmith, *The Vicar of Wakefield* (1762; repr., New York: Pocket Books, Inc., 1957), 5.

10. For a more extensive discussion of Smollett's relationship with sensibility as demonstrated by his treatment of widows in the novel, and for a more extensive discussion of the nature of Sterne's sensibility, see chapter 2. The debate about the nature of Goldsmith's sentiment in *The Vicar of Wakefield* is thoroughly outlined by George E. Haggerty, "Satire and Sentiment in *The Vicar of Wakefield*," *The Eighteenth Century* 32, no. 1 (Spring 1991): 25–38. Although it would be satisfying from a poststructuralist, twenty-first century view to view Goldsmith's sensibility as ironic, I do not see it this way. He may be interrogating aspects of sensibility, including its use of fiction, in *The Vicar of Wakefield*, but I see sufficient overlap in the ideology articulated—and the conventions used to articulate it—in that novel with other texts, including "The Deserted Village," to consider *The Vicar of Wakefield* a sentimental novel.

11. Mary Robinson, *The Widow, or a Picture of Modern Times. A Novel, in a Series of Letters, in Two Volumes* (London: Hookham and Carpenter, 1794), 2:5, 2:6.

12. Mary Robinson is usually considered a radical rather than a sentimental novelist. This classification is generally based on a later novel, *Walsingham* (1797), in which she uses a cross-dressing protagonist to comment on the aristocracy, patriarchy, and their tools, including the system of education for women and primogeniture. Read against *Walsingham* on the basis of subject matter and plot, *The Widow* is conventionally sentimental. Both novels, however, use the overwrought style of late-century sensibility. Robinson understood popular trends well and was very familiar with sentiment's conventions: as Julie Shaffer points out, she used them extensively in her own memoir. Considered as an effort to write what would sell, the sentimental novel *The Widow* may not be radical, but it is typically Robinsonian. Anne K. Mellor, "A Criticism of Their Own: Romantic Women Literary Critics," in *Questioning Romanticism*, ed. John Beer (Baltimore: The Johns Hopkins University Press, 1995): 29–48; Julie Shaffer, introduction to *Walsingham; or, Pupil of Nature* by Mary Robinson (1797; repr., Toronto: Broadview Press Ltd., 2003), 8.

13. Margaret Lee, *Clara Lennox; or, The Distressed Widow. A Novel. Founded in Facts. Interspersed with an Historical Description of the Isle of Man* (London: J. Adlard, 1797), 1:136, 1:137. Technically speaking, Lady Angelina is not impoverished. She is, however, entirely dependent on men to protect her and her child, since she is a widowed mother in a war zone. While she might have access to her own financial resources under other circumstances, she is utterly destitute at this particular moment.

14. Tobias Smollett, *The Adventures of Peregrine Pickle, in which are included Memoirs of a Lady of Quality*, ed. James L. Clifford (1751; repr., London: Oxford University Press, 1964), 430–31.

15. M. Ellis, *Politics of Sensibility*, 135.

16. Sarah Scott, *The History of Cornelia* (1750; repr., London: Routledge / Thoemmes Press, 1992), 210–11.

17. As Smith's biographer Loraine Fletcher contends, Smith is a "radical satirist who is no leveller, and finds it hard to envisage the leaders of a future society." Certainly Smith's portrayal of widows and through them, attitudes toward forms of

wealth and social stability, suggests that she is critical but not revolutionary. Mellor, "A Criticism of Their Own," 30; Loraine Fletcher, *Charlotte Smith: A Critical Biography* (New York: St. Martin's Press, 1998), 174.

18. Sarah Scott, *A Description of Millenium Hall* (1762; repr., New York: Viking Penguin, 1986), 70, 149; Clara Reeve, *The School for Widows. A Novel. In Two Volumes* (Dublin: William Porter, 1791), 2:96; Smollett, *Humphry Clinker*, 220–21; Scott, *History of Cornelia*, 48; Smith, *The Old Manor House*, 448, 521–22. For a more extensive discussion of Madame Miteau, see chapter 3.

19. Reeve, *School for Widows*, 1:219–20; Henry Fielding, *The History of Tom Jones*, ed. R. P. C. Mutter (1747; repr., New York: Penguin Books, 1985); Smith, *The Old Manor House*, 521–22.

20. Sarah Fielding, *The History of the Countess of Dellwyn. In Two Volumes* (1759; repr., New York: Garland Publishing, Inc., 1974), 87.

21. Frances Griffith, *The Delicate Distress*, ed. Cynthia Booth Ricciardi and Susan Staves (1769; repr., Lexington: The University Press of Kentucky, 1997), 1:66, 1:67.

22. Bowers, *Politics of Motherhood*, 16.

23. Frances Burney, *Evelina* (1778; repr., New York: W. W. Norton & Co., 1965), 294.

24. Elizabeth Bergen Brophy, *Women's Lives and the Eighteenth-Century English Novel* (Tampa: University of South Florida Press, 1991), 231.

25. Scheuermann, *Hannah More*, 26; Maximilian Novak, *Daniel Defoe, Master of Fictions: His Life and Ideas* (Oxford: Oxford University Press, 2001), 247, 249.

26. Gary Gautier, "Slavery and the Fashioning of Race in *Oroonoko, Robinson Crusoe*, and Equiano's *Life*," *The Eighteenth Century* 42 (2001): 166; George Boulukos, "The Grateful Slave: A History of Slave Plantation Reform in the British Novel, 1750–1780," in *The Eighteenth Century Novel*, vol. 1, ed. Susan Spencer (New York: AMS Press, Inc., 2001).

27. Van Sant, *Eighteenth-Century Sensibility*, 19, 21; Van Sant's emphases.

CHAPTER 5. SHE PUT MERCURY INTO THE MORNING MILK

1. Records of the Assizes, September 2–3, 1784, ASSI 45:31, 2, Public Records Office.

2. Records of the Assizes, March 17, 1742, ASSI 45:22, 2, PRO; August 6, October 30, 1745, ASSI 45:23, 2, PRO. Although Ann Pearson and several of her neighbors and relatives drank the poisoned beer, no one died.

3. Peter King, "Female Offenders, Work and Life-Cycle Change in Late-Eighteenth-Century London," *Continuity and Change* 11 (1996): 69.

4. Lincoln Faller, *Crime and Defoe: A New Kind of Writing* (Cambridge: Cambridge University Press, 1993), 7.

5. J. M. Beattie, "The Criminality of Women in Eighteenth-Century England," *Journal of Social History* 8, no. 4 (1975): 102–7.

6. Tobias Smollett, *The Adventures of Ferdinand Count Fathom*, ed. Jerry C. Beasley and O. M. Brack, Jr. (1753; repr., Athens: University of Georgia Press, 1988), 16, 12, 267–69.

7. Eliza Haywood, *The History of Miss Betsy Thoughtless*, ed. Christine Blouch (1751; repr., Toronto: Broadview Press Ltd., 1998), 260–64.

8. Elizabeth Griffith, *The Delicate Distress*, ed. Cynthia Booth Ricciardi and Susan Staves (1769; repr., Lexington: The University Press of Kentucky, 1997), 1:22.

9. Frances Sheridan, *Memoirs of Miss Sidney Bidulph* (1769; repr., New York: Pandora Press, 1987), 221.

10. William Wycherley, *The Plain Dealer*, ed. James L. Smith (New York: W. W. Norton & Co., 1979); Aphra Behn and Thomas Betterton, "The Counterfeit Bridgeroom: or the Defeated Widow," in *English Dramas* (London: L. Curtiss, 1677).

11. Peter Linebaugh, *The London Hanged: Crime and Civil Society in the Eighteenth Century* (Cambridge: Cambridge University Press, 1992), xx–xxi; see also Frank McLynn, *Crime and Punishment in Eighteenth-Century England* (New York: Routledge, 1989), xi–xii.

12. Sarah Fielding, *The History of Ophelia* (1760; repr., New York: Garland Publishing, Inc., 1974), 2:109–12.

13. "The Temple Rakes, or Innocence Preserved," in *The Finish'd Rake; or, Gallantry in Perfection (Anonymous); The Secret History of Mama Oello, Princess Royal of Peru (Anonymous); The Masterpiece of Imposture (Elizabeth Harding); The Temple Rakes, or Innocence Preserved (Anonymous)*, ed. Josephine Grieder (1735; repr., New York: Garland Publishing, Inc., 1973), 24.

14. The story of Mrs. Villiard and Mr. D——z, the rich Jewish merchant, appears almost exactly duplicated in a later novel, Sarah Fielding's *Adventures of David Simple* (1744). In Fielding's version, the Jewish merchant has no name and approaches a male jeweler with two daughters to ask for one of the girls in exchange for a huge sum of money. The merchant explains that if he likes her, he will marry her later. After some consideration, the mercenary father insists that the merchant marry the daughter, but announces that she will convert to Judaism, which she does being obedient, areligious, and avaricious herself. Fielding's parental figure is certainly as appalling as that of the anonymous author from ten years before, since the father forces a religious conversion and marriage on his daughter for the sake of money and position, but Fielding's version also diffuses some small degree of villainy. There are no rapes planned or attempted, to begin with. The Jewish merchant, furthermore, hesitates to sue for marriage because of the religious disparity, not because of another wife, and willingly marries the girl after she agrees to convert. While his initial impulses are hardly strictly virtuous, *David Simple* is ultimately kinder to its Jewish character and gentler all around than *The Temple Rakes*. Sarah Fielding, *The Adventures of David Simple: Containing An Account of His Travels Through the Cities of London and Westminster, In the Search of A Real Friend. By a Lady. In Two Volumes*, 2nd ed. (London: A. Millar, 1744).

15. Daniel Defoe, *Moll Flanders* (1722; repr., New York: Penguin Classics, 1989), 137, 139.

16. Moll's mother is not a widow until after her son, Moll's husband, is born, but she eventually does become one.

17. Toni Bowers, *The Politics of Motherhood: British Writing and Culture, 1680–1760* (Cambridge: Cambridge University Press, 1996), 158–59.

18. Frances Burney, *Evelina* (1778; repr., New York: W. W. Norton & Co., 1965), 357; Burney's emphases; Samuel Richardson, *Pamela; or, Virtue Rewarded*, ed. Peter Sabor (1740; repr., New York: Penguin Books, 1988), 498.

19. McLynn, *Crime and Punishment*, 110.

20. Ruth Perry, "Colonizing the Breast: Sexuality and Maternity in Eighteenth-Century England," *Eighteenth-Century Life* 16 (February 1992): 185–215; Felicity Nussbaum, "'Savage' Mothers: Narratives of Maternity in the Mid-Eighteenth Century," *Eighteenth-Century Life* 16 (February 1992): 165–84; Laura Brown, *Ends of Empire: Women and Ideology in Eighteenth-Century English Literature* (Ithaca, NY: Cornell University Press, 1993); Michael McKeon, "Historicizing Patriarchy: The Emergence of Gender Difference in England, 1660–1760," *Eighteenth-Century Studies* 28 (1995): 295–322.

21. Clara Reeve, *The School for Widows. A Novel. In Two Volumes* (Dublin: William Porter, 1791), 2:212.

22. Sarah Scott, *The History of Cornelia* (1750; repr., London: Routledge / Thoemmes Press, 1992), 38–44; Mary Davys, "The Accomplish'd Rake, or Modern Fine Gentleman," in *The Reform'd Coquet; or Memoirs of Amoranda, Familiar Letters Betwixt a Gentleman and a Lady, and The Accomplish'd Rake, or Modern Fine Gentleman*, ed. Martha F. Bowden (1727; repr., Lexington: The University Press of Kentucky, 1999), 172; Kathryn Kirkpatrick, "Sermons and Strictures: Conduct-Book Propriety and Property Relations in Late Eighteenth-Century England," in *History, Gender and Eighteenth-Century Literature*, ed. Beth Fowkes Tobin (Athens: University of Georgia Press, 1994); McLynn, *Crime and Punishment*, 129–31.

23. Eliza Haywood, "Fantomina: or, Love in a Maze," in *Popular Fiction by Women, 1660–1730: An Anthology*, ed. Paula R. Backscheider and John J. Richetti (1725; repr., Oxford: Clarendon Press, 1996).

24. Sarah Fielding, *The History of the Countess of Dellwyn. In Two Volumes* (1759; repr., New York: Garland Publishing, Inc., 1974), 228–76.

25. Eliza Haywood's Lady Mellasin from *The History of Miss Betsy Thoughtless* (1751) also takes refuge in Jamaica, since its "inhabitants thought of little else, but how to divert themselves in the best manner the country afforded; and that they were not too strict in their notions, either as to honour or religion;—that reputation was a thing little regarded among them;—so that in case the occasion that had brought her thither should happen to be discovered, she would not find herself in the less estimation" (523). Although Lady Mellasin then vanishes from the narrative, the idea that she can hide and if discovered, remain respectable, suggests continuing transgression. She will always be wicked, always be criminal, and even if she is more comfortable wherever she is, her character, perhaps her nature, will remain unchanged.

26. Paul Langford, *A Polite and Commercial People: England, 1727–1783* (Oxford: Clarendon Press, 1989), 65–66; Ronald Paulson, *The "Modern Moral Subject," 1697–1732*, vol. 1, *Hogarth* (New Brunswick, NJ: Rutgers University Press, 1991), 279; Jenny Uglow, *Hogarth: A Life and a World* (London: Faber and Faber, 1997), 195.

27. Terry Castle, "The Culture of Travesty: Sexuality and Masquerade in Eighteenth-Century England," in *Sexual Underworlds of the Enlightenment*, ed. G. S. Rousseau and Roy Porter (Chapel Hill: The University of North Carolina Press, 1988), 157.

28. Langford, *Polite and Commercial People*, 66, 169.

29. Catherine Craft-Fairchild, *Masquerade and Gender: Disguise and Female Identity in Eighteenth-Century Fictions by Women* (University Park: The Pennsylvania State University Press, 1993). For a more extensive discussion of the performativity of

gender, see Judith Butler's *Bodies That Matter: On the Discursive Limits of "Sex"* (New York: Routledge, 1993) and *Gender Trouble* (New York: Routledge, 1990). According to this theory of gender, masculinity and femininity are constructs, identities assembled from a variety of signs assigned their gender by any given society. Gender is thereby different from sex, which is biological but no more a determinant of behavior or clothing choice than eye color. If gender is a construct, that is, an agreed-upon set of signals to indicate maleness or femaleness, then it can be manipulated by any member of the society—a man can wear a dress, for example, or a woman wear trousers—to call into question that person's identity and the social norms that depend on clear-cut gender identities.

30. Davys's cross-dressing woman in *The Accomplish'd Rake* is another example of this ambivalence. Although she dresses as a man to pick out a likely man at a masquerade, then reveals herself and sleeps with him to get herself pregnant so she can produce an heir for her husband, her behavior is ameliorated by her awareness of the dishonor of her act and by her laudable concern for the estate. Furthermore, she spends the rest of the novel suffering for this bad decision: she bears a daughter, not a son; her husband dies shortly after; she wishes to become "honest" and marry Sir John since he has fathered her child but he rejects her, and cruelly; she and her child are nearly killed by illness; and she has the misfortune to see Sir John pursuing her beloved sister (178–79, 186, 204–5). Significantly, the nameless woman's behavior is not a referendum on widows, however: her initial transgressions take place when she is married, not a widow. Her big sin during her widowhood is resuming male attire and proposing to Sir John, although again, she has commendable motives. Davys actually uses her widowhood to reinforce her virtues: to show her suffering and atonement, and to underscore that she is an essentially honest woman and a profoundly loving mother and sister (186, 204–5). Furthermore, as Martha F. Bowden points out, the depiction of maternal love is a rarity in Davys novels, perhaps because Davys herself lost two daughters in their infancy and found this topic too painful to write about. That the nameless widow's share of virtues prominently includes a scene of maternal love and for a daughter, especially in a novel where the other significant widow, Lady Galliard, is so unmaternal, suggests an ambivalent attitude toward the cross-dressing and widowhood. Martha F. Bowden, introduction to *The Accomplish'd Rake* by Mary Davys, in *The Reform'd Coquet; or Memoirs of Amoranda, Familiar Letters Betwixt a Gentleman and a Lady, and The Accomplish'd Rake, or Modern Fine Gentleman*, ed. Martha F. Bowden (Lexington: University Press of Kentucky, 1999), xlii.

31. Faller, *Crime and Defoe*, 139, 141.

32. Mary Poovey, *The Proper Lady and the Woman Writer: Ideology as Style in the Works of Mary Wollstonecraft, Mary Shelley, and Jane Austen* (Chicago: The University of Chicago Press, 1984), 19.

CHAPTER 6. A STATE OF ALTERATION

1. Jane Austen, "Lady Susan," in *Northanger Abbey, Lady Susan, The Watsons, and Sanditon*, ed. John Davie (New York: Oxford University Press, 1998), 249.

2. Terry Castle, introduction to *Northanger Abbey, Lady Susan, The Watsons, and Sanditon*, by Jane Austen, ed. John Davie (New York: Oxford University Press, 1998), xxvi–xxvii.

3. Two recent biographers, for example, offer very different theories. David Nokes contends that Austen gave up revising *Lady Susan* because it was not and never would be "substantial enough" to be "refashioned into a full-length novel." Furthermore, he argues, "Turning it into a novel would require investing this brisk social satire with *humanity*, and that was, currently, a commodity in short supply with her" after the death of her father. Claire Tomalin, on the other hand, speculates that "Austen may have frightened herself" with edgy satire. David Nokes, *Jane Austen: A Life* (New York: Farrar, Straus, & Giroux, Inc., 1997), 282, Nokes's emphasis; Claire Tomalin, *Jane Austen: A Life* (New York: Vintage Books, 1997), 84.

4. Jane Austen, *Sense and Sensibility*, ed. Ros Ballaster (1811; repr., New York: Penguin Books, 1995; hereafter cited as *S and S*); *Mansfield Park*, ed. Tony Tanner (1814; repr., New York: Penguin Books, 1985; hereafter cited as *MP*); *Pride and Prejudice*, ed. Donald Gray, 3rd ed. (repr., New York: W. W. Norton & Co., 2001; hereafter cited as *P and P*); *Persuasion*, ed. Patricia Meyer Spacks (1817; repr., New York: W. W. Norton & Co., 1995); *Northanger Abbey*, ed. Marilyn Butler (1817; repr., New York: Penguin Books, 1995; hereafter cited as *NA*); *Emma*, ed. Stephen M. Parrish, 3rd ed. (1815; repr., New York: W. W. Norton & Co., 2000).

5. Margaret Kirkham, *Jane Austen, Feminism and Fiction* (New Jersey: Barnes & Noble Books, 1983); Mary Poovey, *The Proper Lady and the Woman Writer: Ideology as Style in the Works of Mary Wollstonecraft, Mary Shelley, and Jane Austen* (Chicago: The University of Chicago Press, 1984); Claudia Johnson, *Jane Austen: Women, Politics, and the Novel* (Chicago: The University of Chicago Press, 1988); Marilyn Butler, *Jane Austen and the War of Ideas* (1975; repr., Oxford: Clarendon Press, 1987); David Aers, "Community and Morality: Towards Reading Jane Austen," in *Romanticism and Ideology: Studies in English Writing, 1750–1830*, ed. David Aers, Jonathan Cook, and David Punter (Boston: Routledge & Keegan Paul, 1987); Edward Said, *Culture and Imperialism* (New York: Alfred A. Knopf, 1993); Paul A. Cantor, "A Class Act: *Persuasion* and the Lingering Death of the Aristocracy," *Philosophy and Literature* 23 (1999): 134; Alistair M. Duckworth, *The Improvement of the Estate: A Study of Jane Austen's Novels* (Baltimore: The Johns Hopkins University Press, 1994), 84; Susan Fraiman, "Jane Austen and Edward Said: Gender, Culture, and Imperialism," *Critical Inquiry* 21 (Summer 1995): 809; John A. Dussinger, *In the Pride of the Moment: Encounters in Jane Austen's World* (Columbus: The Ohio State University Press, 1990), 85.

6. Michael Steffes makes his case for Austen's possible abolitionist leanings in a reading of her historical context and *Mansfield Park*, although the explicit as well as implicit allusions to slavery appear in many of the other novels, from Mrs. Bennet's commodification of women and men in *Pride and Prejudice* to Jane Fairfax's allusion to the "trade" in governesses in *Emma* to the recuperation of estates in the West Indies held by *Persuasion*'s Mrs. Smith. Michael Steffes, "Slavery and *Mansfield Park*: The Historical and Biographical Context," *English Language Notes* 34 (December 1996): 23–41; David Nokes, *Jane Austen: A Life*, Tomalin, *Jane Austen: A Life*, 85.

7. Leonore Davidoff and Catherine Hall, *Family Fortunes: Men and Women of the English Middle Class, 1780–1850* (Chicago: The University of Chicago Press, 1987), 152–56; Barbara M. Benedict, "Jane Austen and the Culture of Circulating Libraries: The Construction of Female Literacy," in *Revising Women: Eighteenth-Century*

"Women's Fiction" and Social Engagement, ed. Paula Backscheider (Baltimore: The Johns Hopkins University Press, 2000); Amanda Vickery, *The Gentleman's Daughter: Women's Lives in Georgian England* (New Haven: Yale University Press, 1998).

8. Davidoff and Hall, *Family Fortunes;* Maxine Berg, *The Age of Manufactures, 1700–1829: Industry, Innovation and Work in Britain,* 2nd ed. (New York: Routledge, 1994); Bridget Hill, *Women, Work, and Sexual Politics in Eighteenth-Century England* (New York: Basil Blackwell Inc., 1989).

9. Benedict, "Jane Austen," 148; Maaja A. Stewart, *Domestic Realities and Imperial Fictions: Jane Austen's Novels in Eighteenth-Century Contexts* (Athens: University of Georgia Press, 1993), ix, 3.

10. On these issues, Lady Catherine stands in direct contrast to negative characters such as John Dashwood in *Sense and Sensibility,* who is more interested in money than in family, neglects his unmarried relatives, and spends his money tearing up his estate rather than encouraging it to grow, such as enclosing Norland Commons and cutting down all the "old walnut trees" (*S and S,* 190–91). Austen's criticism of selfish landowners was based not in a rational and progressive framework, but a moral and traditional framework (Duckworth, *Improvement of the Estate,* xvi), and John Dashwood's villainy is his using his place in the order for his own pleasure and the pleasure of a wife who certainly espouses the worst of commercialism. Lady Catherine is nothing like him in this regard.

11. Sarah Scott, *A Description of Millenium Hall* (1762; repr., New York: Viking Penguin, 1986), 15.

12. Eileen Cleere, "Reinvesting Nieces: *Mansfield Park* and the Economics of Endogamy," *Novel* 28 (Winter 1995): 119, 121.

13. Vickery's female subjects hail from families "headed," as she puts it, "by lesser landed gentlemen, attornies, doctors, clerics, merchants, and manufacturers." Her sample is one example that the ideological mixing expressed in Austen's widows was a historical reality, as real people mixed socioeconomic groups through marriage. Vickery, *Gentleman's Daughter,* 1.

14. *Emma,* VHS, directed by Diarmuid Lawrence (1997; A&E Home Video, 1998); *Emma,* VHS, directed by Douglas McGrath (1996; Miramax Home Entertainment, 1997).

15. Cynthia Curran, "Private Women, Public Needs: Middle-Class Widows in Victorian England," *Albion* 25, no. 2 (Summer 1993): 227–28; *Essex Pauper Letters,* ed. Thomas Sokoll, Records of Social and Economic History, New Series 30 (Oxford: Oxford University Press, 2001), 542.

16. Stewart, *Jane Austen's Novels,* 17.

17. Duckworth, *Improvement of the Estate,* 3. Curran points out that middle-class widows, whether of the upper or lower end of the middle class, only rarely became dependent on their families ("Private Women, Public Needs," 227). In eliminating even family as well as health from Mrs. Smith's resources, Austen demonstrates how dependent on fundamentals widows, even those accustomed to more comfortable married lives, become upon their bereavement.

18. Benedict, "Jane Austen," 147, 148.

19. Dussinger, *Jane Austen's World,* 116.

20. Fraiman, "Jane Austen and Edward Said," 814.

21. In Lady Russell's attitudes toward what to do with Anne, whom she dearly loves, Austen reveals how the older methods of circulating wealth, such as the use

of women for cementing family lines and estates, were a form of commerce very like the sale of women to which Jane Fairfax refers in *Emma*, and to which *Mansfield Park* refers with its critique of Sir Thomas's desire to sell off, through marriage, Fanny Price. As Jane explains, "There are places in town, offices, where inquiry would soon produce something—Offices for the sale—not quite of human flesh—but of human intellect." When Mrs. Elton replies, "Oh! my dear, human flesh! You quite shock me; if you mean a fling at the slave-trade, I assure you Mr. Suckling was always rather a friend to the abolition," Austen elaborates: "I did not mean, I was not thinking of the slave trade,' replied Jane; 'governess-trade, I assure you, was all that I had in view; widely different certainly as to the guilt of those who carry it on; but as to the greater misery of the victims, I do not know where it lies.'" (*Emma*, 196). For a more extensive discussion of Sir Thomas, Fanny, and the commodification of women, see Eileen Cleere, "Reinvesting Nieces: *Mansfield Park* and the Economics of Endogamy." As Cleere puts it, "With the 'improvement' of his property at stake, Sir Thomas's concern about his slaves and their bodies generates a new level of avuncular interest in his niece and a change of heart that seems like moral regeneration until its economic implications are revealed. Colonialism's economic lessons are introduced within the structure of the Bertram family, and Sir Thomas's East Indian interests transfer themselves to the East room of Mansfield Park" and Fanny Price (123).

APPENDIX

1. Ann Jessie Van Sant, *Eighteenth-Century Sensibility and the Novel: The Senses in Social Context* (Cambridge: Cambridge University Press, 1993), 26–27.

2. It is worth keeping in mind as well that England had nowhere near the number of large cities that it has today. In the early eighteenth century, Manchester had nine thousand people; in midcentury, Glasgow had twenty-three thousand. In 1770, even after the midcentury population boom, Norwich only had barely thirty thousand people and Bristol, Exeter, York, Newcastle, Colchester, and Yarmouth had ten thousand. According to Peter Mathias, as late as 1800, one-third of the English population was still employed in agriculture. That meant that even for widows who lived in what might be called an urban environment, that urban environment could still be quite small in comparison with London, which had seven hundred thousand inhabitants in 1770, or with the populations of Manchester or Bristol today. C. P. Hill, *British Economic and Social History, 1700–1982*, 5th ed. (London: Edward Arnold Ltd., 1985), 4; Roy Porter, *English Society in the Eighteenth Century*, rev. ed. (New York: Penguin Books, 1990), 39; Peter Mathias, *The First Industrial Nation: An Economic History of Britain, 1700–1914*, 2nd ed. (London and New York: Methuen, 1983), 59–60.

3. Society for Bettering the Condition and Increasing the Comforts of the Poor, *The Reports of the Society for Bettering the Condition and Increasing the Comforts of the Poor*, vol. 1 (London, York, Bath, Newcastle, Durham, Hull, Salisbury, Exeter, Manchester, Gloucester, 1798).

4. *The Essex Pauper Letters,* ed. Thomas Sokoll (Oxford: Oxford University Press, 2001); Stanley A. Seligman, "The Royal Maternity Charity: The First Hundred Years," *Medical History* 24 (1990): 403–4, 408.

5. Minutes of the Meeting of the Trustees for Westley's Charity, October 1, 1806, Papers for Westley's Charity, A / AMV 2.2, Somerset Record Office. Hereafter cited as Westley A / AMV.

6. Records of the Yerbury Almshouse, March, 1768, 2074.26:46; Records of the Yerbury Almshouse, August, 1800, 2074.27:67, Wiltshire and Swindon Record Office. Hereafter cited as Yerbury 2074.

7. Flexibility of disbursement depended on the attitude of an organization's managers as well as on their managerial skills. Generally speaking, there was not much leeway for particular circumstance in the provincial organizations, which appear to have been run with little flexibility and considerable haphazardness. The occasional special case would receive extra funds from other organizations, however, such as the Society in London. On rare occasions, the managers granted poor widows an extra £5, such as Margaret Towers received in 1753. The daughters of "the late Rev. Mr. Cooper" also received £10 every year from 1739 to 1766, because they were "Deaf and Dumb" and could not look after themselves. When they turned "Lame" in 1767, they received £15 until one died in 1774, after which the surviving daughter received £10 during the rest of her lifetime. On December 1, 1785, the Managers' Committee granted destitute, seventy-eight-year-old Sarah Maurice the annual aid package £6.6 for herself and an extra £10 to support her son, who was a "Lunatick and Dependent." Minutes of the managers meeting for the Society for the Relief of Necessitous Widows and Children of Protestant Dissenting Ministers, April 6, 1796, OD 2, 3, 4, Dr. Williams's Library. Hereafter cited as OD.

8. W. A. Speck points out that tips to servants by guests of the household, known as "vails," became so high by the middle of the eighteenth century that people hesitated to visit large households because of the great expense of tipping the servants. Starting about 1760, servants' wages were raised to relieve visitors of the need to tip the help by compensating for the loss of vails. W. A. Speck, *Stability and Strife: England, 1714–1760* (Cambridge: Harvard University Press, 1977), 58.

9. Schedule of Uses of the Wolborough Feoffees and Widows' Charity, March 10, 1676, Courtenay 7:2, Courtenay Papers, Devon Record Office. Hereafter cited as Courtenay.

10. It should be noted that some charitable efforts did encourage self-sufficiency on the part of the poor, but these appear to be efforts aimed at children, men, or families. *The Reports of the Society for Bettering the Condition and Increasing the Comforts of the Poor* list several plans for enabling farmers to acquire pigs or cows, or for training poor children to weave or spin. Efforts aimed solely at women, such as lending out linens for childbirth, maintained a woman's position in dependence.

11. Tim Hitchcock, Peter King, and Pamela Sharpe, "Introduction: Chronicling Poverty—The Voices and Strategies of the English Poor, 1640–1840," in *Chronicling Poverty —The Voices and Strategies of the English Poor, 1640–1840*, ed. Tim Hitchcock, Peter King, and Pamela Sharpe (New York: St. Martin's Press, 1997), 11–13; Tim Hitchcock, "'Unlawfully begotten on her body': Illegitimacy and the Parish Poor in St Luke's Chelsea," in *Chronicling Poverty—The Voices and Strategies of the English Poor, 1640–1840*, ed. Tim Hitchcock, Peter King, and Pamela Sharpe (New York: St. Martin's Press, 1997).

Bibliography

Aers, David. "Community and Morality: Towards Reading Jane Austen." In *Romanticism and Ideology: Studies in English Writing, 1750–1830*, edited by David Aers, Jonathan Cook, and David Punter, 117–36. Boston: Routledge & Keegan Paul, 1987.

Andrew, Donna T. *Philanthropy and Police: London Charity in the Eighteenth Century.* Princeton: Princeton University Press, 1989.

Armstrong, Nancy. *Desire and Domestic Fiction: A Political History of the Novel.* New York: Oxford University Press, 1987.

Assizes Papers. ASSI 5, 21, 25, 45. United Kingdom. Public Records Office, London, England.

Aubin, Penelope. "The Adventures of the Count de Vinevil And his Family." In *Popular Fiction by Women, 1660–1730: An Anthology,* edited by Paula R. Backscheider and John J. Richetti, 110–51. 1721. Reprint, Oxford: Clarendon Press, 1996.

Austen, Jane. *Emma.* Edited by Stephen M. Parrish. 3rd ed. 1815. Reprint, New York: W. W. Norton & Co., 2000.

———. "Lady Susan." In *Northanger Abbey, Lady Susan, The Watsons, and Sanditon,* edited by John Davie, 207–72. New York: Oxford University Press, 1998.

———. *Mansfield Park.* Edited by Tony Tanner. 1814. Reprint, New York: Penguin Books, 1985.

———. *Northanger Abbey.* Edited by Marilyn Butler. 1817. Reprint, New York: Penguin Books, 1995.

———. *Persuasion.* Edited by Patricia Meyer Spacks. 1817. Reprint, New York: W. W. Norton & Co., 1995.

———. *Pride and Prejudice.* Edited by Donald Gray. 3rd ed. 1813. Reprint, New York: W. W. Norton & Co., 2001.

———. *Sense and Sensibility.* Edited by Ros Ballaster. 1811. Reprint, New York: Penguin Books, 1995.

Bacon, Jon Lance. "Wives, Widows, and Writings in Restoration Comedy." *Studies in English Literature, 1500–1900* 31 (1991): 427–43.

Ballaster, Ros. *Seductive Forms: Women's Amatory Fiction from 1684 to 1740.* Oxford: Clarendon Press, 1992.

Bannet, Eve Tavor. "The Marriage Act of 1753: 'A Most Cruel Law for the Fair Sex.'" *Eighteenth-Century Studies* 30 (1997): 233–54.

Beattie, J. M. "The Criminality of Women in Eighteenth-Century England." *Journal of Social History* 8, no. 4 (1975): 80–116.

Behn, Aphra and Thomas Betterton. "The Counterfeit Bridgeroom: or the Defeated Widow." In *English Dramas*, 1–59. London: L. Curtiss, 1677.

Bellamy, Liz. *Commerce, Morality and the Eighteenth-Century Novel.* Cambridge: Cambridge University Press, 1998.

Benedict, Barbara M. *Framing Feeling: Sentiment and Style in English Prose Fiction, 1745–1800.* New York: AMS Press, Inc., 1994.

———. "Jane Austen and the Culture of Circulating Libraries: The Construction of Female Literacy." In *Revising Women: Eighteenth-Century "Women's Fiction" and Social Engagement*, edited by Paula Backscheider, 147–99. Baltimore: The Johns Hopkins University Press, 2000.

Berg, Maxine. *The Age of Manufactures, 1700–1829: Industry, Innovation and Work in Britain.* 2nd ed. New York: Routledge, 1994.

Bohls, Elizabeth. "The Gentleman Planter and the Metropole: Long's *History of Jamaica* (1774)." In *The Country and the City Revisited: England and the Politics of Culture, 1550–1850*, edited by Gerald MacLean, Donna Landry, and Joseph P. Ward, 180–96. Cambridge: Cambridge University Press, 1999.

Boulukos, George. "The Grateful Slave: A History of Slave Plantation Reform in the British Novel, 1750–1780." Vol. 1 of *The Eighteenth Century Novel*, edited by Susan Spencer, 161–79. New York: AMS Press, Inc., 2001.

Bowden, Martha. "The Interdependence of Women in *Tristram Shandy*: A Chapter of Eyes, Sausages and Sciatica." *English Language Notes* 31 (June 1994): 40–47.

———. Introduction to "The Accomplish'd Rake, or Modern Fine Gentleman," by Mary Davys. In *The Reform'd Coquet; or Memoirs of Amoranda, Familiar Letters Betwixt a Gentleman and a Lady, and The Accomplish'd Rake, or Modern Fine Gentleman*, edited by Martha F. Bowden, ix–xlvi. Lexington: The University Press of Kentucky, 1999.

Bowers, Toni. *The Politics of Motherhood: British Writing and Culture, 1680–1760.* Cambridge: Cambridge University Press, 1996.

Bowles, Thomas. "The *Bubbler's Medley*, or, a *Sketch* of the *Times*: Being Europe's *Memorial* for the *Year* 1720." August 10, 1720. British Museum Collection of Prints and Drawings, 1689–1790.

Brady, Frank. "Tristram Shandy: Sexuality, Morality, and Sensibility." *Eighteenth-Century Studies* 4, no. 1 (Autumn 1970): 41–56.

Braudel, Fernand. *The Wheels of Commerce.* Vol. 2, *Civilization and Capitalism, 15th–18th Century.* Translated by Siân Reynolds. New York: Harper & Row, Publishers, 1982.

Brooks, Christopher K. "Marriage in Goldsmith: The Single Woman, Feminine Space, and 'Virtue.'" In *Joinings and Disjoinings: The Significance of Marital Status in Literature*, edited by JoAnna Stephens Mink and Janet Doubler Ward, 19–35. Bowling Green, OH: Bowling Green State University Popular Press, 1991.

Brophy, Elizabeth Bergen. *Women's Lives and the Eighteenth-Century English Novel.* Tampa: University of South Florida Press, 1991.

Brown, Julia Prewitt. *Jane Austen's Novels: Social Change and Literary Form.* Cambridge: Harvard University Press, 1979.

Brown, Laura. *Ends of Empire: Women and Ideology in Eighteenth-Century English Literature.* Ithaca, NY: Cornell University Press, 1993.

———. *Fables of Modernity: Literature and Culture in the English Eighteenth Century.* Ithaca, NY: Cornell University Press, 2001.

Burke, Helen. "'Law-suits,' 'Love-suits,' and the Family Property in Wycherley's *The Plain Dealer.*" In *Cultural Readings of Restoration and Eighteenth-Century English Theater,* edited by J. Douglas Canfield and Deborah C. Payne, 9–113. Athens: University of Georgia Press, 1995.

Burney, Frances. *Camilla; or, The Picture of Youth.* Edited by Edward A. Bloom and Lillian D. Bloom. 1796. Reprint, New York: Oxford University Press, 1972.

———. *Evelina.* 1778. Reprint, New York: W. W. Norton & Co., 1965.

Butler, Judith. *Bodies That Matter: On the Discursive Limits of "Sex."* New York: Routledge, 1993.

———. *Gender Trouble.* New York: Routledge, 1990.

Butler, Marilyn. *Jane Austen and the War of Ideas.* 1975. Reprinted with an introduction by Marilyn Butler. Oxford: Clarendon Press, 1987.

Campbell, Jill. "Lady Mary Wortley Montagu and the Historical Machinery of Female Identity." In *History, Gender and Eighteenth-Century Literature,* edited by Beth Fowkes Tobin, 64–85. Athens: University of Georgia Press, 1994.

Canfield, J. Douglas. *Tricksters and Estates: On the Ideology of Restoration Comedy.* Lexington: The University Press of Kentucky, 1997.

Cantor, Paul A. "A Class Act: *Persuasion* and the Lingering Death of the Aristocracy." *Philosophy and Literature* 23 (1999): 127–39.

Carswell, John. *The South Sea Bubble.* Rev. ed. Thrupp, Stroud: Sutton Publishing Limited, 2001.

Casler, Jeanine M. Preface to *The School for Widows* by Clara Reeve. Edited by Jeanine M. Casler. Newark: The University of Delaware Press, 2001.

Castle, Terry. "The Culture of Travesty: Sexuality and Masquerade in Eighteenth-Century England." In *Sexual Underworlds of the Enlightenment,* edited by G. S. Rousseau and Roy Porter, 156–80. Chapel Hill: The University of North Carolina Press, 1988.

———. Introduction to *Northanger Abbey, Lady Susan, The Watsons, and Sanditon,* edited by John Davie, vii–xxxii. New York: Oxford University Press, 1998.

Clark, Alice. *Working Life of Women in the Seventeenth Century.* 3rd ed. New York: Routledge, 1992.

Cleere, Eileen. "Reinvesting Nieces: *Mansfield Park* and the Economics of Endogamy." *Novel* 28 (Winter 1995): 113–30.

Cleland, John. *Fanny Hill, or, Memoirs of a Woman of Pleasure.* 1748–49. Reprint, New York: Signet Classic, 1996.

Cody, Lisa Forman. "The Politics of Reproducing: From Midwives' Alternative Public Sphere to the Public Spectacle of Man-Midwifery." *Eighteenth-Century Studies* 32 (Summer 1999): 477–95.

Cohen, Michèle. *Fashioning Masculinity: National Identity and Language in the Eighteenth Century.* New York: Routledge, 1996.

Cope, Esther. "'The Widdowes' Silvar': Widowhood in Early Modern England." In *"The Muses Females Are": Martha Moulsworth and Other Women Writers of the English Renaissance*, edited by Robert C. Evans and Anne C. Little, 189–99. West Cornwall, CT: Locust Hill Press, 1995.

Craft-Fairchild, Catherine. *Masquerade and Gender: Disguise and Female Identity in Eighteenth-Century Fictions by Women.* University Park: The Pennsylvania State University Press, 1993.

Croxson, Bronwyn. "The Foundation and Evolution of the Middlesex Hospital's Lying-In Service, 1745–86." *Social History of Medicine: The Journal of the Society for the Social History of Medicine* 14 (2002): 27–37.

Davidoff, Leonore, and Catherine Hall. *Family Fortunes: Men and Women of the English Middle Class, 1780–1850.* Chicago: The University of Chicago Press, 1987.

Davys, Mary. "The Accomplish'd Rake, or Modern Fine Gentleman." In *The Reform'd Coquet; or Memoirs of Amoranda, Familiar Letters Betwixt a Gentleman and a Lady, and The Accomplish'd Rake, or Modern Fine Gentleman*, edited by Martha F. Bowden, 123–226. 1727. Reprint, Lexington: The University Press of Kentucky, 1999.

Dawe, Philip. "Courtship for Money / Faisant Amour pour L'Argent." 1771. In "The Satire of Marriage" from the Print Collection of the New York Public Library and the British Museum Collection of Prints and Drawings, 1689–1790.

Defoe, Daniel. *Moll Flanders.* 1722. Reprint, New York: Penguin Classics, 1989.

———. *Robinson Crusoe.* Edited by Michael Shinagel. 1719. Reprint, New York: W. W. Norton & Co., 1975.

Donnison, Jean. *Midwives and Medical Men: A History of Inter-Professional Rivalries and Women's Rights.* New York: Schocken Books, 1977.

Doody, Margaret Anne. "Frances Sheridan: Morality and Annihilated Time." In *Fetter'd or Free? British Women Novelists, 1670–1815*, edited by Mary Anne Schofield and Cecilia Macheski, 324–58. Athens: Ohio University Press, 1986.

Duckworth, Alistair M. *The Improvement of the Estate: A Study of Jane Austen's Novels.* Baltimore: The Johns Hopkins University Press, 1994.

Dugaw, Dianne. "The Anatomy of Heroism: Gender Politics and Empire in Gay's *Polly*." In *History, Gender and Eighteenth-Century Literature*, edited by Beth Fowkes Tobin, 39–63. Athens: University of Georgia Press, 1994.

Duncan, Jeffrey L. "The Rural Ideal in Eighteenth-Century Fiction." In *The Country Myth: Motifs in the British Novel from Defoe to Smollett*, edited by H. George Hahn, 255–72. New York: Peter Lang, Inc., 1990.

Dussinger, John A. *In the Pride of the Moment: Encounters in Jane Austen's World.* Columbus: The Ohio State University Press, 1990.

Earle, Peter. *The Making of the English Middle Class: Business, Society and Family Life in London, 1660–1730.* Berkeley: University of California Press, 1989.

Ellis, Kate Ferguson. *The Contested Castle: Gothic Novels and the Subversion of Domestic Ideology*. Urbana: University of Illinois Press, 1989.

Ellis, Markman. *The Politics of Sensibility: Race, Gender and Commerce in the Sentimental Novel*. Cambridge: Cambridge University Press, 1996.

Emma. VHS. Directed by Diarmuid Lawrence. A&E Home Video, 1996.

Emma. VHS. Directed by Douglas McGrath. Miramax Home Entertainment, 1997.

Erickson, Amy Louise. Introduction to *Working Life of Women in the Seventeenth Century*, by Alice Clark, vii–xiii. 3rd ed. New York: Routledge, 1992.

Essex Pauper Letters. Edited by Thomas Sokoll. Records of Social and Economic History. New Series 30. Oxford: Oxford University Press, 2001.

Faller, Lincoln B. *Crime and Defoe: A New Kind of Writing*. Cambridge: Cambridge University Press, 1993.

Fenwick, Eliza. *Secresy; or, The Ruin on the Rock*. Edited by Isobel Grundy, 37–359. 2nd ed. 1795. Reprint, Toronto: Broadview Press Ltd., 1998.

Fielding, Henry. *The History of Tom Jones*. Edited by R. P. C. Mutter, 1–822. 1747. Reprint, New York: Penguin Books, 1985.

———. "Joseph Andrews." In *Joseph Andrews and Shamela*, edited by Douglas Brooks-Davies, 1–312. 1742. Reprint, New York: Oxford University Press, 1990.

Fielding, Sarah. *The Adventures of David Simple: Containing An Account of His Travels Through the Cities of London and Westminster, In the Search of A Real Friend. By a Lady In Two Volumes*. 2nd ed. London: A. Millar, 1744.

———. *The Governess, Or, The Little Female Academy*. 1749. Reprint, Carnegie-Mellon University: Project Gutenberg.

———. *The History of Ophelia*. 1760. Reprint, New York: Garland Publishing, Inc., 1974.

———. *The History of the Countess of Dellwyn. In Two Volumes*. 1759. Reprint, New York: Garland Publishing, Inc., 1974.

"The Finish'd Rake; or, Gallantry in Perfection." In *The Finish'd Rake; or, Gallantry in Perfection (Anonymous); The Secret History of Mama Oello, Princess Royal of Peru (Anonymous); The Masterpiece of Imposture (Elizabeth Harding); The Temple Rakes, or Innocence Preserved (Anonymous)*, edited by Josephine Grieder. 1733. Reprint, New York: Garland Publishing, Inc., 1973.

Fletcher, Loraine. *Charlotte Smith: A Critical Biography*. New York: St. Martin's Press, 1998.

Fraiman, Susan. "Jane Austen and Edward Said: Gender, Culture, and Imperialism." *Critical Inquiry* 21 (Summer 1995): 805–21.

Gadeken, Sara. "'A Method of Being Perfectly Happy': Technologies of Self in the Eighteenth-Century Female Community." Vol. 1 of *The Eighteenth Century Novel*, edited by Susan Spencer, 217–35. New York: AMS Press, Inc., 2001.

Gautier, Gary. "Marriage and Family in Fielding's Fiction." *Studies in the Novel* 27 (Summer 1995): 111–28.

———. "Slavery and the Fashioning of Race in *Oroonoko, Robinson Crusoe*, and Equiano's *Life*." *The Eighteenth Century* 42 (2001): 161–79.

Gay, John. "The Beggar's Opera." In *Eighteenth-Century Plays*, edited by Ricardo Quintana, 179–237. 1728. Reprint, New York: The Modern Library, 1952.

Gillis, John R. *For Better, For Worse: British Marriages, 1600 to the Present*. New York: Oxford University Press, 1985.

Gilroy, Amanda. "'Candid Advice to the Fair Sex': or, the Politics of Maternity in Late Eighteenth-Century Britain." In *Body Matters: Feminism, Textuality, Corporeality*, edited by Avril Horner and Angela Keane, 17–28. New York: Manchester University Press, 2000.

Godwin, William. *Things As They Are or The Adventures of Caleb Williams*. Edited by Maurice Hindle. 1794. Reprint, New York: Penguin Books, 1988.

Goldsmith, Oliver. "The Deserted Village." In *British Literature 1640–1789: An Anthology*, edited by Robert DeMaria, Jr., 1054–64. 1770. Reprint, Oxford: Blackwell Publishers Ltd, 1996.

———. "The Revolution in Low Life." In *British Literature 1640–1789: An Anthology*, edited by Robert DeMaria, Jr., 1052–1054. 1762. Reprint, Oxford: Blackwell Publishers Ltd, 1996.

———. *The Vicar of Wakefield*. 1762. Reprint, New York: Pocket Books, Inc., 1957.

Griffith, Frances. *The Delicate Distress*. Edited by Cynthia Booth Ricciardi and Susan Staves. 1769. Reprint, Lexington: The University Press of Kentucky, 1997.

Guest, Harriet. "Eighteenth-Century Femininity: 'A Supposed Sexual Character.'" In *Women and Literature in Britain, 1700–1800*, edited by Vivien Jones, 46–68. Cambridge: Cambridge University Press, 2000.

Haggerty. George E. "Amelia's Nose; Or, Sensibility and Its Symptoms." *The Eighteenth Century* 36, no.2 (Summer 1995): 139–56.

———. "Satire and Sentiment in *The Vicar of Wakefield*." *The Eighteenth Century* 32, no. 1 (Spring 1991): 25–38.

Harrison, Bernard. "Sterne and Sentimentalism." In *Commitment in Reflection: Essays in Literature and Moral Philosophy*, 63–100. New York: Garland Publishing, Inc., 1994.

Hay, Douglas, and Nicholas Rogers. *Eighteenth-Century English Society*. New York: Oxford University Press, 1997.

Haywood, Eliza. "The British Recluse; or, The Secret History of Cleomira, Supposed Dead." In *Popular Fiction by Women, 1660–1730: An Anthology*, edited by Paula R. Backscheider and John J. Richetti, 154–224. 1722. Reprint, Oxford: Clarendon Press, 1996.

———. "Fantomina: or, Love in a Maze." In *Popular Fiction by Women, 1660–1730: An Anthology*, edited by Paula R. Backscheider and John J. Richetti, 227–48. 1725. Reprint, Oxford: Clarendon Press, 1996.

———. *The History of Miss Betsy Thoughtless*. Edited by Christine Blouch. 1751. Reprint, Toronto: Broadview Press Ltd., 1998.

Hill, Bridget. *Women, Work, and Sexual Politics in Eighteenth-Century England*. New York: Basil Blackwell Inc., 1989.

Hill, C. P. *British Economic and Social History, 1700–1982*. 5th ed. London: Edward Arnold Ltd., 1985.

Hitchcock, Tim. "'Unlawfully begotten on her body': Illegitimacy and the Parish Poor in St Luke's Chelsea." In *Chronicling Poverty—The Voices and Strategies of the English Poor, 1640–1840*, edited by Tim Hitchcock, Peter King, and Pamela Sharpe, 70–86. New York: St. Martin's Press, 1997.

Hitchcock, Tim, Peter King, and Pamela Sharpe. "Introduction: Chronicling Poverty— The Voices and Strategies of the English Poor, 1640–1840." In *Chronicling Poverty —The Voices and Strategies of the English Poor, 1640–1840*, edited by Tim Hitchcock, Peter King, and Pamela Sharpe. New York: St. Martin's Press, 1997.

Hobbes, Thomas. *Leviathan*. Edited by C. B. Macpherson. 1651. Reprint, New York: Penguin Books, 1985.

Holmes, Geoffrey. *Augustan England: Professions, State and Society, 1680–1730*. Boston: G. Allen & Unwin, 1982.

Holmes, Geoffrey, and Daniel Szechi. *The Age of Oligarchy: Pre-Industrial England, 1722–1783*. New York: Longman Publishing, 1993.

Hufton, Olwen. "Women Without Men: Widows and Spinsters in Britain and France in the Eighteenth Century." In *Between Poverty and the Pyre: Moments in the History of Widowhood*, edited by Jan Bremmer and Lourens van den Bosch, 122–51. New York: Routledge, 1995.

Humphrey, W. Untitled. 1776. In "The Satire of Marriage" from the Print Collection of the New York Public Library and the British Museum Collection of Prints and Drawings, 1689–1790.

Inchbald, Elizabeth. *A Simple Story*. Edited by J. M. S. Tompkins. 1791. Reprint, Oxford: Oxford University Press, 1988.

Irvine, Robert P. *Enlightenment and Romance: Gender and Agency in Smollett and Scott* New York: Peter Lang, Inc., 2000.

Jacobsen, Susan P. "'The Tinsel of the Times': Smollett's Argument against Conspicuous Consumption in *Humphry Clinker*." *Eighteenth-Century Fiction* 9, no. 1 (October 1996): 71–88.

Johnson, Claudia L. *Equivocal Beings: Politics, Gender, and Sentimentality in the 1790s, Wollstonecraft, Radcliffe, Burney, Austen*. Chicago: The University of Chicago Press, 1995.

———. *Jane Austen: Women, Politics, and the Novel*. Chicago: The University of Chicago Press, 1988.

Jones, Vivien. "Eighteenth-Century Prostitution: Feminist Debates and the Writing of Histories." In *Body Matters: Feminism, Textuality, Corporeality*, edited by Avril Horner and Angela Keane, 127–42. New York: Manchester University Press, 2000.

———. Introduction to *Women and Literature in Britain, 1700–1800*, edited by Vivien Jones, 1–19. Cambridge: Cambridge University Press, 2000.

King, Peter. "Female Offenders, Work and Life-Cycle Change in Late-Eighteenth-Century London." *Continuity and Change* 11 (1996): 61–90.

Kirkham, Margaret. *Jane Austen, Feminism and Fiction*. New Jersey: Barnes & Noble Books, 1983.

Kirkpatrick, Kathryn. "Sermons and Strictures: Conduct-Book Propriety and Property Relations in Late Eighteenth-Century England." In *History, Gender and Eighteenth-Century Literature*, edited by Beth Fowkes Tobin, 198–226. Athens: University of Georgia Press, 1994.

Knapp, Elise F. "'Your Obedient Humble Servant': An Epistolary Account of Marriage and Widowhood in Eighteenth-Century Sussex." *Studies on Voltaire and the Eighteenth Century* 304 (1992): 783–86.

Kraft, Elizabeth. "Laurence Sterne and the Ethics of Sexual Difference: Chiasmic Narration and Double Desire." *Christianity and Literature* 51 (Spring 2002): 363–85.

Langford, Paul. *A Polite and Commercial People: England, 1727–1783*. Oxford: Clarendon Press, 1989.

Lee, Margaret. *Clara Lennox; or, The Distressed Widow. A Novel. Founded in Facts. Interspersed with an Historical Description of the Isle of Man*. London: J. Adlard, 1797.

Lewis, Matthew. *The Monk*. 1796. Reprint, New York: Oxford University Press, 1989.

Linebaugh, Peter. *The London Hanged: Crime and Civil Society in the Eighteenth Century*. Cambridge: Cambridge University Press, 1992.

London, April. *Women and Property in the Eighteenth-Century English Novel*. Cambridge: Cambridge University Press, 1999.

Loudon, Irvine. Review of *The Making of Man-Midwifery* by Adrian Wilson. *Bulletin of the History of Medicine* 70 (1996): 507–15.

MacLean, Gerald, Donna Landry, and Joseph P. Ward. "Introduction: The Country and the City Revisited, c. 1550–1850." In *The Country and the City Revisited: England and the Politics of Culture, 1550–1850*, edited by Gerald MacLean, Donna Landry, and Joseph P. Ward, 1–23. Cambridge: Cambridge University Press, 1999.

Mathias, Peter. *The First Industrial Nation: An Economic History of Britain, 1700–1914*. 2nd ed. London and New York: Methuen, 1983.

McDowell, Paula. "Women and the Business of Print." In *Women and Literature in Britain, 1700–1800*, edited by Vivien Jones, 135–54. Cambridge: Cambridge University Press, 2000.

McKendrick, Neil, John Brewer, and J. H. Plumb. *The Birth of a Consumer Society: The Commercialization of Eighteenth-Century England*. London: Europa Publications Limited, 1982.

McKeon, Michael. "Historicizing Patriarchy: The Emergence of Gender Difference in England, 1660–1760." *Eighteenth-Century Studies* 28 (1995): 295–322.

McLynn, Frank. *Crime and Punishment in Eighteenth-Century England*. New York: Routledge, 1989.

Mellor, Anne K. "A Criticism of Their Own: Romantic Women Literary Critics." In *Questioning Romanticism*, edited by John Beer, 29–48. Baltimore: The Johns Hopkins University Press, 1995.

Mulcaire, Terry. "Public Credit; or, The Feminization of Virtue in the Marketplace." *PMLA* 114 (October 1999): 1029–42.

Mullan, John. *Sentiment and Sociability: The Language of Feeling in the Eighteenth Century*. Oxford: Oxford University Press, 1988.

Nokes, David. *Jane Austen: A Life.* New York: Farrar, Straus, & Giroux, Inc., 1997.

Novak, Maximillian. *Daniel Defoe, Master of Fictions: His Life and Ideas.* Oxford: Oxford University Press, 2001.

Nussbaum, Felicity A. "'Savage' Mothers: Narratives of Maternity in the Mid-Eighteenth Century." *Eighteenth-Century Life* 16 (February 1992): 165–84.

O'Brien, Karen. "Imperial Georgic, 1660–1789." In *The Country and the City Revisited: England and the Politics of Culture, 1550–1850,* edited by Gerald MacLean, Donna Landry, and Joseph P. Ward, 160–79. Cambridge: Cambridge University Press, 1999.

Ogg, David. *England in the Reigns of James II and William III.* New York: Oxford University Press, 1969.

Paulson, Ronald. *The "Modern Moral Subject," 1697–1732.* Vol. 1 of *Hogarth.* New Brunswick, NJ: Rutgers University Press, 1991.

Perry, Ruth. "Bluestockings in Utopia." In *History, Gender and Eighteenth-Century Literature,* edited by Beth Fowkes Tobin, 159–78. Athens: University of Georgia Press, 1994.

———. "Colonizing the Breast: Sexuality and Maternity in Eighteenth-Century England." *Eighteenth-Century Life* 16 (February 1992): 185–215.

———. "Women in Families: The Great Disinheritance." In *Women and Literature in Britain, 1700–1800,* edited by Vivien Jones, 111–31. Cambridge: Cambridge University Press, 2000.

Poovey, Mary. *The Proper Lady and the Woman Writer: Ideology as Style in the Works of Mary Wollstonecraft, Mary Shelley, and Jane Austen.* Chicago: The University of Chicago Press, 1984.

Porter, Roy. *English Society in the Eighteenth Century.* Rev. ed. New York: Penguin Books, 1990.

Prest, Wilfred, ed. *The Professions in Early Modern England.* New York: Croom Helm, 1987.

Radcliffe, Ann. *The Castles of Athlin and Dunbayne. A Highland Story.* 1789. Reprint of 1821 edition. New York: Arno Press, Inc., 1972.

———. *The Italian.* 1797. Reprint, New York: Oxford University Press, 1990.

———. *The Mysteries of Udolpho.* 1794. Reprint, New York: Oxford University Press, 1980.

Reeve, Clara. "The Old English Baron: A Gothic Story." *The Old English Baron and The Castle of Otranto.* 1777. Reprint, London: J. C. Nimmo and Bain, 1883.

———. *The School for Widows. A Novel. In Two Volumes.* Dublin: William Porter, 1791.

Ress, Laura Jane. *Tender Consciousness: Sentimental Sensibility in the Emerging Artist—Sterne, Yeats, Joyce, and Proust.* Vol. 59. American University Studies, series 3: Comparative Literature. New York: Peter Lang, Inc., 2002.

Richardson, Samuel. *Clarissa.* 1747. Reprint, New York: Penguin Classics, 1987.

———. *Pamela; or, Virtue Rewarded.* Edited by Peter Sabor. 1740. Reprint, New York: Penguin Books, 1988.

Robinson, Lillian S. "Woman Under Capitalism: The Renaissance Lady." In *Sex, Class, and Culture,* 150–77. Bloomington: Indiana University Press, 1978.

Robinson, Mary. *The Widow, or a Picture of Modern Times. A Novel, in a Series of Letters, in Two Volumes.* London: Hookham and Carpenter, 1794.

Rodgers, James. "Sensibility, Sympathy, Benevolence: Physiology and Moral Philosophy in *Tristram Shandy.*" In *Languages of Nature: Critical Essays on Science and Literature,* edited by L. J. Jordanova, 119–58. New Brunswick, NJ: Rutgers University Press, 1986.

Ross, Ian Campbell. *Laurence Sterne: A Life.* Oxford: Oxford University Press, 2001.

Rowbotham, Sheila. *Hidden from History: 300 Years of Women's Oppression and the Fight Against It.* 3rd ed. London: Pluto Press, 1990.

Said, Edward. *Culture and Imperialism.* New York: Alfred A. Knopf, 1993.

Scheuermann, Mona. *In Praise of Poverty: Hannah More Counters Thomas Paine and the Radical Threat.* Lexington: The University Press of Kentucky, 2002.

Scott, Sarah. *A Description of Millenium Hall.* 1762. Reprint, New York: Viking Penguin, 1986.

———. *The History of Cornelia.* 1750. Reprint, London: Routledge / Thoemmes Press, 1992.

———. *The History of Sir George Ellison.* Edited by Betty Rizzo. 1766. Reprint, Lexington: The University Press of Kentucky, 1996.

Seligman, Stanley A. "The Royal Maternity Charity: The First Hundred Years." *Medical History* 24 (1990): 403–18.

Shaffer, Julie. Introduction to *Walsingham; or, Pupil of Nature,* by Mary Robinson, 7–34. 1797. Reprint, Toronto: Broadview Press Ltd., 2003.

Sheridan, Frances. *Memoirs of Miss Sidney Bidulph.* 1769. Reprint, New York: Pandora Press, 1987.

Skinner, Gillian. *Sensibility and Economics in the Novel, 1740–1800: The Price of a Tear.* New York: St. Martin's Press, 1999.

———. "Women's Status as Legal and Civic Subjects: 'A Worse Condition than Slavery Itself'?" In *Women and Literature in Britain, 1700–1800,* edited by Vivien Jones, 91–110. Cambridge: Cambridge University Press, 2000.

Smith, Adam. *The Theory of Moral Sentiments.* Edited by D. D. Raphael and A. L. Macfie. 1750. Reprint, Indianapolis: The Liberty Fund, 1979.

Smith, Charlotte. *Emmeline, the Orphan of the Castle. In Four Volumes.* London: T. Cadell, 1788.

———. *The Old Manor House.* Edited by Jacqueline M. Labbe. 1793. Reprint, Toronto: Broadview Press Ltd., 2002. 33–523.

Smollett, Tobias. *The Adventures of Ferdinand Count Fathom.* Edited by Jerry C. Beasley and O. M. Brack, Jr. 1753. Reprint, Athens: University of Georgia Press, 1988.

———. *The Adventures of Peregrine Pickle, in which are included Memoirs of a Lady of Quality.* Edited by James L. Clifford. 1751. Reprint, London: Oxford University Press, 1964.

———. *The Expedition of Humphry Clinker.* Edited by Angus Ross. 1771. Reprint, New York: Penguin Books, 1985.

Society for Bettering the Condition and Increasing the Comforts of the Poor. *The Reports of the Society for Bettering the Condition and Increasing the Comforts of the Poor.*

Vol. 1. London, York, Bath, Newcastle, Durham, Hull, Salisbury, Exeter, Manchester, Gloucester, 1798.

Society for the Relief of Necessitous Widows and Children of Protestant Dissenting Ministers. Papers. Dr Williams's Library, London, England.

Speck, W. A. *Stability and Strife: England, 1714–1760*. Cambridge: Harvard University Press, 1977.

Spector, Robert D. *Smollett's Women: A Study in an Eighteenth-Century Masculine Sensibility*. Westport, CT: Greenwood Press, 1994.

Staves, Susan. *Married Women's Separate Property in England, 1660–1833*. Cambridge: Harvard University Press, 1990.

———. "Where is History but in Texts? Reading the History of Marriage." In *The Golden and the Brazen World: Papers in Literature and History, 1660–1800*, edited by John M. Wallace, 125–43. Berkeley: University of California Press, 1985.

Steffes, Michael. "Slavery and *Mansfield Park*: The Historical and Biographical Context." *English Language Notes* 34 (December 1996): 23–41.

Sterne, Laurence. *The Life and Opinions of Tristram Shandy, Gentleman*. Edited by Melvyn New and Joan New. 1760–67. Reprint, New York: Penguin Books, 1997.

———. "A Sentimental Journey." In *"A Sentimental Journey through France and Italy By Mr. Yorick" with "The Journal to Eliza" and "A Political Romance,"* edited by Ian Jack, 1–125. 1768. Reprint, New York: Oxford University Press, 1984.

Stewart, Maaja A. *Domestic Realities and Imperial Fictions: Jane Austen's Novels in Eighteenth-Century Contexts*. Athens: University of Georgia Press, 1993.

Stone, Lawrence. *Uncertain Unions and Broken Lives: Marriage and Divorce in England, 1660–1857*. New York: Oxford University Press, 1995.

Straub, Kristina. "Fanny Burney's *Evelina* and the 'Gulphs, Pits, and Precipices' of Eighteenth-Century Female Life." *The Eighteenth Century* 27, no. 3: 230–46.

Sutherland, Kathryn. "Writings on Education and Conduct: Arguments for Female Improvement." In *Women and Literature in Britain, 1700–1800*, edited by Vivien Jones, 25–45. Cambridge: Cambridge University Press, 2000.

"The Temple Rakes, or Innocence Preserved." In *The Finish'd Rake; or, Gallantry in Perfection (Anonymous); The Secret History of Mama Oello, Princess Royal of Peru (Anonymous); The Masterpiece of Imposture (Elizabeth Harding); The Temple Rakes, or Innocence Preserved (Anonymous)*, edited by Josephine Grieder. 1735. Reprint, New York: Garland Publishing, Inc., 1973.

Thaddeus, Janice Farrar. "Mary Delany, Model to the Age." In *History, Gender and Eighteenth-Century Literature*, edited by Beth Fowkes Tobin, 113–40. Athens: University of Georgia Press, 1994.

Thomas, Ruth P. "Twice Victims: Virtuous Widows and the Eighteenth-Century French Novel." *Studies on Voltaire and the Eighteenth Century* 266 (1989): 433–49.

Thompson, Janet A. *Wives, Widows, Witches and Bitches: Women in Seventeenth-Century Devon*. Vol. 106. American University Studies, Series 9: History. New York: Peter Lang, Inc., 1993.

Tobin, Beth Fowkes. "Arthur Young, Agriculture, and the Construction of the New Economic Man." In *History, Gender and Eighteenth-Century Literature*, edited by Beth Fowkes Tobin, 179–97. Athens: University of Georgia Press, 1994.

Todd, Barbara. "The Remarrying Widow: A Stereotype Reconsidered." In *Women in English Society, 1500–1800*, edited by Mary Prior, 54–92. New York: Methuen & Co., 1985.

Todd, Janet. *Sensibility: An Introduction*. London: Methuen & Co., 1986.

Tomalin, Claire. *Jane Austen: A Life*. New York: Vintage Books, 1997.

Uglow, Jenny. *Hogarth: A Life and a World*. London: Faber and Faber, 1997.

Van Sant, Ann Jessie. *Eighteenth-Century Sensibility and the Novel: The Senses in Social Context*. Cambridge: Cambridge University Press, 1993.

Vickery, Amanda. *The Gentleman's Daughter: Women's Lives in Georgian England*. New Haven: Yale University Press, 1998.

Warner, William. *Licensing Entertainment: The Elevation of Novel Reading in Britain, 1684–1750*. Berkeley: University of California Press, 1998.

Watt, Ian. *The Rise of the Novel: Studies in Defoe, Richardson and Fielding*. Berkeley: University of California Press, 1957.

Weisner, Merry E. *Women and Gender in Early Modern Europe*. Cambridge: Cambridge University Press, 1993.

Westley's Charity. Papers. Somerset Record Office, Taunton, England.

Williams, Raymond. *The Country and the City*. New York: Oxford University Press, 1973.

Wilner, Arlene Fish. "Education and Ideology in Sarah Fielding's *The Governess*." *Studies in Eighteenth-Century Culture* 24 (1995): 307–27.

Wilson, Adrian. *The Making of Man-Midwifery: Childbirth in England, 1660–1770*. Cambridge: Harvard University Press, 1995.

Wolborough Feoffees and Widows' Charity. Papers. Devon Record Office, Exeter, England.

"The World in Masquerade (half in English translation of the other half, which is Dutch)." 1720. British Museum Collection of Prints and Drawings, 1689–1790.

Wycherley, William. *The Plain Dealer*. Edited by James L. Smith. 1676. Reprint, New York: W. W. Norton & Co., 1979.

Yang, Wonkyung. "Childbirth and Female Midwifery in Laurence Sterne's *Tristram Shandy*." *The Journal of English Language and Literature* 44 (Winter 1998): 789–806.

Yerbury Almshouses. Papers. Wiltshire and Swindon Record Office, Trowbridge, England.

Index

middle class, 63–64, 81–82, 88–93,
139–40, 140–41, 149–50, 159, 160
midwifery, 82–84, 170, 189 n. 25,
189 n. 27
Millenium Hall (Scott): city, 61; charity,
111, 145, 171; class stability, 29–31,
60; country, 63; Lady Brumpton,
30, 31; Lady Lambton, 30; Lady
Sheerness, 30, 31, 61; motherhood,
38; Mrs. Alworth, 30, 49–50; Mrs.
Thornby, 30, 38; poor widows, 105,
106, 144; work, 69
Moll Flanders (Defoe), 22, 76, 191 n. 1;
bigamy, 135–36; financial success,
134–35; Moll's mother, 125–26,
194 n. 16; Moll's nurse, 79, 80–81,
134; motherhood, 79, 125–26;
poverty, 118; sensibility, 99–100;
widow as category, 132–34, 135–36;
work, 80–81
Monk, The (Lewis), 32, 34–36, 37, 38,
183 n. 11, 185 n. 37
Mother Needham, 128, 129, 131
Mullan, John, 99–100, 184 n. 23
Mulcaire, Terry, 19, 180 n. 14
Mysteries of Udolpho, The (Radcliffe):
city, 60–61, 62; Madame Cheron,
45–47, 152

New Economic Man, 63–64
Nokes, David, 140, 197 n. 3, 197 n. 6
Northanger Abbey (Austen), 139, 151–52
Nussbaum, Felicity, 127, 181 n. 17

Old English Baron, The (Reeve), 56, 57
Old Manor House, The (Smith),
90, 190 n. 29; city, 62; class stability,
104–5; imperialism, 100–101; motherhood, 37, 38, 50–51; property, 86

Pamela (Richardson): false title of
widow, 130–31; Mrs. Dobson, 81;
Mrs. Godfrey, 126; Mrs. Jervis,
71, 78
parish relief, 98, 111, 114, 149–50, 169
Perry, Ruth, 30, 127, 181 n. 17
Persuasion (Austen), 139; Lady Russell,
139, 157, 160, 162–67; Mrs. Clay,
139, 154, 157–59, 163, 167; Mrs.

Smith, 139, 154–57; slavery, 197 n. 6,
198 n. 21
Plain Dealer, The (Wycherley), 15–16,
121–22
poison, 116, 117, 193 n. 2
Poor Law: *See* parish relief
Poovey, Mary, 17, 135–36, 139
poverty, 83, 93–94, 149–50, 169–76.
See also widows: poverty
Porter, Roy, 172, 199 n. 2
Pride and Prejudice (Austen), 139;
Lady Catherine, 139, 144–45, 146,
147, 166, 167, 198 n. 10; marriage,
164; Mrs. Bennet, 139, 151, 152–53,
197 n. 6
property, 126–27

Radcliffe, Ann, 58, 60–61. *See also
under individual works*
Reeve, Clara, 28–29, 40–41, 88, 108,
182 n. 5, 190 n. 30. *See also under individual works*
Restoration drama, 15–17, 23
"Revolution in Low Life, The" (Goldsmith), 26
Richardson, Samuel, 22, 137. *See also
under individual works*
Robinson Crusoe (Defoe), 57–58; "good
ancient widow," 96–97, 111, 175–76
Robinson, Lillian, 177 n. 1
Robinson, Mary, 192 n. 12. *See also
under individual works*
Royal Maternity Charity, 170. *See also*
charity; widows: charity; widows:
motherhood

Said, Edward, 139
Scheuermann, Mona, 98–99, 113
School for Widows, The (Reeve), 22,
190 n. 30; city, 61–62; class stability,
72–73; country, 63; Donna Isabella,
56, 57, 72–73, 79, 87; limiting
widows' powers, 50; middle class,
81–82, 86–93; motherhood, 78–79,
125; Mrs. Batson, 31–32, 106; Mrs.
Burton, 128; Mrs. Darnford, 66–67,
69, 70, 72–74, 75, 76, 78–79, 86–93,
190 n. 30; Mrs. Gilson, 71, 78,
84–85, 190 n. 29, 190 n. 30; Mrs.

Martin, 72, 73–75, 83, 86–87, 89, 91; Mrs. Strictland, 28, 29, 50, 51, 63, 64, 71, 87, 91, 105–6, 145, 190 n. 30; poor widows, 105–6; remarriage, 51; selfishness, 31–32; sensibility, 88–90, 92–93; Susan Dobbins, 72, 84–85; work, 71–72, 73–75, 77–78

Scott, Sarah, 40–41, 90. *See also under individual works*

Secresy (Fenwick): imperialism, 100–101; Mrs. Ashburn, 45–47, 48–49

Sense and Sensibility (Austen), 138, 164, 198 n. 10; Mrs. Dashwood, 138, 151, 153–54; Mrs. Ferrars, 138, 142–43, 144, 147, 166, 167; Mrs. Jennings, 138, 142, 160–62, 167; Mrs. Smith, 138, 142–43, 147, 167

sensibility, 21–22, 23, 24, 27, 28–29, 30, 43, 44, 49, 51–55, 59, 76–77, 87–90, 92–94, 95–96, 99–112, 141, 168, 181 n. 23, 190 n. 31, 192 n. 10

sentiment, 22, 27, 28–29, 44, 48, 49, 53–54, 55, 56, 59, 70, 75–76, 77–78, 89–90, 92, 97, 99–104, 108–10, 113–14, 148–51, 181 n. 21, 184 n. 23, 192 n. 12. *See also* sensibility

Sentimental Journey (Sterne), 101

sentimental novel: *See* sensibility; sentiment

servants, 30–31, 31–32, 67, 70–71, 72, 78, 79, 88, 107–8, 171–72, 200 n. 8

Shaffer, Julie, 192 n. 12

Shaftesbury, Earl of, 21

Simple Story, A (Inchbald), 85–87, 91

Sir George Ellison (Scott): benevolence, 70–71; charity, 111; Mrs. Blackburn, 54–56, 185 n. 37; Mrs. Ellison, 58–60, 65; Mrs. Maningham, 77–78, 108–9; Mrs. Tunstall, 54–56, 90, 185 n. 37; sensibility, 89–90; widowed housekeeper, 70–71, 77–78, 81; work, 190 n. 32

slavery, 49, 58–59, 113–14, 123, 140, 151, 156–57, 197 n. 6, 198 n. 21

Skinner, Gillian, 21, 27, 76–77, 99–100

Smith, Adam, 21, 181 n. 21

Smith, Charlotte, 101, 105, 192 n. 17. *See also under individual works*

Smollett, Tobias, 28–29, 40, 51, 101–2, 182 n. 5, 192 n. 10. *See also under individual works*

Society for Bettering the Condition and Increasing the Comforts of the Poor, 83–84, 170, 171, 174, 200 n. 10. *See also* charity; widows: charity

Society for the Relief of Necessitous Widows and Children of Poor Dissenting Ministers, 67, 98, 108, 150, 171–72, 173–74, 175, 200 n. 7. *See also* charity; widows: charity

space, 72–73, 74–75, 86–87, 91–92. *See also* city; country

Speck, W. A., 200 n. 8

Spector, Robert D., 182 n. 5

Staves, Susan, 181 n. 19

Steffes, Michael, 197 n. 6

Sterne, Laurence, 44, 101–2, 192 n. 10. *See also under individual works*

Stewart, Maaja A., 27, 50, 152

Temple Rakes, The (Anonymous), 124–25, 128, 194 n. 14

Tobin, Beth Fowkes, 63–64

Todd, Barbara, 15

Todd, Janet, 181 n. 23

Tom Jones (H. Fielding), 22, 91; Lady Bellaston, 41–42, 48–49, 61; Mrs. Miller, 73, 79–80, 83, 106

Tomalin, Claire, 140, 197 n. 3, 197 n. 6

trade, 18–19, 26–27, 29, 90–91, 135, 167, 177 n. 1; women in, 60, 61–62, 135

Tristram Shandy (Sterne), 184 n. 23; "Jew's Widow," 77; midwife, 82–84, 189 n. 27; Widow Wadman, 43–45, 47–48; women, 189 n. 27

Van Sant, Ann Jessie, 99–100, 114

Vicar of Wakefield, The (Goldsmith), 101–2, 104, 192 n. 10

Vickery, Amanda, 147, 177 n. 1, 198 n. 13

Walsingham (Robinson), 192 n. 12

Warner, William, 178 n. 3